THE CUSTOMER CATALYST

THE CUSTOMER CATALYST

HOW TO DRIVE SUSTAINABLE BUSINESS GROWTH IN THE CUSTOMER ECONOMY

CHRIS ADLARD
DANIEL BAUSOR

WILEY

This edition first published 2020
© 2020 Chris Adlard and Daniel Bausor

Registered office

John Wiley & Sons Ltd, The Atrium, Southern Gate, Chichester, West Sussex, PO19 8SQ,
United Kingdom

For details of our global editorial offices, for customer services and for information about how
to apply for permission to reuse the copyright material in this book please see our website at
www.wiley.com.

Wiley publishes in a variety of print and electronic formats and by print-on-demand. Some
material included with standard print versions of this book may not be included in e-books or
in print-on-demand. If this book refers to media such as a CD or DVD that is not included in
the version you purchased, you may download this material at http://booksupport.wiley.com.
For more information about Wiley products, visit www.wiley.com.

Designations used by companies to distinguish their products are often claimed as
trademarks. All brand names and product names used in this book are trade names, service
marks, trademarks or registered trademarks of their respective owners. The publisher is not
associated with any product or vendor mentioned in this book.

Limit of Liability/Disclaimer of Warranty: While the publisher and author have used their
best efforts in preparing this book, they make no representations or warranties with respect
to the accuracy or completeness of the contents of this book and specifically disclaim any
implied warranties of merchantability or fitness for a particular purpose. It is sold on the
understanding that the publisher is not engaged in rendering professional services and neither
the publisher nor the author shall be liable for damages arising herefrom. If professional
advice or other expert assistance is required, the services of a competent professional should
be sought.

Library of Congress Cataloging-in-Publication Data is Available

ISBN 978-1-119-57508-5 (hardback) ISBN 978-1-119-57506-1 (ePDF)
ISBN 978-1-119-57507-8 (epub)

Cover Design and Image: © 2019 John Wiley & Sons Ltd, based on original design concepts by
Alan Clements

Set in 12/18pt Minion Pro by SPi Global, Chennai, India

Printed in Great Britain by TJ International Ltd, Padstow, Cornwall, UK

10 9 8 7 6 5 4 3 2 1

CONTENTS

ARE YOU READY FOR THE C-CHANGE?

DAN STEINMAN

Chief Operating Officer at Gainsight and author of *'Customer Success – How innovative companies are reducing churn and growing recurring revenue'*

Ensuring a customer-led approach to business has been the focus of my career for 30 years. We've called it a lot of different things – Account Management, Customer Relationship Management (yes, CRM), Customer Experience, Customer Advocacy, and most recently, Customer Success. The meaning of the term has morphed a bit but its fundamental essence and purpose has not. However, in the mid-2000's, something major did change – the urgency. The urgency changed dramatically when the subscription pricing model became popular and industries became increasingly digitised. For all the prior years in the history of many industries, vendors had largely been in charge. For example, in the technology sector, purchases for business were usually big-ticket items, implementations literally took years, companies had to buy hardware and data centres in order to run software systems, and the cost of the software was paid up front. In most cases, the customer's money was in the vendor's bank account for 2+ years before a user ever saw the application on their screen. However, the subscription model changed all of that and ushered in a secondary movement called Customer Success. I've been fortunate to be at the forefront of that movement in my roles at Gainsight over the past seven years.

So the Subscription Economy created the need for Customer Success which has become a very large marketplace of its own. All that is interesting and wonderful from the standpoint of vendors, but the most important element hidden behind all of the product development and organisational change is that the power in the vendor-customer relationship has shifted to the customer. This power shift was inevitable simply because the availability of information drastically altered the buying process. Regardless of what percentage you might put on it, it's inarguable that much of the sales process these days is completed before the vendor and customer actually speak. Not only that but some of the most valuable content about a vendor and about their products no longer comes from the vendor – it comes from other customers! Talk about a loss of control. Third-party review sites (both reviewing your products and services as well as your company) are common. Every customer has a voice through various social media channels. LinkedIn makes it so easy to find someone you know who is already using the product or service which you are evaluating. For me in the technology sector, almost none of our customers have data centres or buy hardware anymore because the vendors take on all of that pain and risk. Then we took this evolution one step further and put those customers on a subscription so they can walk away from us without a backward glance. The Customer Economy that we now live in is not a wave, it's a tsunami! And it's turning companies upside down. Every single organisation is being impacted and new ones are being created as we speak.

When it comes to describing the ultimate goal of any organisation today, I think Chris and Daniel have really nailed it in this book with the simple term **Customer Growth.** After all, the bottom line has to be the bottom line. No CEO or Board is going to agree to invest in something that doesn't drive either growth or profitability. If customers hold all of the power, as we claim they now do, then they also hold the keys to our growth and our success. Those running recurring revenue businesses today already know this because they see 50, 60, 70, and even 80% of their revenue coming from existing customers. This message can apply to non-recurring revenue models too. Getting this message out, alongside the practical advice on how to execute on it is critical, and that's why I'm proud and privileged to play a very small part in Chris and Daniel's bold vision for not just a book but a C-change to help organisations become customer-led in everything they do to drive sustainable growth.

Geoffrey Moore, author of 'Crossing the Chasm', states that customers today are the scarce commodity, not the product or service. If that's true, then we should be learning everything we can from the companies disrupting their industries by putting customers first. You'll get some of these inside stories about Starling Bank, Slack, Ritz Carlton, Signify, formerly Philips Lighting and many more in this book. In my opinion, it's critical that this book has not been written by academics sitting in their ivory tower but by those who have been in the trenches strategically and operationally dealing with this seismic shift. Some will ignore this massive business shift – but at their own peril. The fact that you are reading this says that you are not ignoring it but attempting to understand it. I commend you for taking this first step. So – embrace The **Customer Catalyst** spirit and apply the **C-change growth engine** to your organisation. I know it will pay you great dividends. Enjoy!

–Dan

INTRODUCTION

THE CUSTOMER ECONOMY

How do you define a successful business? Most business leaders would agree that *sustainable, profitable growth* has to be one of the most desirable achievements and characteristics of any commercial enterprise. In principle, that sounds simple, doesn't it?

Well, yes – but sustainable business growth is not a one-time effort, and does not happen by accident. It happens because the company creates market demand from customers and prospects and, most importantly, continues – time and time again – to satisfy the needs of its customers. Happy customers not only buy more, they also recommend the company. As a result, customers help accelerate growth. And all of this only really happens when the organisation *truly puts the customer at the heart of everything it does.*

The trouble is, even though most organisations talk a great game when it comes to putting the customer at the heart of their business, they frequently struggle to deliver on that promise. In this book, we will give CEOs, leaders and the whole the organisation the 'How to' with our 10-part C-change growth engine to help them accelerate business growth in the Customer Economy. A toolkit and collection of actions that companies can deploy, according to their own circumstances, is provided to help you achieve this.

Conversely, achieving sustainable profitable growth does not happen when the company pushes products or services at customers that, ultimately, deliver a poor *Customer Experience* (CX). We all have examples where we buy something, either online or in a shop, and it just fails to live up to expectations. We are less likely to buy that brand (or product) again, and we are unlikely to recommend it. In fact, we might go out of your way to unrecommend it because the experience was so poor.

Ironically, many organisations today like to talk about their commitment to corporate social responsibility. They do a great job recycling paper in the office, supporting local charities, maybe encouraging employees to volunteer for worthy causes, etc. All good, positive stuff and long may it continue. But since when did providing poor CX seem like a responsible or ethical business model? It appears the core purpose of business – to satisfy customer needs – somehow got lost in the myriad of other priorities.

So, why do companies talk a good game but struggle to deliver on it? Most companies are structured around functional and operational units, such as finance, sales, product and service. Moreover, the bigger the company gets, the deeper the divides between these siloes. As the gaps increase, it becomes harder to ensure that the business provides the best CX, and to ensure successful customer outcomes.

Employees love their siloes – these siloes give them a profession, a work, identity and even a meaning – for example, 'I'm in sales', 'I work in HR', 'I'm in Trade Finance', 'I cover the Benelux region', etc. People spend years building their careers, and underpinning them with academic and vocational qualifications, training and certifications that establish their credentials and experience. In short, it is an easier and more comfortable option for employees to fall back into their siloes.

But siloes are used by farmers to store grain, and are not great for organisations seeking to drive sustainable customer-led growth. In this book, we will show how we can break down organisational siloes and build customer-led organisations (see Figure I.1).

FIGURE I.1   Siloes are the enemy of customer-centric growth.

Source: Jeanne Bliss. Reproduced with permission

In previous decades, we lived in the product economy. This era was characterised by scant customer choice and customers who were generally more accepting and trusting of company product pitches. In effect, companies were all powerful and could almost pay mere lip service to their customers – at least for the short term.

In 1960, in his seminal paper titled 'Marketing Myopia', Theodore Levitt addressed this phenomenon and brilliantly exposed the fundamental imperative for organisations to become customer-led:

The entire corporation must be viewed as a customer-creating and customer-satisfying organism. Management must not think of itself as producing products but providing customer-creating value satisfactions. It must push this idea (and everything it means and requires) into every nook and cranny of the organization. It has to do this continually and with this kind of flair that excites and stimulates the people in it. Otherwise, the company will be a series of pigeon-holed parts with no consolidating purpose or sense of direction.

In 1974, Philip Kotler, the godfather of modern marketing, continued the same theme: 'All said, marketing is not a short-term selling effort but a long-term investment effort. When marketing is done well, it occurs before the company makes any product or enters any market; and it continues long after the sale'.

On a similar line, Kotler defined *marketing* as 'the science and art of exploring, creating and delivering value to satisfy the needs of a target market at a profit. Marketing identifies unfulfilled needs and desires. It defines, measures and quantifies the size of the identified market and the profit potential'.

In 1992, Don Peppers, a CX originator, commented: 'At many companies, it's easy to point fingers at the service people, or the salespeople, or the account handlers. Customer Experience is *their* job, it's not my job. But I think delivering a better Customer Experience should be considered everyone's job, and everyone needs to know something about what that means.' He argued that employees in product-centric companies are defined by their siloes, and those in customer-centric companies are defined by the CX they collectively provide (see Figure I.2).

Later in that decade, during an Apple all-hands employee meeting in the 1990s, Steve Jobs (see Figure I.3) was asked the following question by one of the company's software engineers: 'I would like for example for you to express in clear terms how, say, Java in any of its any of its incarnations addresses the ideas embodied in OpenDoc.' The employee was effectively asking

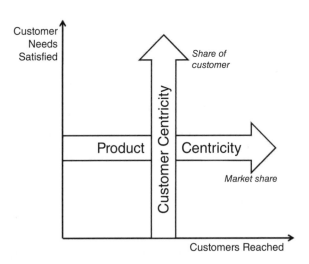

FIGURE I.2 Share of customer versus market share.

Source: Don Peppers. Reproduced with permission.

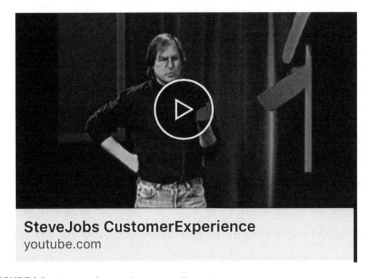

FIGURE I.3   Steve Jobs on Customer Experience.

Source: https://www.youtube.com/watch?v=r2O5qKZlI50. Accessed 18th June 2019. Screenshot by Chris Adlard & Daniel Bausor.

why a particular software development language (Java) was being favoured over another (OpenDoc) in the development of Apple products and services, and ultimately questioning the wisdom (and as most would agree, business genius) of Jobs.

Job's response was incredible in its empathy, clarity and customer-led insight:

One of the hardest things when you're trying to affect change is that people like this gentleman, are right – in some areas. I'm sure there are some things that OpenDoc does, probably even more than I'm not familiar with, that nothing else *out there does. And I'm sure that you can make some demos, maybe a small commercial app, that demonstrates those things. The hardest thing is, how does that fit in to a cohesive larger vision that's gonna allow you to sell $8bn dollars, $10bn dollars of product a year? And one of the things I've always found is that you've gotta start with the Customer Experience and work backwards to the technology. You can't start with the technology and try to figure out where you're gonna try to sell it. And I've made this mistake probably more times than anyone else in this room. And I've got the scar tissue to prove it. And I know that it's the case. And as we have tried to come up with a strategy and a vision for Apple, it started with what incredible benefits can we give to the customer, where can we take the customer. Not starting with, let's sit down with the engineers and figure what awesome technology we have and how we're gonna market that. And I think that's the right path to take.*

As we accept the reality of the Customer Economy, business leaders are now faced with two choices – either to ignore it and carry on regardless, or to embrace it and to think about the implications for their organisation in order to drive customer-led transformation and catalyse growth.

Successful companies of the future will not be organised by divisions and siloes but according to the journey the customer takes with them in the Customer Economy. Indeed, we are seeing this today with companies merging traditional business functions such as customer support and services into a single team such as 'Customer Success'.

As authors of this book, our goal is to help you in your efforts to transform your business to make it as customer-centric as possible, in order to catalyse growth. We have both worked in customer-related fields over the last 20 years. Our paths came together when we both gave speeches on customer-led growth at a 'Customer Centricity' conference at the British Library in London in 2016. We connected immediately with our shared enthusiasm for all things customer-related, which is what gave us the idea to write this book. We would read many customer-related books which have provided a range of perspectives on the topic, often complementary, sometimes contradictory, yet always with valuable insight.

We feel that a strategic, cohesive approach to reengineering the entire organisation around the customer is required. We will share with you from our own experience at the coalface of advising organisations on how to be customer-led. Join our call to arms to lead the mission to create a successful, sustainable, customer-led organisation. It starts here with our 10-part C-change growth engine which leaders across your organisation – from the CEO to managers and all employees – can relate to and implement. Do not think that you will read this and then will be able to deliver a quick fix overnight. Changing ingrained processes and functionally siloed activities to become dynamically centred around the customer requires culture change and an evolutionary approach to transformation. It takes time – however, what we give you is the vision and practical steps to lead the charge!

Practising what we preach in *The Customer Catalyst*, everything that has gone into developing this book is customer-led: from its title to our 10-part C-change growth engine. We wish to help you create a customer-led organisation and ultimately drive growth. Even choosing our title was an evolving process, having been co-created with business leaders and our publisher. This book is genuinely different. We hear you say – 'you would say that, wouldn't you?' But we proudly shout out that this is not a book to buy, use once and put on the shelf. This book serves to help you at all times during your ongoing customer-led business transformation. All too often, business books are thought provoking, but are marked by waning enthusiasm and therefore lack longevity. To drive real business transformation, there must be an evangelistic movement which is marked by a continual commitment to drive change. To help you do that, each chapter of this book tells a story from a different organisation, told by the organisations themselves, and not written in the third person.

We have been roving customer newshounds reaching out across the world to search for the greatest – and most *innovative* – organisations that are pioneering sustainable customer-led approaches. You will hear directly from these business leaders in the book, and then you can see their personal *Customer Catalyst* video stories online at our website: www.theCustomerCatalyst.com. If we are going to build customer-led organisations, it is important to share best practices. So, that is what we are going to do! Read on and join us on *The Customer Catalyst* journey.

GROWTH

When James Bond meets his new quartermaster (Q) for the first time (see Figure G.1), the conversation goes as follows:

'007, I'm your new quartermaster.'

'You must be *joking*!'

'Why, because I'm not wearing a lab coat?'

'Because you still have *spots*'!

'My complexion is hardly relevant.'

'Your competence is.'

FIGURE G.1   Bond meets new quartermaster.

Source: https://www.youtube.com/watch?v=57Uy9jPxxwI. Accessed 18th June 2019. Screenshot by Chris Adlard & Daniel Bausor.

'Age is no guarantee of efficiency.'

'And youth is no guarantee of innovation.'

'I'll hazard, I can do more damage on my laptop sitting in my pyjamas before my first cup of Earl Grey then you can do in a year in the field.'

'Oh, so why do you need me'?

'Every now and then a trigger has to be pulled.'

(Skyfall, 2012)

IT'S THE END OF SALES (AS WE KNOW IT)

Picture the scene: It is close to the end of the fiscal year, and the weekly forecast calls are now held daily. The CEO (Chief Executive Officer); CFO (Chief Financial Officer); CRO (Chief Revenue Officer) are on tenterhooks, waiting for those last few big deals to come in. On the daily sales call, Karsten from Germany explains with clarity and professionalism why Herr Doktor Professor Schmidt is unable to sign the final paperwork until the Works Council has given him approval for this (relatively modest) level of investment in new software. The head of sales is screaming neurotically at Karsten, demanding to speak with whoever it takes to clinch the deal. And so it goes on. The financial year is over, some deals made it over the line (thanks to financial or contractual wizardry, perhaps including some heavy discounts), but many did not materialise. The CEO, CFO and CRO sit around the table to look at the final numbers – they are not spectacular, but there is a good story in there somewhere. Good enough to convince the board, and the sales organisation at the company's upcoming annual kick-off, that things are going in the right direction.

Maybe, but it might not wash the next time around. None of this really resulted in substantial, progressive company growth – especially when the company considers some of the larger renewals that were lost during the year, which almost negated any new business. Maybe the company just achieved inflation-level turnover growth? So, the leadership retrenches, conducts some more navel-gazing and tries to come up with some immediate solutions to this apparently complex problem. Sales directors are replaced, sales executives move on, maybe the CEO gets the boot. Does this sound familiar? According to the Salesforce *State of Sales Report*, 57% of salespeople missed their quota in 2018. Think about your own company: what is the turnover of sales staff? In many companies today, it is not uncommon for salespeople to move on every 18–24 months.

So, what *is* the problem? Why is it so hard to *grow*? According to Lynn Hunsaker, Customer Experience (CX) expert, 'In most companies today, financials are a managerial context: every manager's decisions are shaped by the impact on their budget and bonus or the stock price'. This has an associated knock-on effect: An obsessive, internally-focussed, over-reliance on sales as the primary means of driving company growth, instead of a company-wide, cross-functional team effort, looking outwards and focused on the customer. It is the same root cause as the silo issue described in the introductory chapter.

Salespeople are expensive to recruit, cost a lot to train, demand high salaries and sizeable bonuses, and take time and incur even more cost to replace. Rarely do salespeople consistently meet their targets. Rarely are they incentivised to drive success-ful customer outcomes. And, in the exceptional cases where the sales executive *is* managing the customer relationship, the tendency is for them to throw customer issues over the fence to other departments inside their own company and to avoid those 'hard' customer conversations (unless, of course, not getting involved would be an impediment to closing upcoming new deals in the short-term). In short, the sales organisation (at least in its current format) is becoming less relevant to the growth of the company. It should instead be responsible for closing new deals, not for winning them. And, it should certainly not be constantly inspected as the sole source of company growth. In words similar to those of James Bond: Every now and then, a contract needs to be signed.

SUSTAINABLE GROWTH: DO NOT PLAY THE NUMBERS GAME

FIGURE G.2   Don't play the numbers game.

Source: Finnish Eurojackpot ticket, 2018 by Santeri Viinamäki. https://commons.wikimedia.org/wiki/File:Finnish_Eurojackpot_lottery_ticket_20180206.jpg. Licensed under CC BY-SA 4.0.

Although the product era is over, most businesses today still track their growth using the decades-old, top-down marketing funnel and sales pipeline model. The logic is quite simple. Marketing creates demand in the market for the company's product and services by generating leads through communication and awareness campaigns, and sales follows up by converting these leads into the sales pipeline. The sales teams then continue to progress this pipeline until (some of) it eventually turns into new sales, either from existing customers or new clients. One of the reasons for the popularity of this approach is its apparent simplicity. Indeed, good careers have been built on the back of analysing sales pipeline (and therefore company performance), slicing and dicing this information into a myriad of management reports. When it came to winning new customers in greenfield markets, this model held validity.

But in the Customer Economy of today, all this amounts to a primitive and short-term way of driving and measuring business growth. Why? Several reasons, in fact.

Let us start with the funnel – that is, marketing. The effectiveness of marketing today is typically measured using marketing automation platforms (such as Marketo, Hubspot, Eloqua, etc.). A marketing lead is essentially an individual who has some form of online or offline interaction with a company; for example, he or she has visited the company's booth at a trade show, downloaded a product or service brochure, viewed a company demo or downloaded a trial of a product. Marketing, like all functions, draws comfort from its own silo – by increasing the volume of leads it generates in order to prove campaign return-on-investment (ROI). Unfortunately, the leads are infrequently the type of customers who the sales teams are looking to target (e.g. wrong type of company size or customer profile, wrong demographic, etc.).

Even if marketing does improve on the quality of leads provided to sales, sales may argue (in many cases, legitimately) that most of the work qualifying the lead, or even bringing the lead to the company in the first place, had come via sales. There are, of course, examples where the marketing and sales alignment does work well – but that is usually based on strength of the relationship between people or teams, not due to perfect alignment in terms of shared goals or metrics.

On the sales side, success is measured in terms of opportunity pipeline and closed deals. Especially in the business-to-business (B2B) world, this is not about converting a single lead (i.e. individual person) into a new deal, but rather it is about convincing an ecosystem of customer stakeholders, over a period of time, to sign up to a new deal. Furthermore, most new deals are with existing customers anyway – we all know that it is generally easier to sell to existing clients than to prospects.

In short, the marketing funnel and sales pipeline are not seamlessly connected. They are merged awkwardly with fuzzy logic. Furthermore, in many cases, marketing leads are retrospectively associated with sales opportunities for the sole purpose of justifying marketing investment. An almost inordinate amount of time and money is spent by both marketing and sales running and staffing campaigns and events. This is in the hope that some may deliver the silver bullet that can move the needle in driving demand for the company's products and services. In reality, these campaigns and events do a good job of generating brand awareness and offering customers and prospects networking and relationship opportunities. However, they should not be endlessly analysed, line-by-line, as the principal source of revenue growth.

Neither should sales pipeline receive so much unnecessary attention as *the* source of company growth. Understanding and managing sales pipeline is important, even in the Customer Economy – because renewals and upselling go through a pipeline too. However, the majority of new sales fails to convert, whatever stage it appears in the CRM system.

A salesperson often feels as much pressure to progress the pipeline in the CRM system as he or she does in winning the business! All of this amounts to internally-focused metrics and behaviours which are unsuitable in the Customer Economy.

FIT FOR THE CUSTOMER ECONOMY: AN OUTSIDE-IN GROWTH MINDSET

Having considered the short-sightedness of over-reliance on sales for company growth, and the drawbacks of the funnel/pipeline model for measuring this demand generation, what can a company do differently to drive and measure growth?

As we put it in the introduction, we are now firmly in the Customer Economy. Customers are the real source of company growth, not sales! And customers are served by the whole company, and not by a single department in isolation – be it sales, services or any other function.

So, how does the company consider growth differently in view of this cross-functional imperative? The bottom line is that companies must embrace customer-centric thinking in everything they do. Clearly, this does not happen overnight, and it can be broken down into change programmes executed over many months, quarters and even years.

EVERY CUSTOMER-LED COMMUNITY CLAIMS TO HAVE THE SILVER BULLET

As we explored in the introduction, being customer-led is not a new concept. The difference today, however, is that being customer-centric is no longer an option – it is a necessity for survival and growth. And, as the principle of customer-centricity has existed for a long time, it has taken many forms, having been reinvented on many occasions to suit the zeitgeist. Same person, different attire. For example, when Levitt argued in the 1960s that the essence of marketing was all about satisfying the customer, the marketing purists would, in turn, claim the higher ground that sales was short-term and that marketing was all about building a sustainable business. Hence, today, marketing professionals and leaders still claim to be the ultimate customer champions within any organisation – even if they are viewed upon as a mere executor of product- and solution-led communication campaigns. And even, in the worst-case scenario, when marketers have very little customer interaction at all!

Later followed the CX movement, championed by the likes of Don Peppers, where the idea of satisfying customer needs rather than gaining market share for products and solutions became the 'new' mantra. Ultimately, this movement spawned today's huge global community of CX evangelists and experts, including the likes of Jeanne Bliss, Shep Hyken, Annette Franz, the Temkin Group, the CXPA, etc. Also, it gave rise to many voices in the customer communities and the net promoter system (NPS), pioneered by Fred Reichheld, Bain and Satmetrix. It also led to the seminal book by Kerry Bodine et al., titled *Outside-In*.

In addition to the CX community, there is also a sizeable contingent of Customer Advocacy professionals who champion the cause that a referenceable client base is key to company growth. Bill Lee, author and founder of the Centre for Customer Engagement, rightfully claims the moniker of 'Customer Advocacy & Engagement King', a concept which even now is being reinvented and repackaged by technology vendors such as Influitive who are looking to create a new market category under the theme of the 'Customer-Powered Enterprise'.

Finally, and most recently, is the Customer Success movement, created and championed by the Customer Success platform vendors – first and foremost Gainsight (whose COO wrote the book on Customer Success), but also its competitors such as Totango and consultancy organisations such as TSIA (the Technology Services Industry Association). The Customer Success movement is impressive, amassing thousands of Customer Success professionals at annual conferences in the United States, Europe and Asia. The majority of Customer Success professionals come from a technical support background but have been rebadged and repositioned as customer champions of many organisations, especially in the B2B technology/ SaaS world.

In reality, there is a significant overlap between all of these concepts, ideas and customer communities. By way of example, Annette Franz, CX thought leader, wrote an article in October 2018 to describe the difference between CX and Customer Success. She curated quotes from Customer Success thought leaders such as Gainsight and the Customer Success Association in an effort to compare and contrast the two disciplines. After dissecting the two concepts, she concluded as follows:

> It makes me question if the Customer Success role and discipline are really necessary. What do you think? Customer Experience is the umbrella. Get the experience right – listen to customers, understand the problems they are trying to solve, innovate, and design and deliver a better experience – and Customer Success management becomes obsolete, no? After all, it's all about the customer.

We have seen this before with the crossover between VoC (Voice of the Customer) and Customer Advocacy professionals. VoC teams state that the golden NPS question – likelihood to recommend – is their raison d'être. At the same time, the ultimate goal of Customer Advocacy professionals is to deliver a referenceable client base to advocate at every step of the customer journey. So, what is the difference?

The simple answer is that all of these communities present valid arguments and have important contributions to make when it comes to helping their company drive customer-led growth. Yet, no single community on its own has the silver bullet when it comes to achieving this. In truth, it is the combined set of activities that will help a company achieve its vision for customer-led growth. To coin a phrase, it is a war on all fronts. And, as we mentioned in the introduction, it is no longer a recommendation, it is a necessity. As CX leader Claire Sporton puts it, 'Investors now look for sustainable growth, not short-term wins each quarter. The M&A community are recognising that a commitment to customer centricity is a leading indicator of sustainable business growth.'

THE ANGORA RABBIT: WHY DO CUSTOMER-LED TRANSFORMATIONS OFTEN RUN OUT OF STEAM?

According to Sporton, 'The challenge is that no one would say that the customer is not important – just like the rabbit, everyone will give it a stroke. But when it comes to looking after it, people quickly get bored. And then the fox (the maniacal pursuit of short-term revenue gain) eats the rabbit' (see Figure G.3).

Sporton makes the key point that the pursuit of customer-centric growth needs to be deeply embedded in the organisation: 'There's no business growth unless people change their behaviours. 2-day change programmes don't work. Executive

FIGURE G.3 A White Satin Angora rabbit.

Source: White Satin Angora Rabbit, 2012, by Lanafactum https://commons .wikimedia.org/wiki/File:White_Satin_Angora_Rabbit.jpg. Licensed under CC BY-SA 3.0.

leadership must rigorously champion customer-centric values all the time, ensuring that actions are made, and impact is measured. CEOs must create sustainable, viral change'.

CX leader, Shep Hyken builds on this point 'One of the most important factors in driving growth is to establish a simple, clear and easy-to-remember customer vision statement. And then repeat it over and over again, so that everyone across the company knows it and applies it in their day-to-day activities. Leadership must set an example and constantly defend the culture. Whether it's training, workshops or simply leading by example, the customer vision must be continually re-enforced. Take, for example, Horst Schulze, the founder of Ritz-Carlton (see the Culture chapter). His customer vision statement was simple: 'We're ladies and gentlemen serving ladies and gentlemen.' This statement is still used today, and Ritz-Carlton remains one of the most successful hotel chains ever.

In summary, it is imperative that customer-centricity be hard-wired into the company's DNA, culture, operations, processes, products, systems, etc. – ideally, from day 1; but, if that is not possible, then starting tomorrow.

ARE YOU READY FOR A C-CHANGE?

How does a company robustly and comprehensively embark upon true customer-centric transformation? Here is our 10-part approach to driving customer-centric growth, in the form of the C-change growth engine (see Figure G.4).

The C-change growth engine

The C-change growth engine brings together many new and well-established approaches to customer-led growth. Collectively, this brings about the transformation that any private or public sector organisation needs to secure customer-led growth. While it is unlikely for any organisation to implement all of the C-change components from day 1, the more the organisation can invest energy and resources in this, the more it will see business transformation and growth over time.

FIGURE G.4 The C-change growth engine.

Source: Developed and owned by Chris Adlard and Daniel Bausor.

In the subsequent chapters of this book, we will take each of the C-change growth drivers in turn, providing further explanation and context, together with the latest, greatest and most innovative company case studies in each case. The Customer Catalyst case studies are different, in that they are personal stories from business leaders with honest views on failure as well as success. Also, it is important to note that all the components of this engine interrelate and are not standalone. Hence, we will also explore the interconnectedness of these components and their symbiotic benefits.

Also, we recognise that there are thousands of best-practice case studies which we will not have time or space to cover in this book. We would love to hear your ideas and examples and to showcase these in our Customer Catalyst community at www.thecustomercatalyst.com.

DELIVERING THE C-CHANGE: STRATEGIC ADVICE FROM THE EXPERT CONSULTANT

Rob Millar is Managing Director of Comotion, a leading consultancy specialising in helping organisations transition from having a product-led focus to becoming customer-led companies. His business works across industries to both advise companies on how to build sustainable growth and also to recruit C-level customer-executives to lead the change.

'When embarking on a C-change transformation', remarks Millar, 'the first, and most important, step is to ensure executive buy-in from the very beginning'. In short, every member of the C-suite needs to sign up – not just in principle, but in practice. Often, this process starts with immersion – getting the C-suite to walk in the shoes of their customers, where key VoC insights (see Chapter 1) are used to highlight the reality of what the client is actually saying. 'Ultimately, this is about resonance – if we get the leaders to buy-in to the importance of helping their customers, we will be taking the first step in embedding C-change into the culture of the business', adds Millar (see Chapter 2).

The immediate next steps after immersion are to map out the current- and ideal-state outside-in CX (see Chapter 3). Very quickly, the company can identify basic hygiene issues and draw up a list of quick wins (either at the functional level or across functions). The aim is to build momentum for the transformation by fixing some of these basic issues in order to drive bottom-line improvements and deliver a positive impact on CX.

As the organisation progresses along with its C-change transformation, it can truly start to deliver on its customer commitments. Very often, this means focusing on some of the more complex areas of transformation, meaning changes to technology and platforms (see Chapter 4) to deliver operational efficiencies and underpin process improvements. This can also involve changes to the digital experience – that is, what the end-users see when they interact digitally (see Chapter 5) and across channels to create holistic customer outcomes (see Chapter 6).

Millar continues: 'The steps above are essential to help organisations simply deliver on their existing promise to their customers. Once completed, the next stage is to help the client to differentiate themselves from their competitors'. This means identifying the two or three key things that it should do brilliantly in order to outcompete its competitors. Once identified, we focus on designing a service that provides a tailored and frictionless experience, often backed up by predictive analytics to proactively respond to changing demands around those moments of truth that really matter. Having a measure of Customer Health can provide a fundamental foundation in this process (see Chapter 7).

'Ultimately, the aim is to delight customers and make them successful', remarks Millar. With happy, healthy customer relationships, the client will engage more with the company's brand (see Chapter 8), even co-create with companies (see Chapter 9) and, ultimately, advocate for the organisation (see Chapter 10). 'Customers who advocate on behalf of a company are not only far less likely to churn, but – most significantly – become the best salespeople, and help the business to win new business and acquire new customers'. This is true, sustainable customer-led growth in action.

IS A GROWTH MEASUREMENT SYSTEM FIT FOR THE CUSTOMER ECONOMY?

The C-change growth engine provides an approach to customer-led growth that is fit for the Customer Economy. To measure its effectiveness, a company must develop a measurement system that befits it. Earlier in this chapter, we suggested that using the sales lens as the only measure of growth is short-sighted. More specifically, it is about concentrating on a set of customer-derived growth metrics that can unite a company's cross-functional leadership team, satisfy the CFO's demands and the board, and ultimately guide company functions accordingly. So, we will look at more suitable and effective means of measuring customer-led growth.

In a 2016 McKinsey article by Allen Miller, Ben Vonwiller and Peter Weed, the authors backed up the claim that net revenue retention is the single biggest indicator of likely company growth, especially for technology and SaaS companies. In short, a company with high net recurring revenue means that its existing customers are essentially less likely to defect when it comes to renewing their contracts with the organisation. Also, the net amount of money (i.e. total money less expenditure) brought in from its existing customer base is less likely to shrink, and might actually grow. Companies with a lower net revenue retention rate may try to balance out their losses by winning more new customers, but this is obviously a much harder battle to fight in the Customer Economy. Decades of business wisdom tell us that it is far more expensive to win new customers than it is to sell to your existing ones (as long as they are getting value, of course!). More and more industries work on a subscription basis, as defined by Tien Tzuo in the Subscription Economy; hence, this principle applies in both business-to-consumer (B2C) and B2B worlds.

From an investment perspective, the venture capitalist (VC) community is increasingly looking at net revenue retention as the single biggest indicator of company valuation. Workday and Box are examples of companies that have significantly outperformed other companies at the point of IPO or buy-out, or which have industry-leading net revenue retention rates.

At a macro-level, net revenue retention rates are great indicators of sustainable growth. At an operational level, there are many other ways in which customer-led growth can be measured, as detailed in Table G.1.

Jeanne Bliss, the author of *Chief Customer Officer* and *Chief Customer Officer 2.0*, introduces the idea of 'honoring customers as assets' in her five-step CCO business plan. She cites recent research which shows that, on the S&P 500 Index, 80% of companies listed between 1972 and 2013 were employing so-called 'older' business models where customers are primarily valued for their dollars – and not for their assets, insights and contributions. In other words, a customer is a lot more valuable than the money they bring into your organisation – even if net revenue retention is the key bottom-line performance indicator. Honouring a customer as an asset also means looking at customers' actual actions and their impacts on business growth or loss. This is in contrast to examining what they say they would do (e.g. in a survey) compared to, for example, the amount they spend with the business. In other words, actions speak louder than words.

In this book, we will consider many ways in which customers can positively influence the organisation, whether in the public or private sector, B2B or B2C. Ultimately (but – importantly – not exclusively), we will explore how customers can positively impact an organisation's growth. Later in the book, we will also examine Customer Health in more detail. It is possible to produce a Customer Health Index that measures an organisation's performance against a series of operational key performance indicators aligned to the customer journey. This is unlike the typically applied, inward-looking, set of metrics that consider performance only at a functional-level, which ultimately exacerbate siloed-based thinking.

A NEW BUSINESS FOCUS ON CUSTOMER-ORIENTED GROWTH MEASURES

Almost every company is looking to achieve profitable, sustainable growth. Table G.1 provides some examples of how growth can be measured from a customer-lens or an outside-in perspective (see the Experience chapter for a definition of this). All of these metrics should ultimately roll up to improvement, on both a quarterly and an annual basis, in terms of company revenue and profitability. Notice how none of these metrics focus on the total value or volume of new sales deals won, the primary measure often associated with company growth.

Instead, now everything should be articulated from the perspective of the customer, and not from the view of an individual department's performance. Since most organisations set out to keep the customer at the heart of everything they do, these measures of growth should, in theory at least, align much better with this aspiration.

Every organisation has lots of valuable untapped customer data that is simply not being analysed in the right way. It takes a customer-led mindset, organisational commitment and, sometimes, a lot of effort to establish these customer-oriented measures.

Imagine a different pipeline review call where a cross-functional team is reviewed on the overall health, success and advocacy of the customer, as well as the actual and potential growth of that client or account. Rather than endlessly reviewing individual sales peoples' performances, how about reviewing customer performance (see Table G.1)?

TABLE G.1 Examples of customer-led growth measures.

Customer-led growth measure	Notes and significance
Number of customers by customer type/segment	Everything starts with a solid understanding of the customer base. Many organisations struggle to even count the number of clients they do business with, let alone the characteristics that define them – for example, industry sector(s), size or locations/sites. This is especially true for medium to large B2B organisations that have often made multiple acquisitions. Therefore, they have many CRM or billing systems, or indeed conduct business through channel partners whose customer engagements are not tracked in a consistent way. Having an up-to-date customer list is the first step in achieving customer-led growth and could well warrant a full-time employee position at your organisation!
Average current value per customer	Once the customer list has been established, it is then important to understand the overall recurring revenue (usually annualised) of each customer, as well as the opportunities for growth (e.g. pipeline of new deals). It is also important to understand how this is trending over time to see if the commercial relationship is expanding or contracting. However, revenue metrics alone are not the only measure of customer value. Other more sophisticated measures are also key, such as the value of new business with other customers that the customer has influenced or helped win on the back of their positive referral – that is, their reference value.

TABLE G.1   (Continued)

Customer-led growth measure	Notes and significance
Lifetime value (LTV) per customer	A total of all revenue brought in so far from the customer, plus future committed revenues (bookings) and likely scope for growth. LTV is commonly used as a calculation (1/churn).
Cross-sell and upsell performance (e.g. number of products/ services per customer)	Once the list of clients is established, your portfolio of products, systems and services licensed and/or used by each customer can be plotted against this list. This allows you to perform a white space analysis and understand potential opportunities for growth.
Customer share of wallet (measured in both value and % of growth/ loss)	A comparison of annualised revenue against the client's total spending on comparable/competitor products, solutions and services. Industry analysts can often provide such customer spending data. Or, better still, listen to your customers, and they will probably tell you! This closely relates to the cross-sell and upsell performance discussed earlier.
Customer renewal rates	Increasingly, customers buy products and services on a renewal or subscription basis. Renewal rates, measured in both value and the corresponding % growth/loss or in value from the previous year(s), help organisations further segment their customer base and prioritise them according to their contribution to your business turnover. Many organisations today, for example, Gainsight, already have effective renewal programs in place for this very reason.

TABLE G.1   (Continued)

Customer-led growth measure	Notes and significance
Customer churn rates (measured in both % and growth/loss over time)	As described earlier, a company with low churn means that existing customers are essentially less likely to defect. Organisations may segment their business by geographical or industry sectors, or even product/system usage, to understand which clients are most likely to churn and the impact of this churn on the business.
Net revenue retention	As described earlier, this is one of the single biggest indicators of organisation growth. Companies that are able to retain and ideally grow the revenue from their existing customer base at the lowest possible cost are most likely to grow the fastest. There are many ways to calculate net revenue retention, and we will look to share examples on thecustomercatalyst.com over time.
Gross revenue retention	The gross revenue retention figure is a useful indicator of how much money is retained from a firm's customer base. But at what cost? If the cost to serve is too high, the net revenue retention rate is affected.
Voice of the Customer scores	Net promoter score (NPS) is an old favourite example that provides a quantitative measure of Customer Voice. It has some advantages, but is insufficient on its own as a measure of customer-led growth in the Customer Economy. NPS, like many VoC measures, can ultimately roll up into a Customer Health score.

nitless resources (be it finance, people, technology, etc.), makes sense for them to focus their efforts on their most luable customers – in terms of both current and future otential value.

ustomer segmentation takes many forms, be it industry focus, ompany size, region, cultural fit, etc. Hence, there are many ays to group a company's customer base – sometimes in unexected (albeit very effective) ways. For example, customers can grouped according to the amount of business they helped in as a reference. Often, the smallest revenue contributors are the forefront of co-creation and innovation and therefore t as a lighthouse account for other, often larger, clients eeding customer proof points to spend more money with e vendor.

et the data do the talking! The more relevant, accurate and tegrated your customer data becomes, the smarter decisions ur business can take when it comes to understanding here business focus and attention should be applied. In the ustomer Health chapter, we will examine ways to aggrete customer data to make even more intelligent, real-time d predictive assessments of where business focus should applied.

I

TABLE G.1 (Continued)

Customer-led growth measure	Notes and significance
Value of new and recurring business won and lost through references	This was touched upon earlier wh understanding the value per custo slightly different angle, organisatic and recurring business won thank references. Conversely, it is possib business lost due to the lack of ref or, worse case, negative client refe ultimately prevent deals being wo place.
Customer Health score	In a later chapter, we will explore (more detail. In short, it is possible number of different, varied and nc customer-centric measures into a client. In this way, it is possible to business through the lens of the c journey it takes with your compan

Source: Developed and owned by Chris Adlard and Daniel Ba

CUSTOMER SEGMENTATION AND BUSINESS F(

With a sound understanding of its client base can even get smarter in their growth efforts their customer base to better focus their effc a healthy balance sheet and keeping a good are just smart ways of doing business. Since

WHAT KIND OF BUSINESS RESULTS CAN TRULY CUSTOMER-CENTRIC COMPANIES EXPECT?

We will examine many of the world's most customer-centric companies throughout this book and the results they have achieved. By way of example, leading CX guru Shep Hyken wrote a recent article in *Forbes*, titled 'How to Outperform the Stock Market By 679%'. The main thrust of his argument was that companies that heavily invested in improving and simplifying CX would way outperform those who had not. 'If you invested in the DOW during the 10-year period from 2009 to 2018, your portfolio would have increased by 184%. If you invested in the S&P, your increase would have been 207%. But, if you had invested in the 10 companies ranked in Siegel+Gale's World's Simplest Brands report, you would have outperformed the average of the major indexes by a whopping 679%!'

Dave Jackson, ex-CEO of Clicktools (which was partially acquired by SurveyMonkey before being sold fully to Callidus-Cloud), recognised that cross-functional alignment around the customer journey was essential for growth. In his article 'Avoiding death by stovepipes', he stated that his annual recurring revenue increased by 180% and that his company saw a sevenfold average order value increase and much stronger referrals and advocacy.

CUSTOMER-LED GROWTH TRAILBLAZERS

No one organisation is doing it all right, that is, leading the way in every aspect of the C-change growth engine. However, there are a handful of organisations that have made huge strides in many of the 10 C-change growth drivers and have truly embodied the Customer Catalyst spirit. We mentioned Amazon and Apple in the introduction, the first companies to reach US$1 trillion in valuation/revenue. Microsoft has also joined the US$1 trillion club. While these companies are great examples of customer-led businesses, they are by no means perfect!

However, one company – Zoom – really stands out as a Customer Catalyst reference. Zoom is a San Jose–based web and video conferencing organisation headed by Eric S. Yuan, its CEO. Eric is an ex-Cisco WebEx engineering leader, and he founded Zoom with a simple and clear vision – to make customers happy. Zoom has grown at a phenomenal rate since its inception in 2011. As of June 2019, it boasts annual revenues of over US$330 million and counts over 2000 employees.

Eric is also the highest rated CEO on Glassdoor. This links really nicely to the cultural aspect of the C-change growth engine. Employees do not give CEOs high ratings because they are nice people or because they provide low-cost employee perks like free breakfasts and company SWAG. In fact, such perks can even appear insincere gimmicks and may even be counter-productive.

What really motivates employees? A sense of *authentic* purpose, clear direction and belonging. And what better way to do that? Tell them – and, most importantly, *show* them – that the leadership, and everyone below them in the hierarchy, lives and breathes putting customers truly at the heart of everything they do. Do not just put up aspirational posters claiming 'we put customers at the heart of everything we do'. It means *nothing* without the hard work and dedication of senior leadership and middle management to make it happen.

ZOOM: THE POSTER CHILD FOR CUSTOMER-LED SUSTAINABLE GROWTH

FIGURE G.5   Eric Yuan, CEO, Zoom.
Source: Zoom. Reproduced with permission.

On 18th April 2019, Zoom successfully launched its IPO and is now publicly trading on the NASDAQ, just 8 years after it was founded. Unlike most of today's unicorn public listings, Zoom had broken even for much the fiscal year prior to IPO. It also exceeded market expectations with an initial share price of US$36 at launch. If ever there was a single company that embodies the mantra of sustainable, customer-led growth, it would be Zoom. It has charted its own course by defining its own growth strategy that is completely based on the relentless pursuit of total customer (even user-level) satisfaction.

According to Dan Steinman, COO of Gainsight, 'Eric was very brave to start a company in a market already dominated by very large, successful companies (e.g. Cisco and Citrix). I can imagine that VCs would have questioned the need to create a new company in this space. It was Eric's relentless focus on the customer, not just the technology, that made Zoom's success possible'.

Zoom is a Customer Catalyst pioneer, having covered all 10 elements of the C-change growth engine. According to Yuan, 'I'd rather prioritize great Customer Experience over short-term sales performance. We focus always on existing customers first because our mission is to deliver customer happiness'.

The following are just a few examples of how Zoom is addressing each of the 10 elements of the C-change growth engine:

- *Voice*: Zoom is constantly asking customers for feedback – whether in the form of telephone conversations by CSMs, through the NPS survey (Zoom has achieved an incredible score of 72!) or as part of the beta programmes when it comes to releasing new functions and features. Right from the outset, to every customer not renewing their annual subscription, Zoom asks them their reasons for churning. Yuan would rather give the customer the product for free and, where required, fix any issues raised than lose the customer.

- *Culture*: Zoom takes culture and employee experience as seriously as the Customer Experience itself. Yuan instils a simple philosophy of 'making people happy' – regardless of whether they are employees or customers. The company ethos is all about delivering end-user customer satisfaction, which in itself is an incredibly powerful rallying call for all employees. 'All employees know that we live to serve the customer. Having a great product and a great Customer Success team is just a natural consequence of that'. Zoom works hard to ensure a transparent and positive culture where teams are highly motivated and focused on delivering a great end-user experience. Yuan goes on to say, 'I really appreciate negative employee feedback. Constructive, honest feedback is a rare thing in companies today – and it should be highly prized. It helps us grow and improve'.

- *Experience*: Yuan believes that companies should look at everything from an outside-in, customer perspective. For example, when building a product, development teams always look to ask the question whether the solution will deliver value to the customer. Zoom ensures that the experiences delivered to its customers are as slick and frictionless as possible to drive the best possible client outcomes.

- *Technology*: Zoom uses best-of-breed platforms for many aspects of its business, including a Customer Success platform, which facilitates joined-up cross-functional interaction with its customers. The Customer Success platform is central to both engagement and communication with its clients, and plays a key role in underpinning the digital experience.

- *Digital*: Since Zoom is a SaaS platform, its product is its digital experience. Anyone who has used the platform knows that it is far simpler than the traditional video conferencing systems. According to Yuan, 'It's not necessarily about adding lots of new features, it's much more important to keep things as simple and frictionless as possible for the end-user. For example, we spend a lot of time and effort minimizing the number of clicks or steps the customer has to go through to get the product to work well'.

- *Success*: Zoom has heavily invested in the Customer Success team to ensure that the customer is looked after throughout their journey with Zoom. The CSM team have no sales target and are missioned purely on retention, renewals and customer satisfaction. Yuan points out, 'The customer knows when you're just trying to sell them something'.

- *Health*: Zoom has developed a Customer Health scoring system in its Customer Success platform to keep a real-time check on customer issues, red flags, customer satisfaction and to help CSMs manage and streamline the regular interaction with clients throughout their journey with Zoom.

- *Engagement*: Zoom deploys a number of customer engagement programmes, including their annual conference Zoomtopia (see https://blog.zoom.us/wordpress/2019/04/24/announcing-zoomtopia-2019/), as well as training, webinars and events. They have also established several user groups and advisory boards, all of which form part of their co-creation strategy.

- *Co-creation*: With its growing technology partner ecosystem, it has developed integrations between its own platform and a broad spectrum of industry-leading communication devices, such as Polycom, Logitech and Yealink, and third-party software providers. Zoom has also recently launched its App marketplace, a single place to obtain third-party software applications that make use of Zoom's software development kit and open APIs. Finally, Zoom product development teams also work closely with customers to co-innovate new features and functionality. According to Yuan, 'We only ever turn products from beta to production when we have enough clients that have given the thumbs up'. In other words, Zoom depends on its clients to help innovate, test and release new features.

- *Advocacy*: Yuan recognises that his best salespeople are happy customers. Zoom has built an impressive estate of client advocates (see https://zoom.us/customer/all for some examples). 'Happy customers means lots of recommendations and more new clients', concludes Yuan.

In summary, Zoom is not only the poster child for incredible business performance but also a near-perfect example of customer-led growth, and a company that has truly embodied the Customer Catalyst spirit.

Now that we have provided an overview of the C-change growth engine, we invite you to explore each of the C-change components in turn and to catalyse the transformation of your organisation to a state of customer-led growth.

CHAPTER 1

VOICE

Keep your fingers on the customer's pulse and react accordingly

C-CHANGE GROWTH DRIVERS

- **Organisations should put in place a Voice of the Customer (VoC) programme** to find out what their customers really think about their brand, products and services. This is often the starting point when it comes to driving customer-led growth.

- **Embed your VoC programme into your company's culture.** The VoC programme is not a one-off, single-strand activity. Instead, it should be considered as a continuous customer listening channel. VoC programmes take on board feedback from multiple data and knowledge sources, multiple customer segment groups and personas, and across many regions (national or international).
- **Companies should avoid the classic VoC pitfalls** – for example, by only running a net promoter system (NPS) survey once a year and calling it 'VoC' or just doing it to tick the box of listening to customers. This can produce completely skewed results. Often in such a scenario, the NPS survey delivers invalid responses that ultimately lead to, or simply just validate, poor business decisions. Instead, the VoC programme should be authentic and probe for deeper meaning and root causes.
- **Create an outcome-oriented VoC team**. Once the continuous customer listening channel has been firmly established, organisations should be prepared to drive actions and improvements on a regular and constant business. Some improvements can be executed quickly and have an immediate positive impact on Customer Experience (CX). Other changes are cross-functional and more medium term – nevertheless, they must be planned and actioned over time.

'We have two ears and one mouth so that we can listen twice as much as we speak'.

– Epictetus

'Most people do not listen with the intent to understand, they listen with the intent to reply'.

– Stephen R. Covey

'What good is it, my brothers and sisters, if someone claims to have faith but has no deeds?'

– James 2: 14, NIV

THE ULTIMATE GOAL: A CULTURE OF CONTINUOUS CUSTOMER FEEDBACK AND APPROPRIATE ACTION

It is often said that the key to a successful marriage, a successful business partnership, or indeed any successful work relationship, is communication. And how many times have we heard employee feedback saying, 'we need to communicate better'? It is like a broken record. The key point is that successful communication generally entails two-way dialogue between interlocutors and comprises both verbal and non-verbal forms. The value of listening cannot be overemphasised. Many companies spend so much time and effort telling the world about themselves that they forget how important it is to listen to their customers and, most importantly, to act upon it. However, there are caveats to this concept. First, companies should listen to their customers in the right way – that is, with the intent to both truly understand (and not to gloss over or trivialise) the customer's feedback and to correctly represent it when articulating the consequent actions. Second, everything the customer says should be acknowledged, but not necessarily acted upon. It really depends on who you ask in the customer's organisation, when you ask the person and how you ask it. Hence, it is important to discern and prioritise feedback from customers. Finally, listening to customers should be an integral part of the culture of any organisation. Customer feedback, from any relevant source, should be constantly digested, prioritised and turned into appropriate actions.

Although the C-change growth engine does not prescribe addressing each component in a sequential, step-by-step fashion, one could argue that all good decisions start by listening to what the customer says, and acting accordingly. This is a good, old-fashioned principle that has always helped great companies deliver on their promise of retaining, delighting and growing their customer base. When Finastra, one of the world's largest fintechs, launched its award-winning customer engagement programme, 'Finastra Connect', it analysed customer feedback from a plethora of sources to bucket customers' concerns into key areas of company improvement. All of the improvement areas could be addressed by involving its customers in the Finastra Connect programme offerings.

CX leader Claire Sporton sums up the value of VoC information as follows: 'The Voice of the Customer is core to customer experience efforts and one of the best sources of business intelligence. However, it cannot be the only voice. Employees, suppliers, partners and others all have important perspectives on the experience you offer. Also, other data from, for example, operational and financial sources add colour and context.'

This last point links in very well to the other aspects of the C-change growth engine – in other words, VoC is an essential part of driving transformation in the Customer Economy. It becomes potent when combined with intelligence from other sources such as employees (see the Culture chapter) and operational data (see the Technology and Success chapters).

WHAT IS VOC?

The VoC C-change driver is the essential fuel to power all customer-led decisions of a company. Also, it helps inform the company culture and employee experience. We all know that happy employees mean happy customers, but customer feedback is key to understanding what the problems and issues are in the first place.

According to Confirmit, the VoC and CX platform provider: 'Voice of the Customer refers to the way an organisation collects customer feedback, analyzes the data, distributes it to the right people and takes action on these insights in order to generate financial benefits. Voice of the Customer programmes aim to gather and analyse customer insights, and enable you to take action in order to improve customer experience and deliver positive business outcomes to your organisation.'

The insights–actions–results flow is a clear and simple way of understanding the principle of VoC. Jeanne Bliss, author of the *Chief Customer Officer* book series, builds on this theme in the chapter 'Build a Customer Listening Path'. She suggests that customer feedback comes from multiple sources, throughout the customer journey.

A FREQUENT REALITY: AN ANNUAL NET PROMOTER SYSTEM (NPS) SURVEY THAT MERELY TICKS THE 'CUSTOMER FEEDBACK' BOX

When Fred Reichheld, Satmetrix and Bain launched the NPS in 2003, it quickly became the industry standard tool for measuring customer satisfaction and customer feedback. Today, NPS is deployed universally, in some shape or form, across all industries, and often, is heralded as proof that the company is indeed listening to the voice of its customers. However, rarely are companies using NPS as it was intended. For example, organisations may celebrate their high NPS scores or score improvements without truly understanding what the scores mean. Alternatively, they might solely rely on the 'Ultimate Question', that is, 'what is your likelihood to recommend?' as sufficient, without any attempt to understand the true meaning or context behind the customer scores. They might even be summarising customer feedback from the limited (often statistically insignificant) subset of customer contacts that bothered to respond to the survey. Worse case, no actions are taken as a result of customer feedback, or the wrong decisions are made.

The debate still rages on today – is NPS really fit for purpose in the Customer Economy? Suffice it to say, NPS only receives the level of attention it does because there is no other measure of customer satisfaction that is as universally accepted across all industry sectors and geographies. Also, NPS is easy to calculate by simply subtracting the percentage of Detractors from the percentage of Promoters (those who rate 0–6 from those who rate 9–10). Companies with an NPS score of 0 or less generally need improvement; scores between 0 and 30 are good, with some room for improvement, scores between 30 and 70 are great; and anything over 70 is outstanding.

NPS data can be useful, for example, when looking at customer satisfaction trends over time, or even when comparing one company's NPS scores against its competitors. However, it is highly subjective, and can be very time sensitive (e.g. people are much happier with their laptop when it works than when it breaks down). Also, in the worst case, NPS can be easily gamed by internal teams (e.g. sales), especially when their bonus depends on it! In summary, NPS is still alive and kicking today, even if it has serious flaws, and there are many other measurement system alternatives out there – for example, customer effort scores, customer lifetime value scores or the goodwill index created by Olaf Hermans. Also, we will consider other approaches in the Customer Health chapter.

Furthermore, companies will sometimes overload customer satisfaction questions with too many (often poorly considered) questions. The aim of the questionnaire may not even be to find out what the customer is saying, but instead to prove a point. Even if the hypothesis is not immediately proven, there is a temptation to skew the data to achieve the goal. According to leading CX expert Steven Walden, 'Don't think that if you torture data like this, it will eventually squeal'. Walden continues, 'It is far more important to look at causality, narrative and context behind the data than the numbers themselves'.

At the Customer Catalyst, we believe NPS has validity, but only as just one of many VoC components. It should never be used on its own and in isolation from other VoC sources.

THE BENEFITS OF A MULTIFACETED, REAL-TIME VOC PROGRAMME

By continuously listening to customer feedback across the entire customer lifecycle in real-time, from multiple qualitative and quantitative sources, it is possible to build up a much broader and richer understanding of customer needs. In addition, continuous customer feedback enables you to better consider your business from an outside-in perspective and to break down and ultimately remove instances of functionally siloed, myopic business decisions. This, in turn, helps improve both the customer and employee experience, which helps the company achieve growth in the Customer Economy.

At the highest level, listening continuously to customer feedback helps an organisation understand and segment their customers better. It helps to identify 'at-risk clients', define necessary action plans, and uncover cross-sell and upsell approaches. Ultimately, listening continuously to customer feedback decreases the cost to serve (e.g. C-suite spending time reactively dealing with issues that could have been proactively dealt with much sooner).

Furthermore, when you consider the sub-components of the C-change growth engine, an effective VoC programme will be beneficial in all areas. The following are just some examples (see Table 1.1).

TABLE 1.1   How can an effective VoC programme help drive customer-centric growth?

C-change growth driver	How can an effective VoC programme help?
Culture	Feedback from customers (both positive and negative) can motivate and clarify employees' actions and understanding of their respective roles. It gives them customer-based evidence to empower them and re-enforce a customer-led culture. Above all, VoC can serve as the ultimate rallying call to help employees better understand their roles in the growth of the organisation.
Customer Experience (CX)	By listening to customers (e.g. at customer workshops and feedback groups), it is possible to map out their typical customer journeys from an external customer perspective and to understand where things are working, and where things could be improved. Such sessions can be hugely revealing and very powerful in terms of driving cross-functional change programmes. This approach also helps understand customers better to segment different customer types and their respective journeys.
Technology	Most companies use a plethora of technology platforms – both back-end and front-end systems – to serve their customers. One of the client's frustrations, especially in B2B, but also in B2C, involves having to deal with different systems and processes depending on which part of your organisation the customer is interacting with. VoC feedback helps companies understand where these inconsistencies are occurring.

TABLE 1.1 (Continued)

C-change growth driver	How can an effective VoC programme help?
Digital	Building a frictionless digital user experience, or even a product that makes life as simple as possible for the customer, will help reduce costs, and drive customer satisfaction and growth. Zoom Video Communications lives and breathes this mantra. Not only does Zoom use innovation in the VoC channels (see the following example), but also funnels customer feedback quickly into the design of its user experience.
Success	Customer Success Managers (CSMs) represent one of the fastest growing roles on LinkedIn today. They live to serve the customer and act as the cross-functional facilitator across the organisation. Not only can CSMs gather their own real-time VoC information but they can also help to collate VoC information from other sources to better understand how the company can retain and grow their customer base.
Health	An effective VoC programme will help define the customer journey and ideal CX. Also, VoC will help select the most critical operational metrics that form part of a Customer Health scoring system. Ultimately, the Customer Health score will minimise the need to constantly survey customers as it becomes easier to predict customer behaviours.

(Continued)

TABLE 1.1   (Continued)

C-change growth driver	How can an effective VoC programme help?
Engagement	The Finastra Connect programme, cited earlier, is an example where value-added engagement programmes were developed and launched in direct response to Customer Voice. In other words, by actively listening to customers, new and more effective ways of engaging with them can be achieved.
Co-creation	Effective VoC provides evidence to open up opportunities to co-develop new product and service offerings with the customer.
Advocacy	Customer feedback can uncover, often immediately, hitherto undiscovered satisfied customers who are keen to promote the companies they buy from. They are no longer just users of a company's products and services – they are advocates and fans! Arguably the best form of advertising a company could ask for.

Source: Developed and owned by Chris Adlard and Daniel Bausor.

BEWARE OF THE COMMON VOC PITFALLS!

Richard Owen, former CEO of Satmetrix (the co-originator of NPS) and CEO of OWEN CX, has helped hundreds of customers to successfully transform their business with industry-leading VoC and CX programmes.

Richard believes that VoC is often misunderstood, and that companies commonly consider VoC to only mean taking direct periodic feedback from (often a handful) of customers to improve the perceived quality of its products or services. Such initiatives do not always help an organisation decide how to change the business, even if they might help turn around the CX in places. For example, an annual NPS survey on its own will not provide anything like the depth and breadth of insight required to make smart business decisions.

According to Richard, 'Poor VoC data is far worse than no data'. Richard cites other two other measurement sources of VoC information – operational data (which will be covered in the Customer Health chapter) and employee data (which we will be covered in the Culture chapter).

Also, Richard shares another word of caution. Customers and employees do not always give rational feedback when completing surveys. Surveys can sometimes contain hundreds of cognitive biases. Just because a customer rates himself or herself as a '6' on an NPS survey does not mean that they are not a promoter or advocate of the organisation. Such surveys give us one data point that, when compared to the results of the same survey conducted later, might give us just a small fraction of insight into VoC.

The bottom line, according to Richard, is that, when analysing VoC data and information from a multitude of sources (whether quantitative and qualitative), it is essential to be able to discern noise from signal. Trends are harder to find than anecdotes, but far more important to identify. The skill of the VoC leader lies in extracting the most meaningful, important issues for customers and translating them into actionable programmes of change for the organisation. Some changes are described as 'quick wins' and 'low-hanging fruit'. Others will represent more fundamental, medium–long-term cross-functional change programmes. Either way, if a company wants to succeed in the Customer Economy, its VoC programme should form important bedrock of all its customer-led growth initiatives.

SOURCES OF VOC INFORMATION

Table 1.1 lists out some examples of VoC data. A simple audit of a company's VoC sources, such as this, will help a company understand what information is being gathered and where gaps may exist.

TABLE 1.1 VoC information sources

VoC information source	Description/notes
Weekly/quarterly/ annual business reviews	In B2B especially, customers are providing feedback all the time, in both structured and unstructured ways, to account managers and indeed other functional representatives (professional services, customer support, Customer Success, product management, etc.). Sometimes the information is documented by e-mail, sometimes in knowledge systems, but often it remains in the heads of those people that spoke to the customer. Although this feedback is subjective, it will give some unique and actionable insights, especially when gathered from multiple people in the organisation and the client.
Customer workshops/ focus groups/user groups/customer advisory boards	Giving customers the opportunity to interact with their peers and share their experiences is also an invaluable source of feedback. It can help companies prioritise and democratise important product roadmap and business decisions. Note that companies must be careful not to action everything on the customer wish list but instead prioritise actions that have a win-win benefit. The other key benefit of customer workshops is to map out customer journeys and experiences. This helps you to understand the moments of truth and areas of improvements and to define the outside-in customer journey.

(Continued)

TABLE 1.1 (Continued)

VoC information source	Description/notes
Online customer communities	A similar principle as in the preceding text. The great benefit of online community feedback, however, is that it does not need to be gamed or initiated by the vendor. It is entirely unforced and can be incredibly revealing about a customer's true wishes and intentions.
Executive meetings	In B2B, most company executives like to spend time meeting with their executive counterparts at the customer. Under pressure to drive short-term revenue growth, CxOs prefer the positive meetings that could lead to the prosecution of new business. However, the reality is often the opposite. CxOs are instead frequently brought into customer escalations. In the honeymoon period of new customer relationships or new projects, CEOs will willingly hand out their business cards and offer a 'hotline' to customers in case there are any questions or concerns. This can come back to haunt them. Due to the functionally siloed inside-view of many organisations, the client is left with no option but to escalate to the CEO if things go awry. If the organisation was more

TABLE 1.1 (Continued)

VoC information source	Description/notes
	operationally proactive in its cross-functional client engagement up front, the CEO could spend more time on strategic, constructive client conversations. Either way, the CEO becomes an important source of Customer Voice, and this feedback should be shared with the cross-functional team that is responsible for the ongoing health and satisfaction of the client.
Annual/periodic survey (e.g. NPS)	E-mail surveys are regularly sent out in both B2B and B2C environments. Response rates are generally dropping and customers quickly lose interest if they do not believe a company will respond to or drive consequent actions from their feedback. Surveys are rarely tested with focus groups before being sent out en masse, and responses may be glib at best. That all said, NPS does allow for some trending analysis over time. Also, NPS may, in some cases, give some insight into whether a company is making improvements or not. However, a company that relies on periodic customer surveys (e.g. NPS) does not have a fit-for-purpose VoC programme in place.

(Continued)

TABLE 1.1 (Continued)

VoC information source	Description/notes
Telephone/support surveys on the fly	Sometimes we are asked to complete short telephone surveys post a call centre transaction, or the technical support team might ask for feedback from the customer. Time-sensitive, in-the-moment feedback can be useful, provided it is considered in context with other VoC sources. Customers will generally rate highly when their immediate issues are quickly resolved. When issues are unresolved, it is important to understand the narrative of bad experiences. This may provide very meaningful information about where cross-functional client interactions are not working well (this often relates to billing and invoicing issues).
Social media commentary	Many companies use social media as just another channel of outbound communication. Conversely, companies that are constantly interacting with their customer base have adopted the right spirit, sometimes to help customers, sometimes out of necessity. Examples include travel companies such as airlines and train operators. While much of the client feedback through social channels creates a lot of noise and unspecific or uncoordinated 'panic button' complaints, some key insights can be derived.

TABLE 1.1 (Continued)

VoC information source	Description/notes
Complaints – e-mail, telephone, web	Listening to customer complaints and resolving them quickly is often the key to turning unhappy customers into loyal advocates. A deeply unhappy customer can often present the greatest opportunity for positive cross-functional change.
Paper (e.g. event feedback forms)	When feedback is provided on paper, it should always be digitised and included in the VoC mix. Similarly, insight from surveys and complaint forms should be digitised too.
Website enquiries/feedback	Website enquiries and feedback forms tend to be more transactional in nature. Nevertheless, if your organisation offers this channel via the web, it should at least respond to customer feedback.
Call centre recordings	Call centre feedback should be considered from the perspective of content, duration and sentiment analysis (e.g. tone of voice, vocabulary). The cost of serving unhappy customers is also an important operational metric when considering the need to invest in more proactive ways to predict and resolve issues before they surface.
Employee feedback	In the Culture chapter, we will consider ways in which employee feedback – either about internal ways of working, culture or feedback about customers – can be leveraged to better understand VoC.

(Continued)

TABLE 1.1 (Continued)

VoC information source	Description/notes
Operational data	Given the general survey fatigue that exists today, companies are increasingly turning to more data-based solutions in order to truly understand VoC and to predict customer behaviours and actions. We will cover this in more detail in the Customer Health chapter.

Source: Developed and owned by Chris Adlard and Daniel Bausor.

BRINGING IT ALL TOGETHER – HOW TO MANAGE THIS VOC KNOWLEDGE?

Many companies rely on annual customer surveys because they are relatively easy to execute. In simple terms, gathering and collating the customer responses and feedback can be executed by building an e-mail distribution list, creating a questionnaire through a survey tool and sending it out. When organisations look to gather VoC feedback from across the entire customer life-cycle from multiple customer stakeholders, some of the toughest challenges include identifying the sources; collating the data; normalising the findings and then packaging up the information into a meaningful report to drive appropriate action.

Hence, a successful VoC programme is as much about knowledge management as it is about asking customers for their opinions. The most important issue is that companies employ someone who (either alone or supported by a team) is responsible for managing VoC knowledge and turning it into a strategic, operational and tactical plan that both the C-suite and middle management can work towards.

HOW ZOOM LEVERAGED VOC WITH HELP FROM THE ANALYST COMMUNITY

As covered in the Growth chapter, Zoom is a great example of a successful organisation in the Customer Economy. Its mission to 'make users happy' has not just manifested itself in terms of product and user experience design, but also in the way it constantly solicits feedback from its customers and acts upon it. This, in turn, feeds back into product/user design, thus creating a virtuous circle of customer-centric growth.

Zoom deploys many imaginative ways to gather VoC feedback. One such way is how it partners with industry analyst firms who are also keen to talk to the end users of companies to make accurate market assessments about them. When you compare this to other organisations who struggle time and time again to find enough customers who are willing to advocate on their behalf, it is quite refreshing to see how Zoom has completely turned this issue on its head.

In November 2018, Zoom partnered with leading analyst firm Gartner on its peer insights review programme. It generated 2,456 user ratings from its customer base – an impressive achievement! It received an average feedback score of over 4.7 out of 5, which is extremely high for a technology/software organisation.

Some of the user feedback shared in Zoom's 2018 press release:

'The implementation and training process with Zoom was top-notch. We were able to switch all of our sales team out in 2 days.'

– Services Industry

'Zoom has allowed us to do more with less expenditure. All of the promises the sales team made work. Our students can individually join class sessions or join in a classroom with our equipment. I highly recommend Zoom'.

– Education Industry

'The interface is designed in a very simple way, even for a new user. The cloud version of the product is remarkable in terms of performance and reachability. The new generation is one of the most preferred meeting applications'.

– Manufacturing Industry

CASE STUDY: CLOSE BROTHERS TRANSFORMS CULTURE AND DRIVES BUSINESS PERFORMANCE WITH A BEST-IN-CLASS VOC

'Driving a great customer experience is like regulation; you just need to do it'.

– Martyn Atkinson, Group COO

Close Brothers is a leading UK merchant bank that provides lending, savings, trading and wealth management to businesses and individuals across the UK. Within the banking division, there are five distinct lending businesses, with a broad cross-section of customer types and many regional offices across the UK. With a strong foundation in the corporate values of service, expertise and relationships, and a relentless customer focus, it has achieved impressive growth, even during and following the financial crisis of 2008.

The CX team, led by CX leader Danielle Croucher (see Figure 1.1) and Chief Customer Officer Ian Hunt, is the embodiment of the company's cultural values and raison d'être. During the near-3-year tenure, the CX team have systematically and robustly engineered an ongoing transformation to help it in its quest to become one of the most customer-focused businesses in the UK financial services industry.

FIGURE 1.1 Danielle Croucher, CX Lead at Close Brothers.

Source: Danielle Croucher. Reproduced with permission.

The VoC programme at Close Brothers provides a good example of how to turn valuable, meaningful customer insights into real actions and tangible business results. According to Croucher, 'It's all about listening to customers' feedback, particularly at the moments of truth across their respective customer journeys with the company'. Croucher emphasises the need to go deep at these moments, looking at rich data and information from multiple VoC sources, to understand the customers' pain points, emotions and opportunities in each case.

For Close Brothers, rich feedback means looking at VoC information from a variety of sources – surveys, conversational SMS and journey analytics, sales conversations, ethnographic research, contextual interviews, etc. 'All of the VoC information we use is from primary research', adds Croucher. Her team deploys a user-centred design approach to the VoC programme, which comprises four stages: LISTEN – ANALYSE – ACT – MONITOR. Croucher continues: 'We added the monitoring element to this model because we recognised the importance of dashboarding and management reporting for leaders across the business. Ultimately, we need to keep things as simple and clear as possible for executives to ensure they understand and can act upon any recommended changes'.

The CX team first looks at research from both employees and customers – either anecdotal, observational or from interviews. It then carries out design thinking workshops – either over a period of weeks or in a shorter 5-day sprint window. Post work-shops, it provides a VoC information pack to both executives and other business leaders about the as-is insights and pain points. Also, deliverables include strategic recommendations, to-be journeys or service blueprints, customer segmentation models and personas. And every quarter, a VoC summary is provided to the group board. 'I want our business decisions to be based on customer feedback', remarks Croucher.

Driving customer-led change is, of course, challenging for any company. Close Brothers is fortunate to possess leaders who believe, with conviction, that a truly customer-led company is the most successful business. However, how does a company prioritise VoC-initiated change-requests (relating, e.g., to processes, systems or solutions) above other (predominantly functionally siloed) change programmes? At Close Brothers, as with most companies today, this tension continues. Even investment decisions around, for example, new VoC platforms are not made overnight. Croucher responds to this concern with clarity and confidence: 'In the end, every employee is a part of the customer-value chain. Every decision we take, and every investment we make, all leads back to improving the customer experience in order to drive growth'. Hence, it is not a matter of if, but when.

That all said, Croucher and her team have achieved a remarkable feat, having delivered a consistent and effective VoC operational framework that is universally discussed and respected across the company's businesses. Croucher adds, 'The framework provides the flexibility needed to understand and address both the huge variety and segmentation of customers across all business units, with an operational robustness that befits the professionalism and effectiveness of the CX team'.

The team now enjoys even greater executive commitment, as indicated in the COO quote earlier. The customer has always been in the company's DNA, but the CX team and their VoC programme continue to evolve Close Brothers' maturity, winning the hearts and minds of both executives and employees as they go.

A successful VoC programme, such as the one ran by Close Brothers, is the cornerstone of strategic and operational customer-led transformation. It should be continuous, multifaceted and multi-persona. Ultimately, it should drive actions at all levels across the organisation and should continuously monitor and track organisation performance against its customer vision and objectives. It forms a critical part of the C-change growth engine.

CHAPTER 2

CULTURE

Creating a cultural C-change

C-CHANGE GROWTH DRIVERS

- **The successful organisations in the Customer Economy will not be wedded to the rigid, traditional organisational functions and structures.** These functional boundaries will blur and be guided by a set of C-change growth drivers, aligning the business to an external customer perspective and helping it to meet agile customer needs. This is in contrast to fixed siloes, divisions and business rules of the post–Industrial Age organisations that are becoming less relevant.

- **Chief executive officers (CEOs) and senior leadership need to transform their organisations' cultures with *all* employees being responsible for the customer** and not just domination by the sales function. Cross-functional, customer-defined roles – such as CSMs (Customer Success Managers) will become more relevant. This will demystify false perceptions and erode fear of the customer by employees, which is holding back customer-led growth.

- **Ultimately, every organisation should appoint a chief customer officer (CCO).** Human resources (HR), under the guidance of the CCO, should lead 'C-change' cross-functional working groups to drive customer-led transformation. At the customer or account level, it is important to establish agile, cross-functional, customer-led teams to meet the customer-led mission, values and business objectives of the organisation. Often, these teams are led by new roles such as the CSM.

- **To help instil a customer-led culture, the CEO and CCO must establish a customer vision statement and rigorously promote it at all times.** The single biggest motivator of staff is arguably an unequivocally clear and simple, customer-led rallying call and direction that employees can relate to.

- **Every employee should ultimately understand and be measured on his or her role in fulfilling the customer vision**, and their actions should either directly or indirectly align to improvements in the customer experience (CX). Individual employees' key performance indicators (KPIs) should be linked to Customer Health scores.

In the product and sales era, sales became the primary custodian of the client relationship. Typically, this has happened (in B2B companies at least) because the customer asked for a single point of contact – especially at more senior-level engagements. This, in turn, led to an implicit hierarchy around the customer, where other functions effectively became subservient to sales. Often, this has led to an internally focused culture which is based on a lack of understanding of who the customer is, how to market to them and how to satisfy their needs. For some departments, perhaps the more back-office functions (sometimes even marketing!), the view of the customer is almost akin to the Wizard of Oz (standing behind the curtain in the legendary film) who is all powerful. Yet, once the curtain is drawn back, he is just a human being. Our point here is that customers are human and want to interact with human brands whose values are customer-led. Customers should be understood by the whole organisation, and not just viewed through the single lens of sales. The benefit of this approach is a better insight and understanding of the customer's needs by the workforce as a whole. This leads to a 'C-change', that is, a customer-led transformation for what we term as a stronger 'C' *(customer-led) culture* and holistic CX.

CEOs and their organisations must lead a 'C-change' to remove the cultural fear of the customer which is holding back sustainable, customer-led growth. The whole organisation needs to be part of a '*total customer-led experience*' to match the new blurred lines of who the customer is. Today's customer can be a myriad of personas: They will interact with a number of the company's employees, partners and suppliers whom collectively make up CX and as such, present the brand of the organisation. However, the organisation's own siloes stubbornly persist and prevent a more joined-up, cross-functional CX. In this chapter, we give practical steps to transform to a customer-led culture and '*total customer-led experience*', unifying the organisational functions including HR, marketing and sales.

Whether you are building a start-up or working in a larger organisation, culture is complex and needs to be constantly evolved and managed in order to accelerate business growth. It is hard work and needs planning and dedication. However, when executed well, the rewards are great. A positive and customer-led employee experience leads to the formation of a powerful army of employee advocates who serve as internal catalysts for customer-led growth. Also, companies with consistent, distinctive, customer-led brands and deeply held values tend to outperform others. Organisations need to start top down, but continue bottom up to achieve this.

The CEO needs to understand and lead the mission for a total customer-led experience. They must lead from the top of the organisation and champion being customer-led in everything the organisation does. For example, as you will read in the Voice chapter, leaders should create customer listening paths and regular dialogue to inform, shape and refine the customer-led culture. However, the odds are stacked against this, since there is a tendency for CEOs to come from financial backgrounds, with limited exposure to existing and prospective customers. According to the Global Accounting Network in 2018, 51% of the FTSE 100 CEOs had a background in finance. Peter Cheese, CEO of the 150,000-strong, global professional body for HR and people development, the Chartered Institute of Personnel and Development (CIPD), makes the point about the need to fundamentally change the way organisations are structured in the Customer Economy. 'Leaders need to think holistically in the service of "our customers" and what is the purpose for their organisation'. He added, 'Part of the problem is that too many businesses have lost sight of their purpose and their customers with a singular focus on financial outcomes and the financial stakeholder. Understanding all of the organisation's stakeholders is critical, and in particular, the employees who ultimately are responsible for delivery of the value to customers'. He argues that we have to understand that companies and employees cannot just be understood by looking at numbers. This overemphasis on a financial and cost view of organisations, which has, in the past, often reduced employees to being thought of in cost or economic terms and not valued as people who need to be engaged, invested in, and valued to drive great customer service. Employees are the essential key to customer-led organisations. He summarises the argument by stating that 'we need to move from a *Homo economicus* view of the world back to a *Homo sapiens* view, that is, reset how leaders view the work environment and view their employees as people, with a better understanding of behaviours, motivation, learning, and corporate culture, and how to create diverse and inclusive workplaces first above economics and profit'. We believe that a sustainable, economic and profitable, business model naturally flows from customer-led growth in what is now firmly the Customer Economy.

To create a customer-led culture, the skill sets of senior leadership needs to be broadened to bring strong commercial and customer-facing experience together with good people, as well as behavioural and organisational cultural experience. The culture needs to be shaped and re-enforced dynamically by input from the customer in every facet to create the C-change. Leadership should set a clear customer vision, purpose statement and rallying call that get the whole organisation driving towards a customer-led north star. This rallying call should be constantly repeated, re-enforced and inspected at all levels of the organisation. Such a call can serve as a hugely motivational and unifying force when it comes to gelling the culture of the organisation and the overall employee experience. In the case of Horst Schulze, former CEO of Ritz-Carlton, his rallying call was simple: 'We are ladies and gentlemen serving ladies and gentlemen'.

CEOs TO EMBED A CUSTOMER-LED EMPLOYEE CULTURE

From consulting with customer-led organisations around the world, we believe that leaders should create a 'C-change' by breaking down the traditional, functional boundaries. These functional boundaries need to be relaxed to create cross-functional teams. The overriding principle is that these new teams are designed and rewarded on generating value for customers – rather than an internally-focused approach to deliver pure value for the organisation. We will talk about this move to '*C-change growth drivers*' rather than the current organisational rules later.

Jeanne Bliss, a true CX innovator and author of CCO publications, talks about the need to develop three leadership behaviours to adopt a customer-led culture and foster customer-led growth. First, she urges organisations to unite the leadership team behind a single mission for customer-led growth.

'When I work with leaders embarking on transformation, they jump from their respective siloes in the organisation to fix things that are broken. But first, they need to unite the leadership team to build a single source of truth of how the organisation really works in relation to customers'. Jeanne added, 'Their assessment of business success is based on their silo of the organisation and is the main reason why a customer-led culture and the customer experience fails because the whole leadership team hasn't united in the same direction'.

The second behaviour Jeanne advocates is to give employees the permission to act in support of customer and, there-fore, the right behaviours to facilitate the 'C-change' for a customer-led culture. In terms of quick wins to act as a catalyst for customer-led culture, in the beginning, leaders need to take symbolic actions that remove obstacles for the customer. For example, it could be changing a policy that has been in place for years which everyone knows is unhelpful to customers. Similarly, it could be taking a simple step to streamline CX such as triaging customers to get to the right customer service expert, thereby reducing the time they wait to be served. Such steps form good customer-led behaviours that set a benchmark for customer-led culture.

The third behaviour is for leaders to prove it with actions, and simply relax and trust employees to make good decisions. Jeanne advocates: leaders need to show their commitment to customers to create a customer-led culture with what she terms as 'recipe cards'. These are short posts online or in print around the organisation with explicit actions such as honouring customers as assets. This states that every leader starts his/her meetings with employees by fearlessly sharing the growth or loss of the customer as an asset.

CUSTOMER-LED GROWTH COMES FROM ENGAGED, CUSTOMER-LED EMPLOYEES

In Debra Corey and Glenn Elliott's book *Build It: The Rebel Play-book for World-Class Employee Engagement*, they point out that a group of companies has twice the stock market performance of their peers, innovate more and has half the employee turnover through more engaged employees with customer-led culture. These companies have been outperforming their competitors for nearly 20 years.

Debra Corey sums up nicely the conundrum of creating a customer-led company by saying, 'How can your customers love you if your employees don't even like you?' Corey and Elliott highlight that engaged, customer-led employees create 'better, stronger and more resilient organisations' in three ways: First, engaged employees make better, more informed decisions based on a stronger understanding of their organisation, its *customers* and the context in which they are operating. We believe that this cultural understanding of customers is a fundamental catalyst and foundation to accelerate sustainable growth in the Customer Economy. Second, engaged employees are more productive, which is one of the biggest issues facing businesses today that struggle to get out of the ghetto of flatline growth. They are more productive because they love what they do and do not get distracted by things that do not progress the organisation's mission or goals. Third, Corey says, 'Engaged employees who have a clear understanding of the customer and how their individual and combined roles relate to customer-led growth, innovate and co-create more' (also, see Chapter 9 on co-creation).

Blake Morgan, CX leader, builds on the important connection between employee experience and CX: 'Time and time again, the companies reputed to have the best employee experience (e.g., those reported by the Great Place to Work Institute) are typically those that offer the best customer experience. In fact, companies that invest in employee experience and culture are on average 4.2x more profitable than companies that do not. Companies have to seriously invest in company culture to drive customer-centric growth'.

Blake recounts an employee story from HR solutions leader Workday. 'One of their sales leaders had a daughter who was developing dwarfism and needed specialist care. He was about to leave the company so he could support his daughter, since the company's medical insurance policy didn't cover her care. When he was about to leave, he thought he'd check with the HR team if any exception could be made. Without even batting an eyelid, the HR team amended the corporate medical insurance policy (for the entire company) to cover this case. He ended up staying and became one of the most successful sales leaders the company ever employed'. By going out of its way to make the employee experience as slick and frictionless as possible, CX improved too.

BUILDING AN ORGANISATIONAL STRUCTURE FIT FOR THE CUSTOMER ECONOMY

The new customer-led organisation needs to be agile with cross-functional teams guided by the customer-led mission, vision and values of the organisation. In addition, we are heading towards a place where organisations are structured around the journey that the customer takes with it, that is, around an outside-in view of the company. Innovative organisations today are shattering the traditional functional siloes that have been in place throughout the twentieth century. For example, at Slack, the customer support and services functions have been merged into a single Customer Success department. It is the customer who is the catalyst requiring the status quo to change from this static, functional organisational structure. This is forcing the CEO's skill set to change, having to take charge not only of the common view of CX with (external customers) but also to lead and shape the employee experience. In the customer experience chapter, we will consider ways of improving CX by listening to employees and improving the employee experience.

The nature of the Customer Economy means that CEOs must be far better communicators. They have to hone their listening skills, face-to-face and online, and be able to respond *directly* to *internal customers*, that is, employees as well as *external* customers. This must be done with genuine empathy, insight and authentic leadership to create the 'C-change' to be a successful customer-led organisation. In the past, the CEO only had to do this with internal customers at quarterly employee meetings and town halls. In contrast, now there are higher expectations for CEOs to have strong social media profiles with relevant, customer-led views that appeal to the millennial employees who will be the majority in the next 20 years. Millennial employees are driven to work for customer-led organisations that have a higher purpose and not just short-term quarterly revenues and profit. Greater transparency in the Customer Economy is driving this power shift to customers, including potent customer reviews both inside from employees as well as outside the organisation with external customers. This represents a big opportunity for CEOs to shape customer-led culture as they are the only people who have the mandate to lead cross-functional teams to make it happen.

THE IMPORTANCE OF CUSTOMER-LED BEHAVIOURS AND KPIs FOR EMPLOYEES

This new customer-led workplace means that the CCO must facilitate cross-functional interactions such as the co-operation between HR and marketing functions. HR has the opportunity to develop a more strategic role to create a shift to pan-organisational, customer-led jobs with greater ownership and KPIs linked back to the customer-led mission and objectives of the organisation. Individual employee KPIs must link back to the needs of customers. A great way of doing this is to align employee KPIs with Customer Health scores. The good news is that this is creating new customer-led behaviours. Many companies are moving to smaller, cross-functional, agile working teams that are more collaborative. Such teams are characterised by open lines of communication, allowing them to move faster and adapt more quickly to achieve *customer-led* company and personal objectives. Engaged employees need to have a clear understanding of the customer and how their individual and company-wide roles contribute to the customer-led mission, values and objectives of the organisation. It is these engaged '*C-changed*' employees who are culturally wedded to the customer who will co-create the successful and sustainable, customer-led organisations in the Customer Economy.

In Richard Mosley's paper 'Customer experience, organisational culture and the employer brand' in the *Journal of*

Brand Management, he points out that successful service companies emphasise the role of organisational culture in promoting customer-led behaviours. However, the mechanisms for shaping a customer-led culture (such as internal marketing, often referred to in HR circles as IM – as well as internal branding) have typically relied too extensively on HR taking communication-led approaches to sustain a lasting effect. Senior leadership and HR need to take a holistic approach to shape the total customer-led culture of the organisation, by seeking to ensure that every people management touchpoint is aligned with the broader customer brand values of the organisation.

Since his initial paper, Mosley talks now of how organisations need to focus on three areas to create a customer-led employee brand, which will drive customer-led growth:

1. **Brand values for employees need to be aligned with brand values for customers.** The brand values need to be informed by strategic customers and prospective customers. Leaders need to bake them into the culture and people management so that they are reflected in customer-led employee experience. Since we are now in the Customer Economy, as you will see in the Experience chapter, we argue that the new brand *is* CX.

2. **Customer-led organisational culture.** Leaders need to create a consistent employee experience that reinforces

employees' understanding and support for the desired customer brand experience. Moments of truth that reflect the customer-led brand values need to be rewarded and recounted so that employees see an alignment with external CX.

3. **Meaningful, 'purpose-driven' employment.** Employees are looking for the organisations they work for to have a clear purpose that is not just about short-term revenues and profit. A customer mission statement that is authentic and translated into meaningful actions for employees is one of the most effective rallying calls for any organisation.

Above all, the trend for 'purpose-led brands' needs to be grounded in the value delivered to both customers and employees. So, in other words, the core purpose of the business must be aligned to the external customer and internal customer (i.e. employee) value proposition. However, it comes down to what sustainable value is being provided for customers rather than just short-term internally driven needs of large organisations. A good example of a customer-led employee culture is the global pharmaceutical giant, GSK. Emma Walmsley, its CEO, was brought in to oversee a move to a more performance-driven organisation, but has ensured that this is closely aligned with the underlying purpose of the company, the value they deliver for external customers such as patients and doctors, and the meaningful and progressive employment they provide to those working for GSK.

HR's OPPORTUNITY TO DRIVE EMPLOYEE-LED CX

Technology has disrupted and is continuing to disrupt industries, with shorter product lifecycles and facilitating even more direct connections between organisations and their customers. Like all business functions, technology has enabled HR to be rationalised with the trend for HR technology to allow self-service, challenging the perception of the value of HR. This dichotomy is testing for organisations, as HR is all about maximising the potential of your people and human capital and yet employees see and feel that HR is less present. This highlights an opportunity for HR to take on a far more strategic leadership role in evolving the total customer-led *employee* brand experience bringing in smart human interaction in conjunction with multi-faceted measurement across employee experience, customer understanding and customer-related performance objectives. HR has a key role in leading the 'C-change' and embedding a total customer-led, employee brand experience at every people management touchpoint in just the same way that marketing and sales are using technology to manage every touchpoint on the journey of an external customer. The opportunity lies in close alignment between HR focusing on employees as internal customers and marketing on external customers to co-create broader CX. Commitment to customers' needs to be led from the top by CxOs and especially the CCO, so that everything about the organisation's culture and structure is informed from customer-led insight and experience: the mission is for the customer to be ingrained in every pore of the organisation's skin. HR has the opportunity to be the conduit for customer-led research, insight, customer commitment, customer-informed organisational language, rewards, leadership and education.

Ultimately, this customer-led employer brand experience needs to be continually integrated into what will become, over time, the organisation's customer-led culture, which will drive customer-led differentiation and growth.

THE RISE OF THE CCO

If the Customer Catalyst C-change growth engine is not already part of the organisation's DNA from day one, we believe every company should appoint a CCO in order to embed this into its culture. Companies such as Amazon and Zoom were built from the ground upwards with C-change growth drivers, but they are the outliers. Most companies are on a journey when it comes to customer-led transformation. Some have not left the house; others are getting in the car, some on the main road and others on the motorway. There has to be a C-level person who wakes up every morning with the mission to drive customer-led change across the organisation.

According to Ed Thompson, VP and Distinguished Analyst at Gartner: 'In the past, I didn't think it was necessary for companies to employ a Chief Customer Officer, or someone responsible for driving customer-led transformation and growth. After 10 years, I've come around to the opinion that they really do need to appoint a CCO. Every company is on a journey to customer-centric nirvana, and someone needs to be responsible to help the organisation along with it. I'm seeing such roles appear all over the world from China to the Czech Republic'.

HOW DO YOU DEFINE THE ROLE OF THE CCO?

There is no one definition, as this is an emerging role. Nish Kotak, co-author of the influential 'Chief Customer Officer Report' and managing director of executive search firm Talecco, says, 'A CCO is an executive who is ultimately accountable for both strategy and customer initiatives across the business. It's not just about customer obsession; it's about a balance with financial rigour and operational excellence.'

HOW DID THE ROLE OF CCO START?

Nearly 30 years ago, the role of CCO was introduced by Jack Chambers, CEO at Texas-New Mexico Power, who was far-sighted enough to see the need for creating a customer-led organisation. Since then, the role of the CCO has grown in the USA and has now come over to Europe, where there is now a strong emerging community of CCOs. Digitisation has been a key driver in driving growth of the CCO in the age of the Customer Economy. The CCO is giving customers a voice because they now have power over the buying process as opposed to organisations. According to the 2018 Chief Customer Officer Report, 25% of CCOs stay in their role on an average for 17 months versus 22% who stay for over 3 years. This is in contrast to only 19% staying in the CCO role for 3 years according to the same report in 2017, which demonstrates that they are leading longer-term customer-led growth.

Now, in its third year, the annual CCO report from Talecco has identified the following five key archetypes of CCOs who mirror different maturity levels of customer-led organisations.

1. **The Rising Stars:** They work well in the organisation and realise that the customer is important. This individual can be in any department. However, it is their persistence with the board that has created the role of the CCO for themselves.
2. **The Operational Guru:** This is an individual who is practical and can 'fix the basics' (which we will talk about in the Customer Growth chapter).
3. **Process Practitioner:** Typically, this type of CCO is found in digitally-led organisations focusing on the customer journey with strong process and technical skills.
4. **Engagement Experts:** Often, these individuals come from sales and marketing backgrounds and believe in the whole

vision being customer-led. They have strong business transformation skills and are expert at developing the organisation's values to build customer-led brands 'These CCOs are all about cultural change and are experts at engaging the organisation internally and externally to galvanise change for the organisation to become customer-led', Nish Kotak commented.

5. **Group Influencer:** This is a CCO leader who does not own the whole customer function, but they are the customer champion in a matrix organisation. They will lead the organisation by putting the customer at the heart of customer-led initiatives – initially often with small teams. This CCO will build agile, cross-functional teams including customer insight and digital and customer delivery to facilitate customer-led growth.

Nish Kotak added, 'Where we see the greatest impact of the CCO is the "Engagement Experts" who are typically leading sizeable teams of a hundred plus employees'. In summary, the CCO role is broad in nature, any one of the five archetypes of CCO will need to learn some new skills: from understanding strategy, cultural change, customer data and insight to product management, design and programme management, as well as delivery and measurement. CEOs do not always need a CCO to start thinking about driving customer-led growth, as you can start small with customer change initiatives before embarking on such a hire.

Nish Kotak concluded, 'The journey to customer-led growth is a marathon, not a sprint; however, to get to the end of the marathon, CEOs should really consider investing in the full-fat CCO'.

WHAT ARE THE GREATEST CHALLENGES THAT CCOs FACE?

First and foremost, to drive a customer-led culture and sustainable growth, you need leadership alignment around the customer – starting from the CEO. So, in a change of leadership where a CEO with strong customer-led vision leaves and a new CEO comes in who is not wedded to the customer and is focused purely on cost-saving, the previous work to be customer-led can quickly dissolve. It is hard to defend against this situation. The lesson is that there needs to be a C-change in CEOs being customer-led and having broader management training. This helps CEOs to move away from the short-term, one-dimensional, financially led goals, which just are not going to cut it on their own in the Customer Economy.

Also, the CCO needs to keep abreast of new customer-related technology coming out, such as augmented reality and virtual reality, to enhance CX in both B2B and B2C. Furthermore, customer expectations grow, so CCOs have to meet and exceed their needs. This is especially true with greater sophistication in voice-led CX developments such as Amazon Alexa. Ultimately, anybody who is having an impact on the customer agenda is winning. However, those CCOs who have a customer-led vision and can break down the customer journey and bring bite-size customer change programmes for the organisation are having the biggest impact. Similarly, these CCOs are more likely to have the backing of the CEO, and therefore will succeed.

'We're still on the rise of the CCO but it's still early on in its evolution. Over the next 10 years, the CCO role will morph into other roles. For example, we're starting to see CCOs become CEOs. Whichever organisation they're in and whatever happens, the CCO will always be the advocate of the customer – that is, it's a mindset', commented Nish Kotak.

THE ALTERNATIVE VIEW: EMPLOYING CCOs, CX PROs AND CSMs IS A WASTE OF TIME AND MONEY

Blake Morgan believes that many companies employ CCOs, CX professionals and CSMs to solve the problem of not being customer-centric in the first place. If a company does not have customer-centric values embedded into the culture of the company from CEO downwards, it will never change. Morgan comments, 'These customer-centric roles are brought in to make a change but rarely have any influence, power or budget'. In the past, Blake really saw the value of employing CCOs, but her eyes were opened following a visit to Amazon's company offices. 'Everyone lived and breathed customer centricity. Top executives would spend time in the distribution centres at 2 a.m. to understand how employees in the warehouse were working and the challenges they faced. It is truly in the company's DNA. So why would Amazon need a Chief Customer Officer?' The results for Amazon, as you will see in the Experience chapter, speak for themselves.

Table 2.1 shows some simple ideas for initiatives we have seen from companies embarking on the C-change cultural transformation.

In conclusion, ensure your culture is shaped continually by the 'C-change' engine centred around the 'total customer-led experience'. This must be led from the top and the whole organisation to meet the needs of internal customers, that is, your employees as well as with external customers.

Move from the rigid organisational functions that were built for the mass production needs of the Industrial Age to agile, cross-functional teams that span functions fit for the Customer Economy. These teams will succeed in leading customer-led growth guided by C-change growth drivers and not unbending organisational rules. This will be the foundation to create a distinctive customer-led culture with leadership which is totally attuned to customers, where employees know who your customers are, what they need and how to deliver it to them. It is this customer-led leadership in conjunction with a total customer-led employee brand experience which must

TABLE 2.1   Our C-change culture checklist to instil a customer-led culture.

Initiative	Tick if this applies to your company
Are customer goals and outcomes embedded into your company's vision, mission, vision statement and cultural values?	
Do you have a separate customer vision statement?	
Does every employee understand how their actions form part of total CX?	
Does every employee have incentive plans and KPIs aligned to a Customer Health score?	
Have you built a communication programme to promote stories of employees across all regions and functions about how they have improved CX?	
Do you run cross-functional CX workshops for employees?	
Are employees recognised for good customer-led behaviours?	
Have you surveyed your employee base to understand what challenges and issues they face to drive better CX?	
Do employees understand what actions they need to take to improve CX?	

Source: Developed and owned by Chris Adlard and Daniel Bausor.

be ingrained into the DNA of organisations. It will provide distinctive CX and ultimately differentiate the organisation from the competition to achieve customer-led growth in the Customer Economy.

CASE STUDY: BE MY GUEST! HORST SCHULZE, CO-FOUNDER OF THE RITZ-CARLTON HOTEL GROUP, ON CREATING A CUSTOMER-LED CULTURE TO TRANSFORM GUEST EXPERIENCE

Horst Schulze, Chairman Emeritus, Capella Hotels and Resorts, and former president, CEO and COO of The Ritz-Carlton Hotel Company (see Figure 2.1):

We started with how we wanted our guests to feel when they stay with us. Only when you have your optimum leadership style and culture, then you can look at how you can take it through to your product, that is, in our case – a luxury hotel experience.

FIGURE 2.1   Horst Schulze, Chairman Emeritus, Capella Hotels and Resorts, and former president, CEO and COO of The Ritz-Carlton Hotel Company.

Source: Horst Schulze. Reproduced with permission.

Horst Schulze is a founding member and former president and COO of The Ritz-Carlton Hotel Company which became one of the icons of global luxury in the hotel industry. He is famous for revolutionising the hotel industry and helping to establish one of the most well-known international brands – The Ritz-Carlton® – and the very essence of customer service by creating a culture of 'ladies and gentlemen serving ladies and gentlemen'. Not content with this illustrious career, Horst went on to start another hotel chain, the Capella Hotel Group, which today is arguably setting an even higher standard for luxury and service in the industry. In short, Horst Schulze is a pioneer of customer-led organisational culture with an inspirational leadership story for CEOs encompassing employee engagement and the lifetime values of customers. Horst states, 'If your day-to-day interactions with your customers aren't central to your business culture, you risk losing their trust and business'.

Horst was working for Hyatt and was very established in the organisation. He had been the general manager and regional vice president of over 10 hotels and then in charge of converged operations for the whole United States when somebody called him and said: 'We are starting a new hotel in Atlanta; we have two hotels under construction and we want to start our own brand'. Just over a year later, he and the team opened their first hotel, which was The Ritz-Carlton Buckhead, followed by The Ritz-Carlton Atlanta. The Ritz-Carlton Laguna Niguel was next, followed by The Ritz-Carlton Boston, which had been the first property purchased, along with the name, but was closed promptly for extensive renovations due to its dilapidated state. After 19 years, Horst left the company, and it was a global brand by then. It was voted *not just best hotel*, but the best brand in the world. However, Horst is quick to acknowledge that it was not just down to him, and that the success was founded on a guest-led culture, that is, a customer-led culture – nurtured with many great people, including good bellmen, doormen, maids, waiters, cooks and so on. Together, they created The Ritz-Carlton Hotel Company. Horst Schulze is a customer-led leader who created a C-change in fostering a guest-led culture, which resulted in great service and sustainable growth. He improved on the roles that the extended hotel team played. One of the things that really distinguished Ritz-Carlton at the time was the meticulous approach to how employees related to customers and the very defined way of treating service.

Horst points out, 'I went to The Ritz-Carlton to create the greatest hotel company in the world, that was my vision, that was the dream. I hired people that wanted this. I said to prospective employees, don't join me for a job, join me in this vision. Everything we're going to do is to become the finest hotel company in the world, for the benefit of all concerned from the investors and owners to the customers and employees, as well as society'.

He looked at that mission and said how are we going to be the best? Horst set out for him and his team of employees to be the most efficient they could be for the customer, and also much more efficient than the competition. However, to be more efficient, they had to determine how to do this. As it turned out, his strategy was to focus on customer service from each employee.

> Quickly, it became very clear that I simply had to do better in my selection and hiring of employees. This was in terms of orientation and employee training where it all depended on each employee – and certainly not on me sitting in the office', said Horst. 'It depended on that doorman, how he or she said hello, and about the way that the porter took them from the door to their room. Ultimately, it was about how we did the job in any location where we were operating.

That meant hiring and aligning every employee to what Horst and the team wanted them to be. This gave everybody a purpose and focus on customer service – and why they wanted to be that exceptional company. Also, it showed them how that purpose connected to their lives. Horst did not hire them just for a function, but for them to become part of their organisation and, most importantly, to be part of their guest-led culture. This customer-led ethos was fundamental to the success of Ritz-Carlton; otherwise, they could not do what they wanted to do. Horst added, 'I knew, if I'm hiring and training like my competition, I will be like my competition, but I wanted to be the leader and for us to be better'.

It is important to note that a key component behind the success was that Horst was an early adopter of customer data, which goes back to what we said in the Voice chapter – where the customer is informing all of your business strategy and decisions. Horst was ahead of his time and was a customer survey fanatic before it was fashionable. He just loved data from customers: he wanted to know what guests wanted to feel when they stayed at the hotel. Surveys seemed to imply that guests wanted to feel like they were at home when they stayed at the hotel, but Horst questioned that. Horst hired a world-renowned linguist to precisely inspect the data and word usage and found that guests actually wanted to feel like they were staying in their mother's home. It is fascinating how Horst extended this ethos in everything he and his employees did. Here is a good example of this: an American guest staying at a Ritz-Carlton hotel in another country was disappointed that their room did not have an American TV station that they liked at home. The hotel gardener was talking with the guest and discovered this. So, the gardener worked with fellow team members to make the guest's American TV station available in their room. This level of ownership by the gardener to extend his action beyond his job description is exactly what Horst desired for his employees. This exceptional level of ownership helped the hotel guest feel completely cared for.

Also, Schulze points out that giving employees a sense of empowerment was essential when it came to creating a customer-led culture. While the words are almost a throwaway phrase, Ritz-Carlton practised what it preached. According to Schulze, 'For example, we told employees that they were empowered to make any decision up to the value of US$2000. This really shocked staff! But my thinking was simple – it was worth spending US$2000 to keep a customer! It was all about creating customers for life and driving customer lifetime value'.

When Horst introduced the US$2000 employee empowerment initiative, some hotel owners were very concerned that expenses would run rampant. However, he insisted on this because he knew the trust it extended to employees would be returned with increased customer focus and service, which would ultimately drive sustainable growth. This highlights his customer-led leadership, which manifested itself in the hotel's positive results over the long term.

In order to instil customer-led values across the organisation, Horst created a 'Credo card' at Ritz-Carlton, that is, the mission and values, where he wanted to shape the culture *with 24 service behaviours* (see Figure 2.2). Schulze continues, 'For example,

---

THE RITZ-CARLTON CREDO

"WE ARE LADIES AND GENTLEMEN SERVING LADIES AND GENTLEMEN"

The Ritz-Carlton is a place where the genuine care and comfort of our guests is our highest mission.
We pledge to provide the finest personal service and facilities for our guests who will always enjoy a warm, relaxed yet refined ambience.
The Ritz-Carlton experience enlivens the senses, instills well-being and fulfills even the unexpressed wishes and needs of our guests.

Three steps of service are (1) A warm and sincere greeting. Use the guest name, if and when possible. (2) Anticipation and compliance with guest needs. (3) Fond farewell. Give them a warm good bye and use their names, if and when possible.

THE RITZ-CARLTON BASICS

1. The Credo will be known, owned and energized by all employees.
2. We are Ladies and Gentlemen serving Ladies and Gentlemen.
3. The three steps of service shall be practiced by all employees.
4. Smile–"We are on stage." Always maintain positive eye contact.
5. Use the proper vocabulary with our guests (eliminate hi, ok, folks, etc.)
6. Uncompromising levels of cleanliness are the responsibility of every employee.
7. Create a positive work environment. Practice teamwork.
8. Be an ambassador of your hotel in and outside of the work place. Always talk positively.
9. Any employee who receives a guest complaint "owns" the complaint.
10. Instant guest pacification will be ensured by all. Respond to guest wishes within ten minutes of the request. Follow up with a telephone call within twenty minutes to ensure their satisfaction.
11. Use guest incident action forms to communicate guest problems to fellow employees and managers. This will help ensure that our guests are never forgotten.
12. Escort guests, rather than pointing out directions to another area of the hotel.
13. Be knowledgeable of hotel information to answer guest questions.
14. Use proper telephone etiquette. Answer within three rings and, with a "smile", ask permission to put a caller on hold. Do not screen calls. Eliminate call transfers when possible.
15. Always recommend the hotel's food and beverage outlets prior to outside facilities.
16. Uniforms are to be immaculate. Wear proper footwear and your correct nametag.
17. Ensure all employees know their roles during emergency situations and are aware of procedures.
18. Notify your supervisor immediately of hazards, injuries or assistance needs you have.
19. Practice energy conservation and proper maintenance of hotel property.
20. Protecting the assets of a Ritz-Carlton Hotel is the responsibility of every employee.

FIGURE 2.2 The Ritz-Carlton Credo.

Source: Horst Schulze. Reproduced with permission.

if you were within 10 feet of a guest, the employee should greet a guest warmly and with direct eye contact. Also, if it was going to take longer than 30 seconds for a guest to check in (which is the length of time studies showed a guest was willing to wait before becoming frustrated), guest staff might offer a beverage while the guest waits'. There is much for leaders to learn in fostering a customer-led culture from the Ritz-Carlton Credo, which can be applied to any industry, such as 'Be an ambassador … in and outside of the workplace. Always talk positively' through to 'guest incident forms' to address and resolve customer issues.

When it comes to building an employer brand and employee advocacy, Horst has had a unique approach to driving these. For example, when he opened a new Ritz-Carlton hotel, he would be there to lead training, which really inspired a guest-led culture.

Also, Horst broke down functional siloes and created cross-functional teams to deliver great CX. His mantra was simple – 'Customer service is everyone's job' – and so he embedded this culture to look externally to the needs of guests and not just the needs of his hotels. He is passionate about guest focus and has three simple and powerful steps to make this happen:

And yet in the hospitality industry, these steps are often not followed and not consistently repeated.

Step One: Warmly welcome every customer – see examples in the Credo card in Figure 2.2.

Step Two: Comply with the customer's wishes – Horst always drove a culture to exceed customer's wishes in contrast to many organisations that put barriers to achieving this.

Step Three: Offer a fond farewell.

Also, Horst notes the importance of working with great partners in helping the organisation to deliver great CX. One current partner Horst works with is Arch and Tower, which provides expert consultancy around employee and customer experiences, anchored by strong operational excellence.

Horst concludes by pointing out that a customer-led culture leads to sustainable growth. In order to measure this growth, it is essential to look at data insights in a meaningful way and to drive actions on the back of these insights. Horst had been a data junkie before it was fashionable. He measured and surveyed everything, working with consumer research, testing and customer reviews which in turn drove continuous improvement.

CHAPTER 3

EXPERIENCE

Customer Experience is the new brand

C-CHANGE GROWTH DRIVERS

- **The most successful companies (in both B2B and B2C) relentlessly focus on delivering a great Customer Experience (CX).** In such companies, the CEO, C-suite and other senior executives constantly lead, inspire and align employees across functions around an 'outside-in' customer view.

- **Build an outside-in view of the customer by leveraging Voice of the Customer (VoC) insight,** conducting journey mapping workshops with customers and employees, and then measuring and driving continuous improvement in CX.

- **Do not let technology alone define CX.** CX needs to be human-first with all employees aligning around the customers' wants and needs.

In 1999, Amazon achieved net sales of around US$1.6 billion. In 2017, net sales on amazon.com were US$177 billion. In 20 years, the company has grown 100×, and Amazon is now the largest retailer in the world. With its portfolio of other businesses, such as Amazon Web Services, this organisation is now truly disrupting many other industries such as financial services.

In a brilliant interview by CNBC in 1999, just before the dotcom crash of 2000, Jeff Bezos (see Figure 3.1) pointed out that Internet stocks were very volatile, and it was hard to predict the future successes of these businesses. Most critically, he suggested that getting the fundamentals right around CX was what Amazon truly stood for and would help it navigate the stormy seas to come:

'I believe that if you can focus obsessively enough on customer experience … selection, ease of use, low prices, more information to make purchase decisions with. If you can give customers all that plus great customer service … Then I think you have a good chance, and that's what we're trying to do.'

FIGURE 3.1 Jeff Bezos in 1999 on Amazon's plans before the dot-com crash.

Source: https://www.youtube.com/watch?v=GltlJO56S1g. Accessed 18th June 2019. Screenshot by Chris Adlard and Daniel Bausor.

When a company recruits a new chief marketing officer (CMO), it is often the case that the newly appointed marketing leader will seek to rebrand the organisation in some shape or form. The drive to rebrand the organisation is usually preceded or followed by a discussion amongst the C-suite about the expenditure justification or any potential return on investment. The CMO will typically push for the rebrand, not least because this is his or her own way of making their own mark on the company. However, rebranding is expensive, time-consuming and takes years to establish – even in the smallest company. Systems, processes and offices are littered with old names, terminology and physical brand artefacts. Long-standing employees may still identify far more with the previous organisation, and it requires a huge investment to educate and re-educate the employee base in the new way of thinking.

Despite the many perceived benefits of creating a new brand or investing in brand awareness programmes, the Customer Economy should challenge CEOs and managers to seriously reconsider the investment they are making in rebranding and brand awareness programmes. A company's brand has no secrets. Almost everything anyone needs to know about a company is freely available on the web. Consumers and businesses today, almost always without exception, will read reviews of the company and its products or services before they buy (whatever industry the company operates in) – whether through Amazon, TripAdvisor, analyst firms, technical support forums, etc. – the list is endless. Sometimes, they have even decided which company or product to go for before they have even spoken to your organisation. Potential employees will read reviews on Glassdoor before considering a new employer. Furthermore, bad experiences with a company's brand far outweigh the message the company wishes to tell the market. A shiny new coat of paint will only go so far in hiding the cracks of the building or its structural flaws.

Don Peppers, arguably the Godfather of CX, defines customer experience as: 'The sum total of individual interactions a customer has with a brand over time.'

Ed Thompson, VP and Distinguished Analyst at Gartner, defines CX as 'the customer's perception and related feelings caused by the one-off and cumulative effect of interactions with a supplier's employees, channels, systems or products'.

In the Customer Economy today, the reality is: a company's brand is no longer purely about how the company presents itself to the market; it is more about how the market perceives the company. Never have consumers and customers held so much power in the buying process. The costs for customers to switch are low, especially in the subscription model. In fact, as CX leader Shep Hyken puts it, CX *is* the new brand of today. Hence, it would be far better for organisations to save the huge sums spent on branding to instead invest in time improving CX, which makes the foundations of the brand in the first place.

However, there are signs that things are beginning to change for the better. Even as far back as 2015, ITSMA predicted that investments in CX were becoming a greater priority than those in the brand. ITSMA surveyed over 100 marketing leaders from major global technology and services companies. A significant majority cited that increased investment would be made in CX, engagement, advocacy and satisfaction programmes as compared to the traditional brand activities. If the brand is influenced by company purpose and culture, linking all this back to CX is key.

In 2018, Gartner conducted a CX survey with marketing leaders around the world, and 81% of respondents stated that their organisation would compete on CX in 2019. In short, most businesses today have great intentions when it comes to investing in such programmes, and, hopefully, we will see more investment in them.

When Shep Hyken stated that 'Customer experience is the new brand', the message was powerful. It is partly why many CMOs today are starting to rebadge themselves as chief customer officers (CCOs), not least to cash in on the land grab for new responsibilities. Yet, as we discussed in the Culture chapter, CCOs come from a variety of functional backgrounds. What is the most important attribute of the CCO? The answer: Total Customer Belief.

CX: HUMAN FIRST, TECHNOLOGY SECOND

Digitisation and technology have become unstoppable forces in every industry. We will explore the impact of technology and digital experience in the following chapters. However, an important caveat: without a true understanding of customers, their wants, needs and emotions – serious mistakes can be made. Recently, Facebook employees posted a video from their offices. A 'smart' soap dispenser that senses a person's hands underneath then releases a portion of liquid soap. Unfortunately, it does not seem to work very well for people of colour, as it is unable to recognise darker skin tones. This simple example demonstrates one of the biggest mistakes organisations can make when it comes to defining CX. Companies should never let their own internal ideas, especially around so-called technological innovation, divert them from fully understanding what is happening with their customers. Retaining an 'outside-in' perspective is essential (see Figure 3.2).

FIGURE 3.2 This Facebook office soap dispenser does not work for people of colour.

Source: https://www.youtube.com/watch?v=YJjv_OeiHmo. Accessed 18th June 2019. Screenshot by Chris Adlard and Daniel Bausor.

According to Merje Shaw, managing director of CX Consultancy, Path 59, 'Where most successful start-ups focus on solving a problem through technology they're developing or using, traditional companies often focus very intensely on implementing a shiny new technology (the current favourite being AI). The organisation involved is usually nowhere near ready for this, despite frequently being more digitally advanced than they imagine themselves to be. Identifying a problem and then letting that guide the technology selection would be a far better course of action'.

Take, for example, the rise of self-service checkouts in UK supermarkets. In some cases, customers turn up and there are no manned tills. How does a non-tech-savvy consumer, perhaps a senior citizen, deal with this? Technology has been used to make things allegedly more efficient, but if the experience is made more complicated for customers (or least key customer segments or personas), this will have an impact on business performance and bottom line.

Shaw concludes by saying, 'Companies should always go back to the basics, challenge the assumptions of why things are done a certain way, but never let technology on its own drive decisions for change. Technology is always changing; the human context always remains constant'. In summary, companies should always look to improve the customer's experience, but never dehumanise it.

CX, THE RYANAIR WAY

Ryanair, headquartered in Dublin, Ireland, was founded in 1984 and boasts revenues of over €7 billion euros. It has around 13,000 employees, a fleet of over 400 planes and flies to over 200 destinations. The company has really disrupted the airline industry, and is now the largest European budget airline in terms of the number of scheduled passengers flown. It has a solid safety and punctuality record, and its 'low-fares' mantra has proved to be a massive hit with customers all over Europe. Its low-cost leadership strategy has proved to be very successful in terms of financial performance.

Ryanair, however, has faced a barrage of criticism over the years from many angles. From shocking treatment of airline staff to the story of charging wheelchair passengers extra baggage fees for their wheelchairs, all the way to it avoiding paying traveller compensation for delays and cancellations. The company is searching constantly for ways to cut costs and maximise revenues. Much of this is tolerated by its customers, who understand that 'you get what you pay for', but sometimes it can go too far. Here is a recent example of a customer who travelled with his family on Ryanair (see Figure 3.3). The company had deliberately split up the group so that he would have to pay extra for them all to sit together!

There are many aspects of the Ryanair CX that shock and appall its customers. At the airport, queues always seem to be

Stuart Harris MIoD CIWFM SIIRSM ACIPS · 2nd
Global Director of Facilities at SANNE
3d

Ryan Air what a joke!
I have just checked in for our flight tomorrow for 4 of us and we have been given 6A, 9B, 12D and 22B, but having looked at the seating plan there are lots of seats together, they split you up on purpose to make you pay extra to sit together! Ryan Air should be fined for this behaviour

5,229 Likes · 1,749 Comments

FIGURE 3.3 Stuart Harris' LinkedIn post.

Source: https://www.linkedin.com/feed/update/urn:li:activity:6525673397182177280/. Accessed 18th June 2019. Screenshot by Chris Adlard and Daniel Bausor.

much longer, with less staff helping customers. Customers are penalised for not printing out their own boarding pass and have to pay card fees when paying with plastic, even with debit cards. The back of the seats is either used to display the airline safety instructions or to promote further ways of spending money (e.g. on food items and even scratch cards!). Over 25% of revenues apparently come from ancillary products and services outside of the core flight costs.

In The *Customer Catalyst*, we have argued that the only way of achieving sustainable business growth is to remain customer-led. Ryanair is almost the exception that proves the rule. It is not that Ryanair does not value CX. In fact, every time it is slated for the experience it provides, its PR spokespeople are always quick to respond and robustly defend their strategy – that they save customers money. Despite all this, customers appear to keep going back to them.

Also, there are signs of change at Ryanair, proving that it is looking at ways to improve the CX factor. In 2019, it unveiled the latest round of 'customer care' improvements. These improvements included refunds for customers who found cheaper fares elsewhere and a universal reduction of fares in the subsequent month if it failed to meet its own punctuality targets for the current month. Also, it seeks to resolve all customer claims in 10 days and has opened a 24/7 support centre. Some of these changes have been driven by regulatory pressures, others because the negative impact of poor CX has affected the company's bottom line.

Is the Ryanair approach to growth sustainable? Only time will tell. Our view is that the recent improvements in customer care at Ryanair are a sign of things to come. The European airline industry has already been disrupted, and customers are very price-sensitive. The battleground today, even for the budget airlines, is around making CX better, not on driving down costs and further exploiting customers for short-term financial return.

CX: SATISFICING THE CUSTOMER WITH AN OUTSIDE-IN VIEW

When Kerry Bodine and Harley Manning wrote the seminal publication *Outside In*, their message had the same seismic impact as Humby's phrase 'Data is the new oil' (see the Technology chapter). Today, the phrase 'outside-in' has become a part of the standard vernacular when organisations look at improving CX, and it is heard on a frequent basis across every geography and industry. According to Bodine, 'An outside-in view of CX is one that is built around both the expectations of the customer and the needs and capabilities of the business'. In other words, by understanding the experience that a company provides to the customer – from the customer's perspective – the business is better able to align itself around the needs and wants of the customer in order to drive more successful business outcomes.

Bodine highlights the importance of effective VoC intelligence including ethnographic studies and surveys, as well as quantitative data and journey mapping. All these help organisations understand what CX is today, what it should be like in the future and what needs to change behind the scenes in order to deliver more profitable experiences. She also refers to net promoter score (NPS) as a blunt instrument, but one that still merits investment because of its ease of implantation and understandability to the entire ecosystem of customers, frontline employees, middle managers and executives.

However, Bodine notes that it is impossible for organisations to achieve perfection when it comes to CX. That said, they should always strive to constantly improve. In doing so, they will be successful and drive sustainable growth. Bodine also points out, 'Sometimes you have to make hard choices. Prioritise the moments of truth that really matter most to customers. Don't try to fix everything – because you could end up going around in circles and your efforts will ultimately become unprofitable'. Bodine quotes some of the benchmark organisations best known for great CX, such as Disney and Apple: 'Even these companies have not achieved a perfect customer experience. In some cases, they even do things that annoy customers because they make more commercial sense'. In other words, whilst improving CX is important, there has to be a trade-off in terms of the business needs for revenue or cost savings. Bodine refers to this as approach as 'satisficing the customer'.

CX 101: UNDERSTAND IT IN DEPTH, THEN MAP IT OUT

Having recognised both the trend towards, and the critical need of, adopting CX programmes, how does an organisation typically embark on improving CX, and turn this into business growth?

The first step, as indicated in the previous chapter, is to listen to your customers. Companies must ensure that many sources of the voice of customer information have been digested and analysed, and any key recommendations to improve both CX and any internal processes have been considered. Second, companies must listen to their employees. In the majority of cases, employees know what the customer issues are and how to address them. Third, organisations should run a series of workshops with both employees and customers (and in many cases with partners) to map out the typical customer journey or journeys they would take with your company.

THE POWER OF CUSTOMER JOURNEY MAPPING

Journey mapping workshops are informative and some-times eye-opening experiences for customers, partners and employees alike – and can be tremendous fun for all parties too. Before embarking on any such workshop, it is important to read and analyse many sources of the voice of customer and voice of employee feedback to probe for the right kind of issues, in order to help uncover the so-called customer and employee 'moments of truth' occurring in the customer and employee journey.

According to Annette Franz, global CX, thought-leader and expert in journey mapping, 'Journey mapping is a tool and a process. The process includes current state mapping, service blueprinting and future state mapping, among other things. The majority of companies don't even know what service blueprinting is or that it's a necessity in this process. It's important to note that you can't improve what's happening on the outside (for the customer) if you don't fix what's supporting it on the inside. During service blueprinting, most companies will discover that their processes have definitely not been designed with the customer in mind'.

Journey maps help define the stages of interaction that customers have with your company, who and what they interact with (e.g. which departments – either directly or indirectly, which employees, which partners, which systems, which digital and communication channels), the actions they take and – most importantly – their emotions and feelings. Also, it is important that journey maps look at personas, not just as segments. For example, a persona might be 'A global CIO who has to rationalise his vendor base by 50% in the next 2 months', or 'a single mother of an autistic child', rather than a segment such as 'SME customers with 10 employees' or 'the SUV market'.

There are a few ways to document the customer journey, including customer journey software mapping tools. However, nothing really beats interactive workshop sessions where employees, partners and customers alike can discuss and debate the client experience in person. Using different coloured Post-it notes, it allows workshop facilitators and workshop members alike to simultaneously throw up ideas and suggestions on to the board. It is an excellent way of breaking down organisational siloes and show team members what CX really looks like (see Figure 3.4).

Workshops allow groups an opportunity to map out customer journeys for a variety of personas, and thus the output of these sessions is often a series of journey maps representing a more holistic view of the customer's experience. No two customer journey maps are ever really identical, even if there can be a lot of commonality in the themes and issues raised by different customers.

Whilst the journey map is the expression of the customer's experience, a service blueprint is a description of what is happening inside the organisation. In some cases, the internal workings are very messy but CX is relatively seamless. A strong customer culture goes a long way in overcoming these issues! However, it is important not only to consider how CX can be improved but also how the internal teams, systems and processes can align better to improve it.

Once the 'as is' state has been mapped out, journey maps and service blueprints can be created to understand what the future ideal state should be. Then, it is a case of coming up with a cross-functional action plan to help close the gap. Some improvements can be made relatively quickly – for example, it might be an annoying jingle sound or choice of music on a

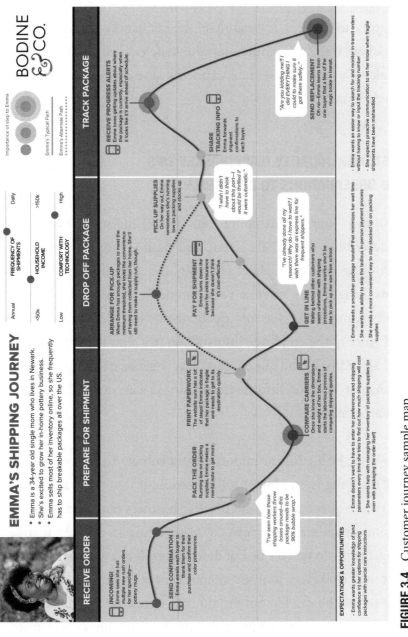

FIGURE 3.4 Customer journey sample map.

Source: Kerry Bodine. Reproduced with permission.

call centre system that needs replacing. Others might be more complex to address, for example, the company's app does not work very well, or customer questions such as 'why do I need to speak with three different departments to resolve an apparently simple issue?'

CUSTOMER JOURNEY MAPPING: KEY TIPS AND OBSERVATIONS TO GET IT RIGHT

Customer journey mapping can be an indispensable way of describing both the current and desired future-state CX. According to Carla Hall, Founder and Director of Cudos Consulting, 'They offer a very simple yet powerful way of synthesising (often lots of) qualitative voice of the customer and voice of the employee information (e.g. emotions, feelings, verbal feedback) and quantitative data (e.g. observational, operational or systems information) into an easy-to-understand, visual format'.

However, Hall adds an important disclaimer, 'Customer journey mapping is an almost futile exercise if it is not translated into consequent actions and positive business outcomes'. Many organisations make the mistake of investing in journey mapping, merely to tick the box of describing CX at a given moment in time. However, journey mapping is an iterative exercise that should be carried out on multiple occasions – not least to measure actions against positive customer outcomes. Also, it is crucial to have leadership fully behind the programme, in the same way as it is for driving a customer-led company culture. Indeed, this is true for all other elements of the C-change growth engine.

VoC and voice of the employee feedback are both essential ingredients when it comes to understanding CX. 'Understanding the types of issues raised by both employees and customers *before* carrying out a journey mapping workshop allows you to probe for the right things during the workshops', adds Hall.

According to Annette Franz, 'Transforming the customer experience is as much about inside-out as it is about outside-in. I've seen it time and time again: if you fix 90% of what's going wrong with the employee experience or what the employee is finding painful or inefficient to do in delivering the customer experience, you'd fix most of the CX issues before you even need to speak to the customer'.

From a practitioner standpoint, having CX mapped out with employees before speaking to the customer also provides an easier starting point and framework for discussion with customers. 'It is difficult taking a blank canvas to customers because they struggle to properly articulate their journey', adds Hall. Customers are not always able to recall all the interactions they had with a company until they are prompted.

The customer feedback stage typically comprises one or two parts – either purely qualitative or both qualitative and quantitative. In the first part, customer journey workshops would typically involve a facilitated discussion about events, or so-called 'moments of truth' along the journey, together with associated thoughts and emotions. The second part would look at more operational or statistical data – for example, hold time for a call centre, time to resolve the issue, percentage of problems resolved, money saved, etc.

Following the outside-in perspective, it is then time to turn back to staff to understand how the customer journey maps can be translated into action plans and roadmaps for delivering cross-functional change. For example, how would a call centre representative engage differently with an angry customer? What type of training would he or she need? Or, if the product is full of software bugs, how long would it take to fix them, and which departments need to be involved?

In conclusion, Hall re-emphasises the point that journey mapping is an indispensable part of defining CX, but that is an iterative process that must be repeated and checked against business outcomes over time: 'It's not a one-off exercise! Go back to either the same clients, new customers, or a mix of both to see what progress has been made'. Going back to the same clients can be useful to demonstrate that positive changes have been made. In

B2B, this might form part of Customer Advisory Boards (as covered in the Customer Engagement chapter).

AVOIDING COMMON JOURNEY MAP PITFALLS

Saul Gurdus is the founder of Method Garage, a company that helps companies define their Customer Success strategy through data and design. In his recent blog 'Customer journey mapping: 5 traps and tips from the trenches', Saul pointed out five common pitfalls to avoid when carrying out journey mapping:

1. Don't just map journeys for the sake of it. Do it to solve a specific problem, for example, 'we've noticed that customers who have problems in the on-boarding stage almost always churn. How do we fix it?'
2. Avoid customer interaction by proxy. In other words, do not just assume you know what customers think and feel because you have read the last NPS survey results. Customers need to be part of the sessions in person – nothing beats the face-to-face contact.
3. Eliminate the check-box approach, that is, touchpoint inventory – done! Do not just list out the functional interactions at each stage and assume all these stages have equal weighting and importance. It is not an inside-out mapping exercise, but the world from the customer's perspective.

4. Do not map in a closet. Do not just map out customer journeys with a crack customer team. Involve the employees, and run a series of workshops. Gain multiple perspectives; get their buy-in for a change. Use workshops as a way of catalysing cross-functional dialogue.

5. Avoid stopping at the current state. Do not just rest on your laurels. Map the journey, make improvements, perform the journey map session again, make more improvements. It should be a continuous drive for improvement.

Customer journey maps: Are they all they are cracked up to be?

Despite the massive popularity of customer journey maps, they are not without their sceptics! We know that every customer and every consumer is, at some point, different. Similarly, every customer interaction is ultimately different (especially if you consider feelings, emotions and perceptions, etc.); people are more complex than simple personas! Can everything really be simplified into a set of generic customer journey maps and frameworks? Does this really benefit the business or the customer?

In our view, the short answer is *yes* – but, in an ideal world, companies would have a journey map catalogue for every customer and every persona at every moment in time. Clearly, this is an almost impossible task. However, by carrying out a decent number (let us say 20-30, in the best-case scenario) of customer and employee journey mapping workshops, the company and its employees will begin to develop a broader and more informed view of the customer journeys (and experience) today. Also, they will develop a deeper under-standing of the current cross-functional service blueprint, as well as future state journeys and blueprints. Further-more, nothing should stop Customer Success managers from taking any generic maps and understanding what tuning might need to be done to reflect the journeys of the clients for which they are responsible (see the Customer Success chapter).

Driving operational excellence with customer journey maps

Even though maps are like snowflakes, (i.e. no one map is exactly the same) after performing a series of customer workshops, it is still possible to spot trends and patterns across customer journeys. These maps can be translated into generic customer journey stages that can help define the cross-functional customer interactions (either direct or indirect) and, ultimately, provide a framework for operational measurement and change that is aligned to CX. We will cover this in more detail in the Customer Health chapter, but suffice it to say that most companies can define a generic, or set of generic, journey maps that serve as cross-functional frameworks for transformation.

For example, following a series of customer workshops and advisory boards, Finastra, a leading fintech, could produce a generic customer journey framework. Customers from multiple regions and multiple personas could unanimously agree that the following list of 10 generic stages represented a perfectly satisfactory strategic-level overview of their customer journey.

Awareness and consideration

Needs assessment

Proof of concept

Partner engagement

Purchase

Solution implementation

Post-sales support

Training and communication

Renewal and repurchase

Recommendation and endorsement

In the Customer Health chapter, we will explore Finastra's Customer Health index, which was based entirely on these 10 generic journey stages. Also, Finastra could build on this even further by mapping customer survey data to these 10 generic stages, that is, comparing the operational view with feedback data.

THE POWER OF CUSTOMER ADVOCATES ALONG
THE CUSTOMER JOURNEY

In the Customer Advocacy chapter, we will consider in more detail the power of customer advocacy in growing a company's brand and business. Mark Organ, Chairman of the Board at Influitive and an authority on customer advocacy, puts it like this: 'The best place to reinvest your customer advocates is in the customer experience itself'. Organ argues that the best CXs are those that are infused with a company's own customers. Hence, Influitive has coined the term 'customer-powered enterprise (CPE)', and describes it as follows:

> 'A customer-powered enterprise (CPE) is an organisation that leverages its customers not only to inform all aspects of its business strategy but also to fuel its sales, marketing, CS, and product efforts. When executed right, these efforts will significantly accelerate sales and increase customer lifetime value'.

Many B2B organisations are already adopting the CPE strategy, including Ceridian, a cloud-based human capital management SaaS solution. Ceridian's world-class XOXO programme reinvests customer advocates along the entire customer journey – during marketing, sales, pre-sales and post-sales support.

Howard Tarnoff was the originator of the XOXO initiative, and, over a five year period, one could see an improvement in sales efficiency by 20%, a gross margin increase of 8% and an increase in the company's NPS by 47 points. Also, Tarnoff could integrate a number of market-leading platforms such as Gainsight, RO Innovation and Influitive to align internal teams along the customer journey and underpin a world-class CX.

VIRGIN MEDIA: DELIVERING SUPERIOR CX IS IN THE DNA

Since its inception, the Virgin brand has been heralded as a force for positive disruption, dynamism and leading-edge innovation across many sectors – from music, airlines and health clubs, through to telecommunications and financial services. Most people relate the Virgin brand to the ethos and demeanour of its founder and leader Richard Branson – relaxed, unpretentious and authentic, yet sophisticated, edgy and driven to excel. When it comes to delivering great CX, the Virgin brand has embodied this since its foundation.

Amelia Mansell, Director of customer experience at Virgin Media, describes the culture as 'genuinely authentic'. She goes on to say that: 'Delivering a great customer experience is in the DNA of the company. It begins with organisational culture and the experience the company creates for its people'. In the words of Richard Branson: 'Clients do not come first, employees come first. If you take care of your employees, they will take care of your clients'.

FIGURE 3.5   Richard Branson, Founder, Virgin.

Source: Visual Eye http://www.visualeye.biz/. Reproduced with permission.

FIGURE 3.6   Amelia Mansell, Head of customer experience, Virgin Media.

Source: Amelia Mansell. Reproduced with permission.

FIGURE 3.7   Virgin Media Trinity App.

Source: https://vimeo.com/205946515. Accessed 18th June 2019. Screenshot by Chris Adlard and Daniel Bausor.

Mansell explains: 'If employees enjoy working at Virgin Media and take pride in the Virgin brand, they will be prepared to go the extra mile for the customer'.

Virgin Media offers four multi-award-winning services – broadband, TV, mobile and home phone – to residential and business customers across the United Kingdom and Ireland. It competes with the likes of BT and Sky. Virgin Media's dedicated, ultrafast network delivers the fastest widely available broadband speeds to homes and businesses. Virgin Media is expanding this through its Project Lightning pro- gramme, which could extend the network to up to 17 million premises.

As a business, Virgin Media constantly strives for competitive advantage through delivering a differentiated suite of 'quad-play' products and great customer service.

The rising expectations of today's customers in an increasingly digital world means Virgin Media continues to develop and understand how emerging digital technologies can be used to the best – and most appropriate – effect for its people and customers. This is illustrated by the development of a mobile application for field technicians, which was achieved through a journey-led approach to understand what tools and information Virgin Media field technicians needed to support them in delivering great CX.

Virgin Media employs field technicians to install and service new broadband, TV and phone services to homes and businesses across the United Kingdom. The company's technicians are very much the face of the Virgin Media brand with these customers. Good interpersonal skills are essential for technicians, and the in-house teams receive regular training to help them maintain the highest standards of technical expertise, courtesy and professionalism. Mansell explains: 'Our customers may only ever meet one of our people when we install our products or make a service visit when something doesn't quite go to plan. So it's really important that we give a great experience at these points'.

The Virgin Media customer experience team was keen to understand how it could make things as simple and efficient as possible for the field service technicians to deliver the best possible CX. The team initiated a number of facilitated multidisciplinary employee focus groups, in which the as-is and future-state customer journeys were discussed and mapped out. Most importantly, the team looked at how the future-state CX journey could be translated into service design blueprints.

The team engaged a technology partner, Virtusa, to help with this exercise, not least because many of the 'moments of truth' underpinning both the technicians' and customers' experience were technology-driven. According to Stephen Wood, Vice President of Innovation at Virtusa, 'The series of workshops allowed us to produce a journey map for each of the different levels of network, since the use cases were slightly different. But interestingly, this approach also helped us identify the common root causes of issues across the different network levels'.

Once the common issues were understood, it helped Virgin Media's CX team introduce a series of important preventative measures to make life as straightforward as possible for field technicians. Providing the right tools and technology was a critical success factor, which resulted in the team working with Virtusa to develop a new mobile application for technicians. The application provided a single place to find and fix technical faults, map Wi-Fi spots, check signal strength and Wi-Fi speeds, and find the required technical documentation. Mansell continues: 'We called this mobile app *Trinity* – the application was all about using engaging technology and exploiting our rich datasets to provide the right information to our engineers to setup the home environment, and support our customers in getting the most out of their experience with our services'.

Not only was this a brilliant example of a good employee experience leading to good CX, it was also a great showcase for co-creation. Many of the ideas (and indeed prototypes) for the features and functions of the Trinity app were originally sourced from technicians themselves who had, up to then, created their own workarounds and gadgets to fix issues they had faced. 'By pooling ideas from multiple technicians, we could deliver a truly innovative and useful piece of the technology that engineers actually asked for. It wasn't a top-down mandate, it was true grassroots innovation', remarks Wood.

In Chapter 5 (titled 'Digital'), we will consider some of the best practices around user-led design innovation, including how customers and users create their own pathways that are typically not defined by straight lines and theoretical models. Great technology-driven CX is based on real-use cases, and not ones dreamed up in isolation in the lab.

Mansell reflects on lessons learnt when it comes to improving CX. Reflecting on some of the points in the Technology chapter, one of the biggest challenges has been to ensure that technology and platforms make life as easy as possible for employees to serve the customer. While the Trinity app is an example of positive advancement in technology, sometimes adding new technologies to a complex legacy IT estate can result in workarounds or compromises which can make life more complicated, rather than easier, for employees. The Trinity app, for example, is part of a broader 'single customer view' solution that signals the health of the network for multiple employee groups – both in the field and in the office, although work is ongoing within the business to rationalise and unify platforms.

As Virgin Media embarks on the next phase of its digital transformation, another lesson learnt confirms the need for holistic, customer-centric, journey-led design, supported by brilliant technology-led solutions – and not vice versa. Previous experience has shown that starting with technology first can lead to solutions that are not fit for purpose and can be detrimental to CX. Delivering a fully-integrated customer and digital experience is more about cross-functional alignment than it is about using the most current technology. As we presented earlier, CX should be human first, technology second.

Mansell provides three key recommendations to CEOs and executives seeking to deliver great CX. First, start with the employee. Not only will they become your biggest advocates, they have a wealth of first-hand knowledge about what is needed to deliver positive CX. Second, consider decisions from the customer perspective, fostering a customer-centric culture. Decisions are often made on internal assumptions or business-focussed outcomes without due consideration for the customer's reaction. Making decisions with a customer lens may not feel ideal in the short term but can result in favourable outcomes in the long term. Finally, it is always good to regularly speak to customers directly or spend time with front-line teams. Listening to customers and hearing the Customer Voice first hand is key in keeping up to date with what customers really want and what experiences they are expecting from a business.

Not only does a great employee experience mean great CX, it also results in a more efficient and effective operational model. Mansell concludes: 'And as an added bonus to Virgin Media, getting it right first time and providing a great customer experi- ence will also help drive our costs down'. Looking to the future, Mansell believes that Virgin Media will continue to turn up the dial on customer centricity. She continues: 'Our north star is to be the most recommended brand by our customers and our people; advocacy by our employees and customers could be the single biggest indicator of the health of our business!'

CX: POWER TO THE PEOPLE

Joe Strummer, lead singer of The Clash, famously said: 'without people, you're nothing'. His words are etched on murals, including in his old stomping ground of Notting Hill, London. In this chapter, we have considered the importance of an outside-in perspective when it comes to defining the ideal state CX. However, it is as much about driving change and action, and this starts with the employees. Hence, the inside-in perspective, as we explained in the Culture chapter, is of equal importance. The Virgin Media case study is a great example here. According to CX leader Claire Sporton, 'It all comes down to people. Technology and data alone will not improve CX. It's about aligning employees (and the employee experience) to customer outcomes and, ultimately, business results'.

CHAPTER 4

TECHNOLOGY

Well-integrated technology platforms and data provide the essential cornerstone for great customer experiences

C-CHANGE GROWTH DRIVERS

- **Build a customer operations team** that can consider technology investments and usage from a customer-led perspective, as opposed to an internal, functionally siloed one.
- **Back-end technology and systems should be as simplified, unified and joined-up as possible** to provide the slickest and

most effective platform to underpin great Customer Experience (CX).

- **Do not fall into widget traps**. It is far better to invest in a robust, well-integrated platform that supports integrated, frictionless CX than it is to buy new technology features and functions without understanding the bigger customer picture.

- **When it comes to providing great CX, data is the new oil**. Most organisations already possess an abundance of data, they just need to be refined properly and used in a way that satisfies regulatory requirements.

Underpinning great CX, which is driven from an external, customer-journey-derived view of the organisation, is technology. Joined-up CX means ensuring the systems and processes at both the *back-end* (i.e. what goes on behind the scenes inside the organisation) and at the *front-end* (i.e. what the customer sees), or a mix of technologies covering both aspects, are as integrated, seamless and quick as possible, in the eyes of the customer. Without integrated systems and processes, in both B2C and B2B environments, customers quickly cotton on to the fact that doing business with the respective company can be laborious, inconsistent and even painful.

While the C-change growth engine encourages organisations to adopt an iterative step-by-step approach to customer-led transformation and growth (rather than a linear one), companies should map out their CX and customer journeys before choosing which technology and platforms to keep, remove and add. The ideal state CX should determine the choice of platforms, not the other way around.

A SIMPLIFIED, INTEGRATED BACK-END

In this chapter, we will consider some of the ways in which organisations can align their technology and platforms around CX. The challenge for many organisations in achieving this goal, however, can be immense. Almost without exception, every large- and medium-sized organisation, irrespective of industry sector, has built up layers of complex and interconnected infrastructure often over decades, including business and IT software applications, servers, routers, firewalls, databases, IT security systems and infrastructure management. Also, technical debt is a major issue – with more software applications, more (often redundant) lines of code are generated, meaning more processing time and therefore slower system speeds. Most organisations are desperately trying to simplify their technology estate while migrating large amounts of applications and data to the cloud. Providing joined-up, slicker and faster CX requires a lot of investment in people, and sometimes financial investment in a new technology to replace multiple old ones.

Making things simpler for the customer has not always been in the DNA of technology departments. No IT professional deliberately sets out to give either the internal or end customer a bad experience, but technological systems have traditionally (often with the best intentions) been delivered in siloes. This is either because individual business functions have in the past demanded their own technology systems, or because technology teams themselves have imposed their own (often isolated) views, based on perceived technological or business benefits. In either case, the systems delivered are unlikely to have factored in the impact on the end customer.

Delivering world-class, cross-functional processes and simplifying the technological complexity that underpins these processes are not always the popular choices for business, operations and technology teams. However, this is really the key to improving CX. It is too easy to think that introducing new fancy features, cool functions and latest widgets will solve a bigger issue. However, what the customer wants is a frictionless experience that is as quick and painless as possible.

Ed Thompson, Vice-President and Distinguished Analyst at Gartner, emphasises that companies should imitate best practice before trying to innovate. The best practice is about keeping things as simple and repeatable as possible. 86% of new efforts to delight the customer don't work! Also, they should consider rationalising their product and system portfolio, because this makes it easier to focus on efforts and deliver the right experience with technology. Finally, they should look to accelerate the delivery speed. Customers want things both fast and frictionless'.

We explore these ideas in this chapter.

PROLIFERATING TECHNOLOGY AND TOO MANY CHOICES

For example, to illustrate the issue of choice and complexity, let us consider Scott Brinker's ongoing work to map out the Marketing Technology (Martech) landscape (see Figure 4.1). He first launched his Marketing Technology Infographic in 2011. At the time, it contained around 150 vendors. The 2019 edition contains over 7000. Figure 4.1 shows a screenshot of the latest version. The choice of systems is bewildering. Imagine then how many more options there might be available to other business functions!

In theory, these systems present marketing departments with multiple ways of carrying out their day to day activities, such as driving more demand, improving project management, delivering effective advertising campaigns or running more successful events. They even purport to help teams deliver better customer and digital experiences, maintain healthier customer relationships and more successful client outcomes.

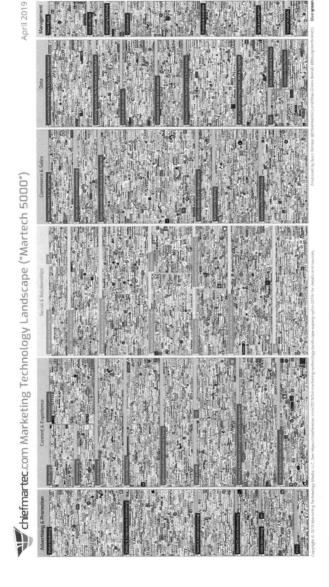

FIGURE 4.1 The Martech 5000 (now over 7000 vendors in 2019).

Source: *Scott Brinker*. Reproduced with permission.

As mentioned, when it comes to providing great CX, it is more important to think about how to integrate and simplify technology before investing in new tools to deliver additional features and functions. That said, in some cases, certain applications can deliver a significant business advantage. Therefore, it should be considered as part of delivering better CX, a key component of the overall drive to customer-led growth. Later in this chapter, we will consider how to align technology around the client experience and provide some examples of best-of-breed applications.

SALES AND MARKETING: STOP USING TECHNOLOGY TO GAZE DOWN FUNNELS AND ALONG PIPELINES!

In the Growth chapter, we discussed why looking at sales as the primary source of growth is short-sighted and why the 'funnel-pipeline' model is no longer fit-for-purpose in the Customer Economy. It is interesting to note that the marketing automation platforms (e.g. Marketo, Pardot and Eloqua) that underpin most programmatic marketing campaigns today purport to offer 'better customer experiences'. In fact, in most cases, they merely provide more sophisticated ways of tracking individuals' (primarily digital) interactions with a vendor. Indeed, the leading analyst firm Gartner puts them in the 'customer relationship CRM lead management' category. This is a far more accurate description of such systems. In the worst-case day-to-day scenario, these systems merely offer a sophisticated form of e-mail delivery and web registrations. The net result? More siloed thinking and marketing further disconnected from CX – the opposite of what marketing, according to Levitt, originally set out to do!

Even customer relationship management (CRM) systems, once heralded as the vanguard of customer-led business strategies and customer-centric technology decisions, have been misused to the point of creating bad CX. Most organisations using systems such as salesforce.com are often faced with multiple and differently structured CRM instances, multiple customer sets and missing/outdated customer data. Often, this has been due to company acquisitions.

In a recent interview, Jeremy Cox, SAP Principal Analyst at Ovum, suggested that traditional CRM systems would simply not be able to address the biggest customer-facing challenges.

In fact, according to Ed Thompson, VP and Distinguished Analyst at Gartner., 'the vast majority of CRM projects have no benefit to the customer'.

A CRM with no benefit to the customer? Yes, you heard it correctly. That is almost always the case in most organisations. This is almost unbelievable when one thinks that Gartner itself defines CRM as: 'The practice of designing and reacting to customer interactions in order to meet or exceed customer expectations and so increase customer satisfaction, advocacy and loyalty'.

The ITSMA survey 2015 mentioned in the VoC chapter and their subsequent research would indicate that investment is moving away from traditional brand and demand-generation activities into more customer-centric programmes. When it comes to technology, we believe that marketing teams should shift their entire thinking to more customer-aligned systems.

CROSS-FUNCTIONAL, CUSTOMER-LED PROCESSES TO DRIVE TECHNOLOGY DECISIONS

Investing in new technology systems does not, on its own, ensure seamlessly integrated CX. To deliver on this project, a significant investment must be made in integrating existing systems into the new applications and reducing underlying technological complexity. Organisations must recognise that, to achieve this, they will have to make significant investments in cross-functional alignment as well as technological simplification and integration.

Mashreq Bank is a leading Middle Eastern bank. Nitin Bhargava, its Chief Technology Officer and Head of Business Technology, has overseen the integration of multiple applications and data systems to provide a 360-degree customer view (see Figure 4.2). This allows both internal teams and, ultimately,

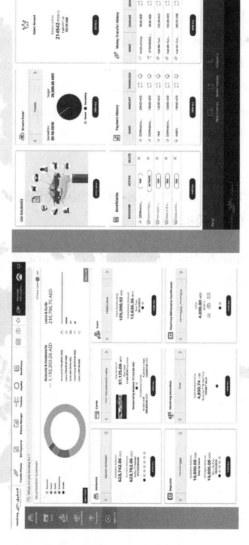

FIGURE 4.2 The client 360-degree view programme at Mashreq Bank.

Source: Nitin Bhargava, Mashreq Bank. Reproduced with permission.

customers to see an entire financial portfolio in one view. This includes current accounts, pensions, insurance, stocks and loans. Even today, banks struggle to simplify the experience in this way for either the internal or external customer. By making this experience as frictionless as possible, it also becomes easier for customers to consider new products and from the bank. This leads to new revenue opportunities for the bank – a win-win! It is important to note that this project represents a significant time and financial investment in defining cross-functional processes and to integrate back-end and customer databases systems accordingly.

WHEN IT COMES TO SEAMLESS CX, DATA IS UNQUESTIONABLY THE NEW OIL

When Clive Humby coined the phrase 'data is the new oil' over a decade ago, his main point was that data, like oil, is a valuable commodity as a raw material, but even more valuable when refined. Also, Clive meant that those who procure, control, manage and effectively use data are those that will win in their respective industries. As technology has proliferated, organisations have generally acquired more data. This does not automatically mean that, by having more customer data, companies have better insight about their customers or end-consumers. Clive points out that the CRM revolution 20 years ago made great inroads into understanding and serving customers better. However, he believes that CRM has now moved away from its core purpose and become more of an internal system to manage the business, or best case, make certain interactions (e.g. call centres) operate more efficiently. In fact, CRM systems have, in many ways, only exacerbated the problem of silo-based thinking. Also, they are rarely used to codify the emotional interactions between customer and vendor. For example, in B2B, CRM systems are used primarily to store numerical data about customers with minimal contextual or relationship-oriented information about them.

Ultimately, data should be used to give organisations a far better insight into their customer base, to make smarter decisions about how to serve them better and, therefore, ultimately to drive more sustainable growth. Clive reiterates the point that the digitisation of every industry is changing the dynamics of every business, and the smart use of customer data has become the single biggest source of competitive advantage in this area. 'If you're a retailer or a bank, you should be scared of Amazon. If you're a bank, you should be scared of open banking. And if you're a private health provider, you should be scared of Fitbit', notes Clive.

Clive concurs with the idea that the brand of any organisation is now defined by the experience and perception of the company by its customers. Moreover, understanding a customer base means better customer segmentation. And all of this is driven by better data insights. In addition, different customer groups perceive and interact with a company in different ways. The only way to establish a clear view of your customer segments, their wants and their needs is through joined-up data. Therefore, in the same way that it is necessary for organisations to integrate systems, it is essential to do the same with data, too. The winners of tomorrow will be those who can get as close to their target customer groups as possible by using their own data, and data they can procure outside of their organisation to better understand and serve their customers.

Clive Humby quotes numerous examples in his career where a customer-aligned data view can be monetised. By way of a simple yet effective example, he conducted a project at a specialist UK off-licence chain (Ashe & Nephew). On this assignment, his data analysts could substantially increase sales of both beer and wines but putting the staff who liked beer more than wine in the shops where beer was a more popular consumer choice. Similarly, they put staff who liked wine more than beer in the shops where wine was the more popular choice. By understanding the customer segmentation and journeys better, management could provide better CX because the staff was simply more enthusiastic and knowledgeable about the products they were selling.

What is the benefit of a joined-up, data-driven customer view? In B2C, Clive Humby expects a 25% sales uplift; and in B2B even more. Furthermore, it's it is not just about driving sales; it is also about increasing efficiency and lowering the cost to serve. Retail organisations can typically improve the efficiency of their supply chain by up to 8%. In short, all this is a key contributor to customer-led growth.

THE IMPACT OF REGULATION ON A DATA-DRIVEN, JOINED-UP CUSTOMER VIEW

Having up-to-date, joined-up client data is the right goal for any organisation, as is data that allows companies to get even more sophisticated in their analysis, segmentation and service to customers. Interestingly, in the Health chapter, we explore ways in which such data can be leveraged to get more predictive.

One of the biggest considerations, if not challenges, in achieving a robust, data-driven customer view is regulation. In every industry, companies must adhere to strict privacy and compliance regulations that govern the collection and use of customer and consumer data. Clive Humby notes, 'A fundamental consideration in the way we acquire and manage data concerns the permissions companies need to use it. Ultimately, the customer has to be in control'.

By way of example, let us take the EU-driven data directive, the General Data Protection Regulation (GDPR). This regulation came into effect in May 2018 and applies to all EU citizens. It aims to guarantee every EU individual with the right to:

- Be informed about a company's products and services
- Be completely erased from any company's records
- Self-select the type of information it wishes to receive from the company
- Choose whether their digital/online behaviour is tracked (e.g. through company or third-party cookies).

Philosophically speaking, this presents quite a different perspective on data as compared to that in the world of Google, Amazon and Facebook. Such organisations are truly leveraging data, often in extraordinary ways, to provide more personalised CX and drive company growth. These organisations believe that data is the new oil. Marketing automation platforms generally aim to apply similar thinking, even if their goal is primarily to drive campaign leads, not to improve CX.

The news is littered with examples of companies who are fined for the misuse of customer data. The fines themselves often represent a mere fraction of the commercial benefit that such companies have achieved or were looking to achieve. A recent story concerned Bounty, a UK-based pregnancy and parent advice service. For decades, UK mothers have received a 'bounty-pack' (containing nappies, vitamins, baby wipes, etc.), (sometimes only hours) after giving birth in National Health

Service hospitals up and down the country. Bounty encourages mothers to join the 'Bounty Club', which offers free guidance and help to new mothers. Very recently, Bounty received a fairly hefty fine for selling their data to third-party companies without explicit customer consent.

Smart companies are those that are not only able to use data to establish a more intelligent customer view and ultimately drive better decisions, but also those that can navigate and satisfy regulatory constraints. Clive Humby believes that, over time, 'the commercial benefit of a joined-up data-driven customer view will outweigh the regulatory demands, and companies will be willing to pay customers and consumers for the right to use their data'.

A related example is TSB Bank. In 2019, the bank launched the UK's first refund system to cover all types of transaction fraud. According to the online publication RegTech Analyst: 'As part of this new service, customers will be protected from unauthorised transactions on their accounts or customers being tricked into authorising payments to fraudsters. Customers are also covered for third-party fraud loss which occurs on their TSB account. Currently, consumers are only refunded for fraud losses in limited circumstances. However, TSB customers will now be refunded any loss they've suffered from their account as a result of third-party fraud'.

This is a great example of a company that has not only embraced the regulation that protects consumers but has also gone a stage further to improve CX by protecting them from something that could have hit them financially.

TYING IT ALL TOGETHER: A CUSTOMER OPERATIONS TEAM

Most organisations have a dedicated sales operations team. These teams tend, worse case, to focus solely on how CRM systems such as salesforce.com can provide more accurate sales performance information, or, best case, on how such systems can be better integrated with other (primarily pre-sales focused) systems such as marketing automation platforms. The role of the sales operations team is important – but since companies incorrectly place disproportionate emphasis on sales to drive growth, there a very few individuals looking at systems and data from an end-to-end customer perspective. This job should certainly not be left to IT departments, who are often too many steps removed from the end-customer.

Indeed, the larger the organisation, the greater the likelihood that *each* of its business functions will have its own operations leader or staff. Clearly, every function needs systems, processes and data to support its own activities. For example, HR needs systems and processes to pay employees and track their performance, finance needs to pay invoices and monitor departmental budgets, sales need to measure pipeline, support needs to track cases, etc.

However, in this scenario, who is tracking the 360-degree cross-functional view of the customer? In a recent blog post, Customer Success leader Jason Noble argued for the need to establish a customer operations team to do just that. A customer operations team could be the team responsible for any cross-functional combination of systems, tools or processes that allows for a customer-led view of the business. Some examples include:

- Customer segmentation data analyses and recommendations
- Customer data consistency across multiple data repositories
- Management of a Customer Success system and other customer-centric tools
- Development, ongoing maintenance and reporting of a Customer Health index (CHI)
- Customer risk scorecards and reporting
- Voice of the Customer system creation and reporting.

Jason concludes his suggestion by stating that 'your customer operations function allows you to access and view all of this data in a customer-focused way. It allows you to shift your Customer Success management from being reactive to proactive to predictive (using the data to feed into trigger points that you've defined as part of your customer journey)'.

The 'knowledge management' discipline has existed for decades, but is even more relevant than ever in the Customer Economy. According to the leading academic institution Henley Business School, 'Effective knowledge management improves individual and organisational performance by creating channels for knowledge to flow across organisational boundaries'. Having valid, up-to-date, insightful knowledge about customers is essential – and much of that is held in the minds of customer-facing employees and back-office staff alike.

The customer operations team should effectively become the nerve centre for all knowledge about customers, to help the business make the necessary plans and actions to become truly customer-led.

USING JOURNEY-ALIGNED SYSTEMS TO PROVIDE A 360-DEGREE CUSTOMER VIEW

While it is generally acknowledged that the CRM movement has not delivered on the promise of technology-powered, joined-up, cross-functional CX, it has nevertheless helped some organisations join the dots better between functions and given them a more customer-centric view into their business. In the Health chapter, we will consider how Finastra, one of the world's largest fintechs, has used its CRM system as the central platform underpinning a 30-point, real-time Customer Health

Index (CHI) – taking information from other applications and sending it back into the central CRM system.

Indeed, CRM systems such as salesforce.com have a phenomenal ecosystem of partner systems that, when integrated into the main CRM system, can help companies build a richer, end-to-end, customer-journey-aligned view of the customer. Table 4.1 considers business software applications that can be utilised at different stages of the customer journey. All the data captured by the individual applications can be sent back to salesforce.com to create this 360-degree customer view.

Advanced reaps a plentiful customer harvest from essential CRM groundwork

'We will continue to drive our success by further investing in our products and continuing to provide excellence in innovative technology and customer support, leading us to our goal of becoming a world-class organisation', Gordon Wilson, CEO of Advanced.

Advanced provides enterprise and market-focused software systems that simplify the complex and make a difference, improving the lives of millions of people in the UK. Advanced is recognised as a British business success story, having grown to a £750 million company in just 8 years. Following

TABLE 4.1 System examples aligned to customer journey stages.

Customer journey stage	Description of stage	Examples of journey-aligned CRM-integrated systems	Journey-aligned customer and company benefits of the system
Awareness and consideration	Before any individual or organisation decides to buy a product or system from a company, they interact with an organisation's brand in many ways – mainly digitally, through a company's own websites and the web, and offline in physical environments such as industry conferences. It is possible, to varying degrees, to track some of this activity to measure interactions before a customer chooses to buy.	Marketo, Eloqua, Engagio	*Customer:* More targeted and relevant products and services, more engaging information and communications *Company:* Can track the interactions of customers and prospects before they decide to buy and gauge their potential interest

(continued)

117

TABLE 4.1 (Continued)

Customer journey stage	Description of stage	Examples of journey-aligned CRM-integrated systems	Journey-aligned customer and company benefits of the system
Need assessment	As part of the consideration process, customers will weigh up the pros and cons of a company's products and services based on their own needs and wants, and compare to competitor offerings.	Revegy, Qvidian	*Customer:* Can make a more informed choice and the relevant internal business case where needed *Company:* Can better plan its resources accordingly, understand the customer better and tailor its offerings accordingly
Proof of concept	Customers can see live demonstrations, analyse trial versions or receive tester examples of a company's products or services before they buy.	Pre-sales adviser	*Customer:* Gets to touch and feel product or service before proceeding *Company:* Gets another chance to convince the customer to engage and buy
Partner engagement	Partners may present additional value-added offerings to a company's products or services (e.g. insurance protection on flights, delivery partners for tech companies).	PRM salesforce	*Customer:* Receives a richer experience *Company:* Fulfil missing parts of customer needs

Purchase	Making the purchase process as seamless and easy as possible. Minimising the number of purchasing steps.	RFPIO	*Customer:* Makes it simple to do business *Company:* Accelerates transaction time
System implementation	Once the customer has bought, how easy does he or she find it to use the product, service or system? How soon was the customer able to see a return or benefit from his or her investment?	Microsoft Project	*Customer:* Receives value faster *Company:* Fulfils on its sale promise to customers
Post-sales support	Things rarely go completely according to plan; most companies offer some form of post-sales support. The efficiency and effectiveness of the support organisation is a necessary component of any customer journey.	Zendesk	*Customer:* Gets issues resolved quickly *Company:* Reduces cost to service customer
Training and communication	Helping the customer make the best use of your product and service, and access online communities, training workshops, etc.	Cvent Instructure	*Customer:* Extracts maximum value from investment *Company:* Provides a richer client experience

(continued)

TABLE 4.1 (Continued)

Customer journey stage	Description of stage	Examples of journey-aligned CRM-integrated systems	Journey-aligned customer and company benefits of the system
Renewal and repurchase	In the subscription dynamic today, where consumers and business customers alike buy on a subscription basis, how can companies make it easy to buy additional products and services or renew their relationships?	Sage, Quickbooks	*Customer*: Enjoys the ease of doing business *Company*: Makes it harder for the client to switch, drives increased revenue from client
Recommendation and endorsement	How likely and how easy is it that consumers and customers will recommend an organisation and its products and services?	RO Innovation, Influitive, Trustradius	*Customer*: Feels empathy to your brand *Company*: Recruits the best salesforce it could ever hope for

Source: Developed and owned by Chris Adlard and Daniel Bausor.

its acquisition by Vista Equity Partners in March 2015, the business has undergone significant transformation and investment in its people and solutions, creating a solid platform for further impressive growth.

Advanced employs 2000 people and has a loyal customer base of more than 20,000 organisations. Led by Gordon Wilson, Advanced has undertaken what is arguably the largest transformation of any UK company, helping the £220 million turnover business leap from 135th position in the Sunday Times Top Track 250 to the 97th place.

Since joining the company nearly 2 years ago, CEO Gordon Wilson has exemplified industry excellence, driving the creation of a new, consolidated leadership team, investing in the development of a dynamic and driven workforce as well as revolutionising Advanced's structure to reinvent every aspect of the business.

When Vista Equity Partners acquired Advanced in 2015, the company effectively comprised 13 separate sub-organisations (born primarily out of previous acquisitions). Working closely with Vista, Advanced's leadership team soon initiated a number of strategic change programmes across the organisation, including rationalisation and unification of systems, processes and functions.

By mid-2016, after (just) 6 months of hard graft, the multitude of CRM installations had been consolidated into a single instance of salesforce.com. This entailed cleaning and importing 13 sets of customer data against a common data format set (e.g. customer names, site locations, job titles and job roles), removing duplicate entries and even ensuring a consistent product naming convention.

Such a project may not appear as groundbreaking, innovative or stimulating as, for example, deploying a robot or delivering a cutting-edge virtual reality project. However, its strategic and operational importance, as an integral part of delivering enhanced CX, is immense. Very few organisations today apply this level of hygiene to their back-end systems (because it is often too big a problem to fix!), and the rest, therefore, sadly have far less chance of delivering frictionless, joined-up CX.

Once the essential groundwork had been carried out, Advanced was able to reap massive rewards. Peter Sadler, Director of Customer and (interestingly) Product Marketing at Advanced, led many of these transformation programmes (see Figure 4.3). Sadler points out: 'We can now communicate with our customers in a way that is far more meaningful and relevant'. Many B2B organisations today, in a race to deliver campaigns to market, resign themselves to using marketing automation platforms to bombard their clients with uncoordinated and poorly targeted e-mails. Thanks to this approach, Advanced software

FIGURE 4.3   Peter Sadler, Director of Customer and Product Marketing at Advanced.

Source: Peter Sadler. Reproduced with permission.

can now deliver far more timely and relevant communications to its customers. 'We now send monthly targeted e-newsletters to our clients, only about the things they're interested in', remarks Sadler. Blisteringly simple, brilliantly effective.

But the fruits of their labour did not stop there. When GDPR came into effect in 2018, Advanced was already well prepared. 'It really wasn't that painful for us. Our customer data sets were relatively clean. Our contact permissions and opt-ins were in good order', adds Sadler. Compare this to most organisations, where GDPR has been nothing short of a nightmare! Advanced could also use this exercise to grow the quantity of opted-in relevant decision-maker contacts in their customer database from 200 to over 7000 contacts – in just 2 years.

'The excellent working relationship between our Chief Marketing Officer and Chief Sales Officer has been a critical success factor throughout this journey', notes Sadler. How many times do we see a disconnect between these functions? Very often, it is because marketing is not aligning its efforts around customers, and sales is not seeing the value that marketing brings, thus creating a vicious circle of mistrust and misalignment. In this refreshingly simple yet effective example of co-operation, there is one thing that has truly united the functions: The customer! Cast your mind back to Levitt's quote in Marketing Myopia: The entire organisation should be focused on generating and satisfying the customer. Advanced provides a great case in point. The customer, once again, is the ultimate rallying call – not just as a visionary statement, but as an operational reality.

Yet more fruits have since been harvested: The CRM system is also the central platform from which all customers access their support portal. The portal allows customers to log helpdesk issues, search the knowledge base, download hints/tips and video tutorials, etc. But that is still not all! Advanced has built a CHI, and implemented a predictive analytics tool and a sales engagement tool on top of its CRM system. In short, the CRM system is not only being used as it was originally intended – to manage customer relationships – but also a whole lot more.

In the Health chapter, we will consider the power of CHIs. Suffice to say that Advanced's CHI has allowed it to both understand the customers that need the most support and to identify and predict at-risk customers where cross-functional action plans and executive support are applied to ensure that risks are mitigated ahead of time. The predictive analytics tool (Sidetrade) helps the company identify the next best sales actions for clients (e.g. delivering important communications about products and solutions, or training and support). Also the sales engagement tool (SalesLoft) helps provide more consistent CX during the pre-sales phase. In other words, sales is able to offer more accurate and relevant information about product and solution capability in order to set the right expectations with customers. This ultimately leads to better delivery, as well as happier and more referenceable clients.

In the future, further innovation will be driven on the back of the renewed CRM platform. Enhancements to the customer portal will help Advanced to further enrich its customers' experience. Like the concept of the Customer-Powered Enterprise from Influitive, Advanced hopes to further facilitate intra-customer interaction for the purposes of training, sales and support. 'Moving forward, we'll also be looking at ways to proactively recommend new products, solutions and features to our customers, based on the behaviours and actions they display', adds Sadler.

Sadler's top three tips for customer-led technology transformation:

> 'First, there is no alternative to rolling your sleeves up and getting into the detail of your customer database. Second, you can achieve a lot, quickly, but you have to actively work together across functions as the impacts of each decision have to be understood. Third, you have to think about things from the customer point of view, really from their point of view and challenge yourself consistently'.

Sadler's top three lessons learnt during this transformation:

> 'First, as our tech stack has evolved, we have had to revisit elements of the CRM platform such as our product hierarchies, again you have to take the lid off and get back into the detail. Second, we had to revisit the integration we did between the CRM and our marketing automation platform; it didn't track and report communications as we needed. It was painful to start again but has been very much worth the effort. Third, we got the balance of people who actually had the ability to issue customer communications wrong at first. The system and the process were tight, and it was hard as there were some groups of people who were used to communicating who suddenly couldn't, and we had to make sure we had additional people in place through which the business could communicate'.

In summary, none of these positive changes, of course, happened by the technology itself. It is a great testament to both the executive leadership and operational leaders at Advanced, such as Sadler. It really smacks of a well-run company that is committed to continuous improvement. Most importantly, Advanced is a company that recognises the supreme value of its customer base to the growth of its organisation.

THE RISE OF CUSTOMER SUCCESS PLATFORMS, BRANCHING OUT ACROSS THE C-CHANGE GROWTH ENGINE

Customer Success platform vendors such as Gainsight have created unparalleled market awareness for their brand and systems, and experienced impressive growth in the last 5 years. In the Customer Success chapter, we will consider Customer Success as a business discipline and examine the reasons for its significant growth in popularity over this period.

The Gainsight Customer Success platform is branching out across all areas of the C-change growth engine and seeks to cover the entire customer lifecycle. It is helping its customers to build a 360-degree view of their customers, drive better CX, improve the business outcomes of their clients and drive adoption of their systems by their clients. Figure 4.4 considers many components of Customer Success which the Gainsight platform is addressing.

FIGURE 4.4 Elements of Customer Success.

Source: Gainsight. Reproduced with permission.

Where CRM has failed to deliver on the CX that companies are looking to create, platform vendors such as Gainsight are offering a new way of achieving this. It is possible that Gainsight could be the platform of the future for customer-centric growth.

Clearly, any new technology requires investment and a business case. Companies such as Mainstay have produced detailed assessments of the ROI associated with investments in Customer Success platforms. In their recent white paper titled 'Measuring the ROI of Customer Success Management Systems', Mainstay reported the following key insights:

- Every company that adopted Customer Success management programmes reported a significant boost in sales revenue as it retained more customers and sold more products and services to existing customers. Revenue was on track to increase by more than US$11 million over a 3-year period.

- On average, companies in the study reduced churn to about 2–3%, a 5–10-times reduction from before Gainsight.
- On average, companies said they significantly boosted engagements with customers, reaching 250% more customers with some form of outreach activity – from 900 to 2800 outreaches per week on average.
- While greater customer retention rates drove revenue gains, companies also reported improvement in selling more products and services to existing customers.
- Beyond revenue enhancement, companies reported significant cost-cutting benefits from adopting automated CSM systems, averaging US$1–5 million per year in operational savings when compared to manual CSM programmes.

TECHNOLOGY TO SUPPORT THE CUSTOMER VIEW

When it comes to choosing the right technology for a business, there are countless possibilities, strategies and approaches. When it comes to creating an outside-in, customer-centric view of a business, the same logic applies.

As mentioned in the introduction to this chapter, the C-change growth engine encourages organisations to adopt a piecemeal, step-by-step approach to customer-led transformation and growth. However, wherever possible, it makes sense to under-stand ideal state CX first, before deciding on the ideal platform strategy.

By building a dedicated customer operations team, companies can begin their journey to develop an outside-in, integrated and customer-led view of their technology platforms and customer data. This view will also help organisations become more sophisticated and predictive in customer-led decision-making.

And a final note of caution by Ed Thompson, VP and Distin-guished Analyst at Gartner: 'Customers often know more about all things digital than employees. Part of the challenge for busi-ness and technology leaders is delivering systems and digital experiences that make it easier for employees to serve their cus-tomers and to train them on new ways of working'. In other words, choose technology platforms that underpin great CX, but also one that employees can get behind.

CHAPTER 5

DIGITAL

Delivering a frictionless digital experience

C-CHANGE GROWTH DRIVERS

- **Organisations that provide the simplest and most friction-less digital experiences will be those that win.** This is simply because digital is one of the main, if not the sole, means by which customers experience your brand today – especially with the generations of people who have grown up in a digital world.

- **For many organisations, the entire product and service offering for customers is digital**. Examples includes SaaS organisations and digital banks. Hence, a great front-end, digitally delivered Customer Experience (CX) is everything. Learn from CEO of Starling Bank, Anne Boden, how the bank has won over half a million customers in less than 3 years with one of the world's first digital-only challenger banks.
- **Maintain a relentless focus on simplicity**. Consider new technologies such as artificial intelligence (AI) and robotics – but only ever use them as part of a well-defined digital CX that makes life as simple and easy as possible for your customers. Learn how UC Berkeley simplified the digital experience by responding to user behaviours.
- **Omnichannel digital experiences should always be deployed in a joined-up way**, from an outside-in, customer perspective, and properly integrated with back-end technology, platforms and data.

While the technology, platforms and data that underpin frictionless CX play a critical role, the front-end digital experience (i.e. what the customer sees) is critical. This is because the race to digitisation across all industries has become the primary means by which customers interact with a company's brand, products and services. Younger generations, such as the millennials and those of school-age today, have grown up in the digital world, and therefore consider CX as almost exclusively digital. These generations are wired to think differently about how they buy products and services – and have little patience for interactions that fail to deliver almost immediate satisfaction. Digital experience truly transcends the boundaries of B2B and B2C alike. For all these reasons, providing a joined-up, frictionless digital experience is now of paramount importance.

DIGITAL EXPERIENCE IS THE NEW PRODUCT

For many organisations, the digital experience *is* the product or service itself. Software-as-a-service (SaaS) companies, for example, are effectively selling software on a subscription or usage basis. This trend became mainstream from the moment Marc Benioff kicked off the CRM revolution with the launch of salesforce.com 20 years ago. His mantra was simply 'no software', meaning customers could subscribe to a digital service or experience without the need to even install CDs. Today, the notion of producing and shipping CDs and installing them on PCs and servers seems archaic, but 20 years ago this was the primary means by which software was distributed to businesses and consumers.

Even in the sectors that were traditionally characterised by inefficient, laborious and manual processes, the digital experience has become the new service offering and has dramatically changed CX (and, in most cases, for the better). For example, UK public sector services have massively improved in the last 10 years. Tax returns, passport and driving license applications, and council tax payments are all quick and painless, and the digital experience is relatively frictionless. Now, everything can be accessed by a single portal (https://www.gov.uk), which advertises the simple message 'Simpler, Clearer, Faster'. Hats off to the UK public sector teams and technology partners for this service – it is simply excellent. Digital experiences provided by public sector services in other countries may not (yet) have reached or surpassed this standard.

Ironically, in many cases, it is the private sector that is playing catch up. Many companies that have traditionally been hardware-centred have found the move to digitisation hard, and the digital experience is, therefore, leaving a lot to be desired. Pyronix, a UK-based manufacturer of high-end electronic security equipment (e.g. intruder alarms) for use in residential, commercial and industrial sectors, is one such example. It invented the 'PIR' – the passive infrared sensor, which is used in intruder alarms around the world today. Like cars, the Pyronix alarm system units have, for many years, been packed with embedded software code. Embedded code, often written in feature-poorer (albeit more robust) software languages such as C++, can be relatively easily scanned for software bugs and security flaws, and therefore is generally more reliable. However, in its attempt to move into the modern age, in recent years, Pyronix has started to offer alarm management systems via smartphone apps. Suffice it to say, the reliability and usability of the Pyronix apps leave a lot to be desired; and the overall digital experience is poor. Its app reviews are littered with angry customers who feel cheated, especially given the relatively high cost of the alarm system as compared to the alternatives. What the business does not seem to have fully understood is that, by offering a poor digital experience, overall CX is massively compromised. There are plenty of smaller competitors out there who have built their companies based on excellent digital experiences who will cannibalise Pyronix's reputation and revenues if the company does not address this issue quickly.

PRODUCT MANAGERS ARE BECOMING CUSTOMER CHAMPIONS

In the introduction, we considered how we have moved away from the product and sales economy, to the Customer Economy. This in no way means the death of products and services, quite the opposite, in fact. It simply means that the company cannot survive and grow by being product- or service-led; it instead needs to be customer-led! The role of a product manager will no doubt exist for many years to come, but by way of example of the organisational changes discussed in the Culture chapter, traditional product roles are beginning to change. Pramod Chandrayan, Chief Product Officer at India's Easygov (India's version of the UK's gov.uk), puts it like this:

'The role of a product manager is to be a champion of the customer-first philosophy, to deeply understand the personas and sentiments of its customers. He or she should empathise

with the customers a lot, which makes them a real winner. They identify with their customers, often interacting with them through all possible channels – either physical or digital – to understand their requirements and map these to their product design and development strategy. For product managers, customer delight is paramount. So, they work really hard to design a system which provides an awesome user experience. The first impression of a consumer when any product gets into their hand should be nothing less than a wow! This is the dream of any great product manager'.

This is precisely what Steve Jobs was talking about in the Introduction. Start with CX and work backwards. Do not start with the product!

A GREAT DIGITAL EXPERIENCE ACCELERATES PROFITABLE AND SUSTAINABLE GROWTH

There is another important dimension to all this: money! In simple terms, the better the product works from the outset, the less human intervention is required, and the more profitable and sustainable growth can be. In the following chapter, we will consider the phenomenal movement over the last five years – that is, Customer Success. Apart from the unparalleled demand for software developers/engineers (which is another proof point of the digitisation of every industry), Customer Success Managers (CSMs) are one of the most sought-after roles in the world today (according to LinkedIn – another game-changing software platform!). There are more Customer Success roles than there are people to fill them. Customer Success has been driven by the move to subscription-based business models, especially SaaS. We explore this in more detail in the following chapter, but, in summary, CSMs are recruited to 'drive successful customer outcomes'. In many cases, this means fixing things in products to ensure they work properly for the customer (in addition to managing client relationships in the process). If these things are not fixed, the customer will not renew, and revenue is impacted.

However, CSMs are relatively expensive. Imagine if the digital (product) experience was so slick and so simple to use that it did not need a CSM to help make it work. According to Dave Jackson, Customer Success leader and ex-CEO of Clicktools (which was partially acquired by Survey Monkey before being sold fully to Callidus Cloud), 'For B2B SaaS organisations, Customer Success should be built into the product from the outset'. Dave goes on to say, 'We don't speak to a CSM when we use Facebook or Amazon, it just works!' While it is correct that human intervention, especially in B2B organisations, may well never be completely removed, the balance is shifting more and more towards self-service.

Zoom is another great example of this – the product just works, and there is a far less need to talk with a CSM or technical support to resolve issues. According to Eric Yuan, CEO of Zoom,

'When we talk about user happiness, first of all, your prod-uct has got to work, right? Every time a customer is using Zoom, they really like it. That's the number one thing; your product has got to work. Every time after the meeting is over, customers say, "Yes, this experience is great." They enjoy using your product'.

When it comes to providing a slick digital (product) experience, Jackson adds 'Common practice is not always best practice'. In other words, many organisations seeing the Customer Success phenomenon are quite likely to recruit more CSMs before thinking about how to build great CX into the product from the outset.

However, for those companies that do get this right, the benefits are huge. Not only can growth become more sustainable and profitable because customers are more satisfied, but they are also more likely to renew and advocate. Consequently, this approach drives up the company valuation. Product (software) revenue is generally regarded more highly by investors than services revenue. Product revenue can scale exponentially (i.e. countless new users can be added to platforms without signif-icant new investment in infrastructure, people, systems, etc.) as compared to services revenue (which scales in a more linear fashion).

THE SAME RULE EVEN APPLIES TO PHYSICAL PRODUCTS!

It is fairly easy to make the connection between the digital (product) experience and overall CX, but a good product experience is also essential! Blake Morgan, a leading CX guru, recently pointed out some products that deliver on the promise of great CX. Morgan cites Dyson in a recent *Forbes* article:

'What is now one of the most recognisable vacuum designs started by realising the difficulties of vacuuming and listening to customers' complaints. Sir James Dyson was annoyed with standard vacuums – he didn't like having to constantly buy and change bags or straining to manoeuvre the vacuum. He soon realised many other people felt the same way, so he designed a bagless vacuum with a swivel-ball joint that makes it easy to go around corners and furniture. Dyson products are continually evolving with customer feedback to turn vacuuming into a more pleasant and comfortable experience'.

DELIVER A GREAT DIGITAL EXPERIENCE BY KEEPING IT SIMPLE

Heathrow Terminal 5 (see Figure 5.1) is generally well regarded by travellers around the world. It is almost always possible to get from terminal door to gate in 20 minutes or less. The terminal building feels light, calm and efficient. The automated,

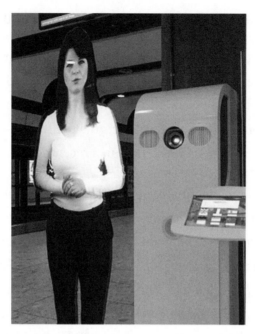

FIGURE 5.1 Heathrow Hologram.

Source: https://www.youtube.com/watch?v=CGfnPh7gn4c. Accessed 18th June 2019. Screenshot by Chris Adlard and Daniel Bausor.

technology-driven processes are slick, and overall CX is generally very good. Once you venture onto the transit train between departure gates, you are greeted by a virtual reality representative telling customers which platform to stand on for the next transit. Some would argue that this use of technology is unnecessary, and that the overall experience is not really improved with it. Others believe it is a more interesting and engaging way of keeping passengers updated. Either way, the reason CX works well is primarily due to the factors mentioned earlier.

James Thornett, a digital experience guru who has led digital experience projects for the UK government, Tesco and the BBC, puts it like this: 'In so many companies today, when it comes to digital experience, there is still a lot to do in just sorting out the basics. Too many companies are doing digital projects because they're technically feasible, not considering what is needed, and not considering what customers actually want'. The hologram example illustrates this point well. Thornett continues 'AR, VR, AI, etc., means nothing if the Customer Experience is poor. Always start with what the customers need, not what the technology can do'.

AI: WILL IT TRANSFORM CX?

A great foundation for digital experience is great CX – this means simple and frictionless. Also, it means being human. However, there is no doubt that AI is having an impact on the digital experiences that customers have. For example, real-time personalisation is becoming the norm in digital interactions. The more you interact with Google and Twitter, the more the platforms serve up increasingly relevant content suggestions. Google Maps is probably the best car navigation software on the planet now, because it is constantly analysing huge volumes of data sent directly back from smartphones to advise (and, most importantly, update) drivers on the best route to take at any given moment. Chatbots are getting more sophisticated – when customers type in questions online, chatbots can often solve minor, incidental issues (e.g. by finding relevant or associated knowledge base articles), which saves the customer from having to speak to a support agent over the phone.

Even Tesla announced recently that it will be launching a fleet of Robotaxis to replace and outdate the likes of Uber. The power of AI and robots is only set to increase. However, the key question is always this: will it positively impact CX, or not? If yes, it will be adopted; if not, it will not be adopted, and another technological white elephant would have been created.

A GREAT DIGITAL EXPERIENCE CREATES A VIRTUOUS CIRCLE OF CONTINUOUS CUSTOMER FEEDBACK

A well-executed, simple and frictionless digital experience goes a long way in delighting customers. But that is not the only benefit. Also, it provides incredible new insights into customer and consumer behaviour that were previously either hard or not possible to ascertain. Thornett points out, 'Digital experiences are constantly collecting data and everything can be tracked and measured throughout the customer journey'. Whether it is mouse clicks, or mouse movements (e.g. circling behaviour indicates frustration that things are taking too long), eyeball tracking, keystrokes, session time, etc., everything can be analysed – and in increasingly sophisticated ways. Thornett continues: 'In the past, getting customer or user data involved workshops and surveys and needed a lot of interpretation which was prone to error and subjectivity. It's much easier now to see what customers really think because we can observe their actions and analyse real data'.

DIGITAL PRESENTS ENDLESS POSSIBILITIES TO RE-IMAGINE CX

Every industry has now been affected by the unstoppable march of digitisation. Some sectors have already been radically disrupted, while others still offer plenty of scope for transformation. Thornett compares the experiences provided by supermarkets' online stores to the disruption that is taking place by fintechs. 'When you buy groceries online, everything is organised in the same way as it appears in the shop. Why can't you shop based on the type of person you are and the use cases that are most relevant to you? This is already happening in the financial services industry today – completely new ways of managing your finances and spending have been launched that were simply not there in the physical branch'.

DIGITAL EXPERIENCES ARE OMNICHANNEL

A joined-up digital experience, just as joined-up CX, will leverage multiple means of communication and interaction with customers across the lifecycle of their experience with a company's brand. Omnichannel just means using a variety of means in an integrated way. Examples of channels could include text messaging, websites, social media, call centres, mobile apps, e-mail and credit card transactions. It requires a lot of work from technology, CX and marketing teams to ensure that these front-end digital experiences are well knitted and make life as seamless as possible for the client. This applies equally in B2B and B2C. Also, it is important to note that the back-end systems, that is, those covered in the Technology chapter, should be considered as part of the integration process, too. For example, billing information and customer profile information might be stored in two different systems. The customer expects the company to have a unified view of his or her information, whether he or she interacts via text, e-mail or through a call centre. This is not always the case, and many companies have a lot of work to align the front-end omnichannel experience with both itself and back-end systems.

HOW TO CREATE A GREAT DIGITAL EXPERIENCE?

As we described in the previous chapter, the first step is to define what great CX looks like. Second, you need to work out how digital technologies can be best used to deliver this CX. The technology itself should not define the experience. Thornett has a simple yet effective mantra: 'First make it work well, then make it look good'.

To illustrate the point, let us take the example of Kent State University (KSU) in Ohio. In 1962, the university was so fed up with students walking across the grass to their lecture buildings and classrooms, that they asked mathematics students to calculate the quickest routes from specific points to other points on the campus. Once they had calculated these routes, an elaborate network of intersecting straight-line concrete paths was laid. However, it was not long before students started creating their own pathways across the lawned areas, which were rarely straight and often curved in nature. In other words, the users (the students) trod the pathways they felt most appropriate to their intended destinations. In 2003, UC Berkeley learnt from KSU's mistakes and took a different approach. First, they waited for the students to create their own paths; then, they concreted them over! This is a great example of user-led design.

Thornett applies this philosophy when designing and building digital experiences. First, it starts with assembling the right team of experts. Typically, the team comprises both service design and user research (those that research, conceptualise, define service blueprints and analyse data), and user experience designers (those that design the user interface, carry out front-end software development, design the content, and deliver it from a technology standpoint).

Second, he lays four simple phases – 'Discover, Define, Develop and Deliver'. He believes that, at certain points of the lifecycle, it is important to apply 'divergent' thinking, and, at other times, 'convergent' approaches. For example, when the service design team begins to conceptualise new ideas, the goal is to really think outside the box and consider as many ideas and possibilities as possible, based on customer feedback. Then, they need to distil their ideas into actionable plans that the user experience team can work towards. The same then applies to the user experience team. They first think divergently about the ways in which the service design blueprint can be delivered (with technology, there are, of course, many ways to achieve the same thing), and, in the end, they act convergently to deliver on time.

Finally, once the digital experience is delivered to the end-user, the process starts again – new research is generated, and new CX usage data is provided. This helps both the service design and user design teams to continually improve the systems they provide, and to deliver ever more frictionless CX.

According to the European Design Council, 'One of the greatest mistakes is to omit the left-hand diamond and end up solving the wrong problem'. In other words, listen to your customers (as we explained in the VoC chapter); observe their behaviours, wants and needs; and then deliver the solution. Technology teams should never dive into solving problems without carrying out adequate customer and user research first. Figure 5.2,

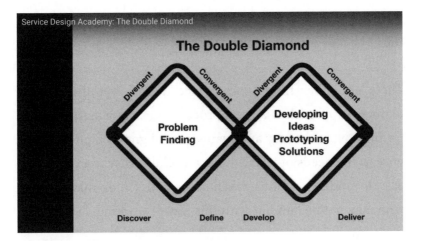

FIGURE 5.2 Double Diamond.

Source: https://www.youtube.com/watch?v=mRd7OVmiyZw. Accessed 18th June 2019. Screenshot by Chris Adlard and Daniel Bausor.

a graphic from the Service Design Academy, provides an overview of this process, showing the four stages of the design review board, with the 'double-diamond' divergent/convergent approach.

As discussed, all technology decisions should be driven from an outside-in perspective, as part of delivering the best CX. First and foremost, the primary aim is to deliver great digital experiences for employees and customers alike. The front-end part of this equation comprises the user experience and product features (i.e. what the user sees – as we have covered in this chapter). The back-end part covers the technology and data platforms (as described in the previous chapter). These components need to be considered together, not in isolation. And all of them should consider other elements of the C-change growth engine.

There are other models to service design, but the double-diamond approach is a great process to use as a starting point for improving the way an organisation aligns its digital experience to the needs of its customers. It is also easy to explain and easy to understand for stakeholders and senior management who may not be familiar with this way of working.

DIGITAL EXPERIENCE REGULATION NEEDS TO PLAY CATCH-UP OR OTHERWISE INNOVATION WILL JUST WORK AROUND IT

In the Technology chapter, we considered the impact of regulation on data privacy. Also, we pointed out that there is a balance to be achieved between driving innovation and securing regulatory compliance. However, the smartest digital innovators see regulation as an opportunity, and not as a handicap. The pace of change is so fast that innovation will find the quickest and simplest route to either satisfy or (legally) circumvent regulatory constraints.

Even companies from highly regulated environments, such as large banks, are now looking at hitherto unimaginable ways of driving innovation that still satisfy regulatory demands. One example is their ongoing quest to mass migrate IT systems

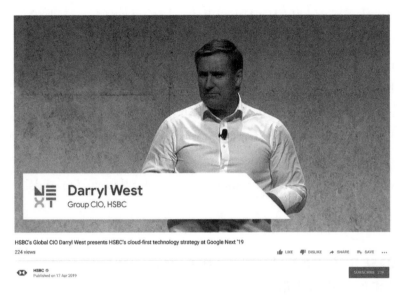

FIGURE 5.3   Darryl West, HSBC, at Google Next Conference.

Source: https://www.youtube.com/watch?v=NS2mgBW_eS0. Accessed 18th June 2019. Screenshot by Chris Adlard and Daniel Bausor.

and applications into a cloud environment (such as Google Cloud, Microsoft Azur and Amazon Web Services). Darryl West, HSBC's Global Chief Information Officer, spoke about HSBC's move to cloud at the Google Next Conference in April 2019 (see Figure 5.3). West cites many ways in which the movement to the cloud is helping the bank. For example, in the case of global liquidity reporting – that is, where banks look to find their current balance (in this case, across 28 different countries) – HSBC can now do this in 2.5–3 hours, as compared to the pre-cloud duration of 9–14 hours. This drive to innovation has been very well received by UK regulators.

But that is not all – West also cites a new project, a new platform for SME business banking. HSBC is developing a cloud-first, mobile-first banking system or application with Google Cloud. It promises to offer enhanced security and will leverage both AI and machine learning. Also, it will deliver enhanced customer journeys. For a large, traditional bank such as HSBC, this is a game-changing example of innovation driving new CX which will challenge – but ultimately satisfy – regulatory demands.

CASE STUDY: HOW STARLING IS DIGITALLY TRANSFORMING THE WAY WE BANK

Starling was founded in 2014 and became a full-fledged digital, mobile-only licensed bank in 2016. As of June 2019, it boasted more than 600,000 consumer accounts in the UK and has secured funding of over £233 million (see Figure 5.4). According to CEO Anne Boden, 'Our vision is bold. We're changing the way consumers and businesses are banking and look to revolutionise the banking industry. We're giving customers unprecedented value for money, a new level of Customer Experience' (see Figure 5.5).

Boden started Starling out of a desire to change the way banks operate and service their customers. 'Banks have operated the same way for hundreds of years, the banking system is basically broken, and the customer is often the one that suffers', remarks

FIGURE 5.4   Starling Bank, Bank Cards.

Source: Starling Bank. https://www.starlingbank.com/news/vertical-debit-card-launch/. Reproduced with permission.

FIGURE 5.5   Anne Boden, CEO of Starling Bank.

Source: Starling Bank. https://www.starlingbank.com/people/anne-boden/. Reproduced with permission.

Boden 'Taking customer data, for example, banks use this to sell more things to the consumer. In our case, we use the data and the corresponding use of AI and machine learning to help customers manage their finances better'.

Starling has no physical branches and can be accessed via Apple and Android mobile devices. The digital experience it provides is based on the way in which customers use or spend money in their day-to-day life – and therefore does not follow the same protocol that traditional banks used when they took retail banking online. Traditional banks have often failed to deliver great experiences, and their retail banking applications are almost universally criticised by younger generations, especially those who have grown up in a digital world. Starling offers a powerful yet simple digital experience that is appealing not just to the millennials but also to older generations. In addition, Starling has formed a partnership with the UK Post Office, so that its retail banking customers can deposit and withdraw cash at all 11,500 post office branches throughout the UK.

Also, Boden points out that Starling is as much about providing a digital banking platform as it is about offering banking facilities to consumers. By building a platform characterised by Open APIs (Application Programme Interfaces), it can bring new functions and features to its customers with incredible speed and agility. One of its fintech partners is Moneybox, which allows Starling customers to round up their purchases and invest their spare change. Another partnership is with Flux, which helps its clients to view detailed receipts for their transactions and gives them access to loyalty schemes. Companies that manage the platform, and the data within it, are those that will own the market for decades. No wonder that investors have been clamouring to get a slice of the Starling action!

The digital experience, built on principles of simplicity and transparency, is also applied to the way in which Starling customers interact with the bank. Starling Bank still makes use of call centres, but combines this with WhatsApp-style chat interfaces. Boden continues 'We're simply emulating the way customers typically interact with their friends or colleagues today'.

Also, creating a positive and ethical company culture at Starling has been an essential part of delivering the best positive CX for customers. Starling takes pride in avoiding hidden customer charges and any hard sell to clients, and it invests a lot in simply listening to what its customers have to say! It even publicly specifies a detailed set of company values on its website, entitled 'Treating customers fairly'. Indeed, one of the reasons for Starling's phenomenal rise, according to Boden, is because 'Customers trust us'.

At the back end, Starling has leveraged Amazon Web Services to provide the speed, agility and scale that befits a company experiencing such massive user growth. It runs hundreds of core-banking microservices on the Amazon platform. As we covered in the customer experience chapter, it is incredible to think of how Amazon has completely transformed the retail sector, and now offers its infrastructure to help transform other sectors. Will Starling do to banking what Amazon did to retail?

Starling's phenomenal growth has been built on delivering a great digital experience and word of mouth. Its best salespeople are its customers. Only recently, in 2019, has Starling begun to invest more substantially in advertising (e.g. in the London Tube, at bus stops, etc.). Additional investment such as this can only further legitimise the Starling brand as a mainstream banking player. However, the brand is more about the experience that Starling provides than its advertising spend.

In summary, by building a bank from CX upwards, Starling is completely transforming the way we do banking today. And this is really just the start.

In conclusion, digital experience plays a vital role in providing a seamless, end-to-end CX. For many organisations, the digital experience is the product (e.g. fintechs, SaaS companies). However, as digitisation accelerates across every industry, digital is becoming the predominant force. The next battleground will be between balancing digital and human experiences.

CHAPTER 6

SUCCESS

Success breeds success

C-CHANGE GROWTH DRIVERS

- **The Customer Success Manager (CSM) plays a critical role in ensuring cross-functional alignment around the customer.** This is because customers are demanding ever slicker, more integrated experiences. Hence, the CEOs and leaders should increasingly redirect investments from sales into Customer Success to drive sustainable business growth.

- **The role of the CSM is evolving from merely a post-sales function**. The CSM is now responsible for ensuring a successful customer experience across the entire customer lifecycle – even before the customer has bought anything from the respective organisation, and especially during the onboarding and implementation phases. The CSM role is also valid in both B2B and B2C environments.

- **CSMs should be incentivised and compensated first on successful customer outcomes, and second on securing customer renewals**. They should not be given sales incentive targets as this drives the wrong behaviours.

Customer Success, like all aspects of the C-change growth engine, serves to drive sustainable business growth. According to Wikipedia (see Figure 6.1):

'Customer Success *is the function at a company responsible for managing the relationship between a vendor and its customers. The goal of Customer Success is to make the customer as successful as possible, which, in turn, improves customer lifetime value (CLTV) for the company'*.

FIGURE 6.1 Definition of *Customer Success*.

Source: https://en.wikipedia.org/wiki/Customer_success

Gainsight, arguably the leading voice on the subject of Customer Success, describes it in three ways: a philosophy, a department, and – most importantly – a discipline (i.e. CSM, VP, Customer Success, etc.). Customer Success is an evolving discipline and increasingly intersects with other elements of the C-change growth engine, just as other C-change growth drivers increasingly intersect with each other. Ultimately, all of the C-change growth drivers must blend together in support of sustainable, customer-led business growth.

THE PHILOSOPHY

The shoots of the Customer Success philosophy, as it is recognised today, first appeared around 2004 at salesforce.com, when the company discovered that its churn rate was 8% per month. But the movement really started to take hold from 2009 with the formation of Gainsight, a Silicon Valley–headquartered software-as-a-service (SaaS) company known for its Customer Success platform. In 2016, the seminal book *Customer Success* was launched. Written by Gainsight's CEO Nick Mehta, COO Dan Steinman (who wrote the foreword to *The Customer Catalyst*) and Lincoln Murphy, the book really marked the moment when both Gainsight's market position and today's Customer Success phenomenon was truly cemented. Gainsight is a privately listed company but boasts over 500 employees with customers across the globe. It is widely regarded as one of the leading technology companies in Bay Area. Gainsight runs three industry conferences a year – one in Bay Area, one in Europe and another in the Asia Pacific region. These events, known as 'Pulse', a phenomenon in their own right, are now attended by thousands of CSMs and the associated ecosystem of partners, executives, analysts and other industry commentators.

The Customer Success philosophy came about because of the explosion in the number of SaaS-based businesses. Their customers buy either on a subscription or consumption basis; so, if they are not happy, they will either not renew or will no longer use the company's products or services. In other words, switching is easier than it used to be. While the idea of satisfying, retaining and growing customers is nothing new, the move to the 'everything as a service' model has emphasised the need to become customer-obsessed. In many ways, Customer Success has much in common with other customer-centric philosophies such as Customer Experience, Customer Advocacy and Customer Engagement.

That said, Customer Success does place particular emphasis on the post-sales customer experience – the bit after the customer chooses to buy (i.e. the second part of the customer journey that we discussed in the customer experience chapter). Also, it has been recognised for focusing the minds of Customer Success teams and executives on driving the business outcomes for the customer. This has effectively injected some more science and quantification into the mix, much of which has been enabled by Customer Success platforms such as Gainsight and Totango.

While Customer Success started in the SaaS world, it has moved increasingly into non-SaaS businesses (in both B2B and B2C). It has begun to address some of the topics and practical project considerations that customer experience practitioners have been grappling with for decades. Indeed, Gainsight defines Customer Success as a combination of both Customer experience and Customer Outcomes, that is, $CS = CX + CO$. Also, Customer Success is expanding its reach by considering issues such as product-led customer experience. The theory here is that, by building a self-service, frictionless product experience (similar to that described in the Digital chapter), there is less need to recruit and deploy CSMs, especially for the more mundane tasks. It is part of the reason why Gainsight has recently acquired Aptrinsic to help their customers drive better digital (product) experiences. Aptrinsic helps companies to automate and streamline and development of software products. This, in theory, should make life easier for the customer (especially if he/she does not have to talk every week to the CSM for each vendor solution he/she is using!)

THE DEPARTMENT

Increasingly, the Customer Success function is eclipsing other business functions such as customer support and customer services. In some cases (e.g. Slack), customer support and services have been merged into a single Customer Success department. This is just one example of how businesses of the future will be structured around the customer journey and not around their own internal siloes.

In March 2019, Customer Success leader Scott Gilbert published a blog defining the key functions and business components of Customer Success. He listed them out as follows:

- Professional/implementation services
- Knowledge management
- Customer/technical support
- Renewals
- Customer Success operations

Note carefully that all the functions described here relate to the entire post-sales engagement with customers, and therefore reflect just part of the overall experience. However, this broad, all-inclusive view of Customer Success is an accurate description of how the function is developing today.

THE DISCIPLINE: CSM AS THE CUSTOMER'S ULTIMATE CHAMPION

While the Customer Success philosophy and department purports to only look at the post-sale customer experience, we at The Customer Catalyst believe that there should be a single 'scrum master' role. This individual should be responsible for orchestrating the cross-functional interaction with a single customer (or a small subset of clients) along the *entire* customer journey. This applies to both new areas of growth with existing customers and new clients (or prospects) alike. This indicates both pre-sales and post-sales responsibility. In the case of B2B, there are primarily two areas where this could sit: (1) sales, and more specifically, account management, and (2) Customer Success management. There are pros and cons to both approaches. To make matters slightly more complicated, the CSM role might even sit in sales!

However, on balance, just as the executive team needs a cross-functional, externally focused leader, which is the chief customer officer (CCO), individual customers need a single orchestrator (or scrum master) who is characterised as both cross-functional and customer-first. We have seen models where both sales and CSMs have joint overall 'orchestration' responsibility – but, generally, this causes friction.

The entire raison d'être of the CSM, as orchestrator of the customer journey and experience, is to ensure that the customers' desired outcomes are achieved. The CSM should not be measured by internal performance metrics such as sales pipeline or marketing funnel. They are the equivalent of the scrum master in the agile software development teams. Sales will be the natural outcome of good behaviours and leadership exhibited by the CSM. As mentioned in the Growth chapter, it is the end of sales (as we know it).

In today's Customer Economy, the CSM, as the ultimate orchestrator of cross-functional interactions, has primary responsibility for the overall customer relationship, and is supported by other functions. Even in the B2C world, CSMs could play this role by looking after groups of customer segments or personas, rather than it being solely the responsibility of sales or marketing. The CSM is a facilitator of cross-functional interactions along the entire customer lifecycle. Given the key role of the CSM, the demand for CSMs is growing and is, as mentioned in the previous chapter, far outweighing the availability of CSMs. Perhaps even a good, new home for sales?

AN OUTSIDE-IN PERSPECTIVE TO CUSTOMER SUCCESS IS ESSENTIAL

Whether it is mapping the customer journey, developing growth metrics or telling the customer's story, it is essential to always walk in the shoes of the customer. The same applies to Customer Success. All too often, CSMs will define customer outcomes that are internal performance metrics. For example, CSMs may look at the number of open support cases, churn rates or opportunities for cross and upsell. While it is key to measure these things (especially when it comes to measuring growth), the CSM also has to drive the customer's own outcomes. The CSM is the ultimate customer champion and should be encouraging cross-functional team members to align their goals to those of the customer!

ESTABLISHING A CSM MATURITY ASSESSMENT

Recently, the Technology Services Industry Association (TSIA), a leading industry think tank, has launched a Customer Success maturity assessment named the 'LAER efficiency model' (see Figure 6.2) – this stands for Land, Adopt, Expand, Renew. It helps companies to understand how far along the Customer Success journey they have travelled, in terms of their key performance indicators (KPIs), critical practices, compensation models, organisational structure and culture. This model looks in depth at Customer Success maturity and highlights some of the linkages between the other disciplines included in the C-change growth engine. At Gainsight's European Pulse conference in late 2018, most of the 1000+ attendees classed themselves in the 'Experimenting' category – meaning there is still a lot of work to be done!

We have examined the elements of this model in the Culture, Technology and Health chapters of this book. It is also worth emphasising the parts of this model that are critical

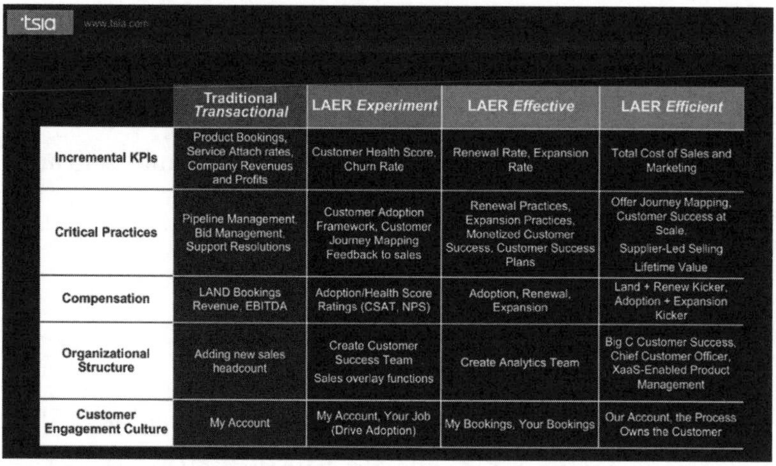

	Traditional *Transactional*	LAER *Experiment*	LAER *Effective*	LAER *Efficient*
Incremental KPIs	Product Bookings, Service Attach rates, Company Revenues and Profits	Customer Health Score, Churn Rate	Renewal Rate, Expansion Rate	Total Cost of Sales and Marketing
Critical Practices	Pipeline Management, Bid Management, Support Resolutions	Customer Adoption Framework, Customer Journey Mapping Feedback to sales	Renewal Practices, Expansion Practices, Monetized Customer Success, Customer Success Plans	Offer Journey Mapping, Customer Success at Scale, Supplier-Led Selling Lifetime Value
Compensation	LAND Bookings Revenue, EBITDA	Adoption/Health Score Ratings (CSAT, NPS)	Adoption, Renewal, Expansion	Land + Renew Kicker, Adoption + Expansion Kicker
Organizational Structure	Adding new sales headcount	Create Customer Success Team Sales overlay functions	Create Analytics Team	Big C Customer Success, Chief Customer Officer, XaaS-Enabled Product Management
Customer Engagement Culture	My Account	My Account, Your Job (Drive Adoption)	My Bookings, Your Bookings	Our Account, the Process Owns the Customer

FIGURE 6.2 The LAER (Land, Adopt, Expand, Renew) efficiency model, TSIA.

Source: TSIA. Reproduced with permission.

in the overall impact of the Customer Success programme, as follows.

ONBOARDING IS THE SINGLE BIGGEST SUCCESS FACTOR IN CUSTOMER SUCCESS

According to Lincoln Murphy, Customer Success leader and co-author of the book *Customer Success*, 'the seeds of churn are planted early'. In other words, if the CSM sets the right expectations and then ensures the customer derives value quickly post-purchase, the customer will be far less likely to defect. The CSM needs to be on the ball throughout the customer journey to ensure the customer experience is as smooth and painless as possible and to help the customer achieve time to value as quickly as possible. This creates a much tighter relationship, based on trust – and customers know that the CSM has their back!

IT IS NOT ALL A BED OF ROSES: HOW TO SOLVE THE TYPICAL CHALLENGES CSMs FACE

Table 6.1 looks at just some of the major challenges that Customer Success teams face today, and how they can handle or

TABLE 6.1   Example of how to overcome common CSM challenges.

Key CSM challenge	How to handle/overcome
Lack of executive customer vision or strategy	Most CEOs want their company to be customer-centric. However, many fail to turn that high-level statement into meaningful strategic change initiatives and cross-functional change programmes across the organisation. CSMs have powerful weapons to influence the thinking of the C-suite: the Voice of the Customer and the Voice of the Employee from cross-functional working groups. The CSM's role is to champion their voice back inside the organisation and influence positive change by communicating customer stories and employee stories that ultimately impact customer experience. Often now, great companies will recruit a CCO to drive these initiatives top-down, not just bottom-up.

(continued)

TABLE 6.1 (Continued)

Key CSM challenge	How to handle/overcome
Every customer journey is different	The CSM is the ultimate champion, and it is his or her job to develop a deep understanding of the customers for whom they are responsible. By segmenting the customer base, it is possible to deal with the challenges of volume. The CSM should first establish which the key accounts are for the business and prioritise those first (e.g. based on at risk of churn, potential growth opportunities, analysis of the 'ideal customer' profile). Once key clients are identified, the CSM should then map out the customer journey for each of their priority customers with the cross-functional engagement team responsible for the client.
Customers comprise multiple personas	Also, for B2B at least, developing a deep understanding of customers means understanding the customers' organisational structures, hierarchies and knowing who to talk with. Much of this relates to the principles of good old-fashioned account management. As the CSM takes on more of the traditional sales responsibilities, he or she needs to build a good network of relationships across the customer. For B2C, understanding customer personas means developing a deep understanding of the profiles and audiences, and their wants, needs and feelings. It is not just about understanding demographic or socio-economic data.

TABLE 6.1   (Continued)

Key CSM challenge	How to handle/overcome
Communication and programmatic engagement need to be tailored	We will cover this in more detail in the Engagement chapter. Highly targeted communication (either account or persona specific, or both) needs to be planned and executed carefully. In the case of B2B, the mass e-mail approach is a very blunt instrument and does not give the customer any sense that the vendor is really aligning their efforts to them. The same applies to programmatic customer engagement activities – for example, workshops, advisory boards, focus groups, etc. CSMs should help drive proactive engagement with the client to drive co-creation and advocacy.
Functions are too focused on internal metrics	We will explore Customer Health in the following chapter. Customer Health scores allow companies to turn operational data into journey-aligned metrics that can be linked back to the performance and activities of each function. The role of the CSM is to work with each function to articulate the link between the customer and the employee, for the customers for whom he or she is responsible. Over time, every employee should possess both internal KPIs and customer-journey-aligned KPIs. Internal teams should also see the customers' own success measures and link to those.

Source: Developed and owned by Chris Adlard and Daniel Bausor.

overcome them. As we launch The Customer Catalyst, we are keen to hear as many stories from the trenches about the challenges faced, and how they can be handled.

HOW DO YOU MONETISE THE CSM?

As the CSM role becomes more in-demand across many industries, business leaders are increasing financial investment in these roles. Microsoft, for example, recently went on a major recruitment drive to hire over 2000 CSMs around the world – a decision that was led by the chief financial officer, who was convinced of the need to protect, maintain and grow subscription revenues. Given the high cost of employing and deploying CSMs, executives are increasingly looking at ways to monetise their investment. One possibility is to charge back the CSM to the customer or charge back Customer Success as a service to customers – a bit like a value-added insurance policy, this applies equally to B2B and B2C. By way of an interesting example, security alarm system companies (e.g. Pyronix), mentioned in the digital chapter, offer both installation and annual Customer Success plans (via a network of approved installers) to ensure the ongoing maintenance of systems (even if it is something as simple as changing batteries in the PIRs!). What this company lacks in digital experience, it compensates for in Customer Success. Over time, these Customer Success plans will no doubt become more sophisticated. Imagine a business model where alarm system manufacturers do not charge you for installation. You simply pay on a consumption basis for the ongoing safety and protection of your home, and you can switch to a new supplier at any moment. Maybe that would prompt a company like this to up its game in terms of digital experience.

Another factor to consider around monetisation is more internally focused. The CSM community has long debated the need for variable compensation models, that is, where CSMs receive additional salary and bonus for successful client outcomes, renewal protection or customer sales growth. At The Customer Catalyst, we believe that variable compensation models can work – but only if they are aligned to what is important to the customer and, at the very most, whether a renewal was secured. The CSM should not be rewarded for account growth or new customer sales, in monetary terms at least, because this may drive completely wrong behaviours. Customers cotton on to compensation models very quickly – they can smell a target-drive salesperson a mile off. It would be a travesty to introduce that type of behaviour into the CSM world. Also, sometimes, a CSM, with the customer's business outcomes in mind, might actually recommend a customer exiting the relationship if it is in the client's best interest. Consider amazon .com for a second; the company makes it just as easy to walk away as it does to buy! In other words, compensating a CSM on renewals might be the right thing to do – but the company is truly customer-centric; it will not push for either a short-term sale or even a renewal if it is simply the wrong thing to do (financially, ethically or tactically).

THE ROLE (AND LACK) OF CUSTOMER SUCCESS LEADERSHIP

As covered in the Culture chapter, we believe that every company should appoint a CCO. The CCO should report directly to the CEO and have ultimate responsibility and executive empowerment to drive the cross-functional transformation needed to achieve customer-led growth.

It is also important to appoint someone in charge of Customer Success, who (we would recommend) reports to the CCO. For smaller organisations, the role might be a hybrid of the two. This individual needs to be able to make the bridge between managing the team (or teams) of CSMs and executive leadership. The CSM team should be one of the best sources of customer intelligence and voice, which should be systematically and continuously articulated back to the executive team. This ensures that the right business decisions – for the ultimate benefit of the client – are made. Unfortunately, just as there is a global CSM skills shortage, there is also a lack of Customer Success leaders. We believe that the Customer Economy will ultimately force businesses, academia and vocational education or industry organisations to redress this supply and demand imbalance.

ALLOCATE SOFTWARE: A WORLD-CLASS CUSTOMER SUCCESS PROGRAMME IMPROVING PATIENTS' LIVES

'Over the coming months, we will continue to grow the business while remaining focused on building innovative solutions and delivering an excellent customer experience. We always look forward to meeting and listening to our customers and partners to ensure we continue to evolve to meet their changing needs'.

– Nick Wilson, CEO, Allocate UK

Allocate Software is a leading international provider of workforce and resource planning software and services, supporting the operational and administrative needs of healthcare, defence and maritime sectors. Allocate Software is headquartered in the United Kingdom, with 538 employees, including over 190 in research, development and product management functions. It provides services and support to its international customer base through regional offices in the United Kingdom, Sweden, Germany and Australia.

In the healthcare sector, Allocate is enabling the delivery of safe and effective care at optimal cost. In simple terms, Allocate helps public and private health organisations allocate the right healthcare professionals to the right place at the right time. The company has customers in 11 countries, and its software is used by over 800,000 healthcare professionals, across 800 organisations.

Its Optima, Software-as-a-Service (SaaS), platform optimises the complex staffing requirements of large healthcare organisations. Alongside automating sophisticated scheduling and ensuring accurate pay for staff that have complex pay rules, it is unique in providing additional benefits to improve the safety of staffing, given changing patient needs, the management of contingent workforce and the engagement of staff through a dedicated app. Optima is used to plan the working lives of half million staff across all workforce groups including doctors, nurses, therapists, care staff, operational staff and administrators.

Verity Dods, Head of Customer Success for Allocate UK (Figure 6.3), remarks: 'At the end of the day, this is about improving the lives of individuals around the world with better healthcare provision'. Dods, a trained nurse, now runs a team of over 10 CSMs. That said, the software provided by Allocate is used either directly or indirectly by a variety of customer personas – including roster administrators, matrons, project leads, bank leads, procurement, CEOs, directors of nursing, finance directors, HR directors, medical directors, consultants, junior doctors, nurses, leaders and delivery teams.

Given the importance of client retention, satisfaction and the interconnectedness and value of referrals and advocacy in the healthcare sector, Allocate's quest to maintain high retention and low churn led to the formation of the Customer Success

FIGURE 6.3 Verity Dods, Head of Customer Success for Allocate UK.

Source: Verity Dods. Reproduced with permission.

team 3 years ago. Allocate then developed a Customer Health score (the ERMI – Electronic Rostering Maturity Index) for its customers to baseline and benchmark their performance against a set of consistent metrics. It then launched a Customer Success programme inside the organisation and formed a series of cross-functional customer-focused teams.

Verity has overseen a number of key actions to help develop a truly world-class Customer Success programme. First of all, it was important to assign CSMs to the right volume and types of customers and to segment these customers fairly and appropriately. Second, it was about arming the Customer Success team with the right tools and data to do their job. CSM teams were then missioned to closely engage with the entire account team and wider business, including account managers, professional services and marketing. The CSMs have to be always on the front foot with customers – staying connected to the effective use of software and benefits realisation, as well as understanding and communicating where additional modules in the portfolio might help meet customers' emerging needs

Focused customer experience activities are co-ordinated by the CSM and form part of the Account Success Plan. Optima customers receive a comprehensive programme which includes system training, out-of-hours upgrades, support and, of course, the services of the CSM.

Allocate's mission states that 'We care about helping people deliver the best healthcare', and it is obvious that this purpose is a significant motivating factor for CSMs who can clearly see the impact their work has on the workforce delivering care. Additionally, CSMs are rewarded for improving Customer Health scores. This also makes good business sense as satisfied customers typically seek out new modules. CSMs also have shared responsibility with other functions to drive product and other feature usage.

The CSM is present as part of the cross-functional team at each stage of the entire customer lifecycle, from onboarding to expansion and advocacy. Figure 6.4 provides a simple yet

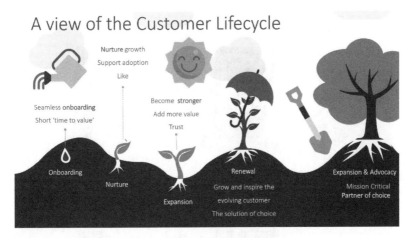

A view of the Customer Lifecycle

Nurture growth
Support adoption
Like

Become stronger
Add more value
Trust

Seamless **onboarding**
Short 'time to value'

Onboarding

Nurture

Expansion

Renewal

Grow and inspire the
evolving customer

The solution of choice

Expansion & Advocacy

Mission Critical
Partner of choice

FIGURE 6.4   A view of the customer lifecycle at Allocate.

Source: Allocate. Reproduced with permission.

powerful overview of this journey and the key goals of the CSM. Words such as 'nurture', 'trust', 'grow', 'inspire' and 'partnership' provide a clear view of the company's vision for happy customers. The use of organic/natural symbols (such as water, seeds, sun and trees) represents the importance of sustainable growth and authentic customer commitment.

Customer Success has evolved to work more strategically along-side cross-functional teams to develop a wider customer experience programme – everything from great customer support and help to move customers from on-premise software to the cloud, to a proactive approach to managing customer relationships (see Figure 6.5).

Our Customer Experience Improvement Programme

FIGURE 6.5 The Allocate Customer Experience Improvement Programme.

Source: Allocate. Reproduced with permission.

Recently, Allocate launched an app for clinicians which allows them to view their roster, request annual leave, swap shifts and book additional shifts to boost their income. Many organisations choose to launch the roll-out of the app alongside the introduction of this latter feature. In these organisations, the use of booking has been shown to bring a positive increase in staff engagement along with a decrease in shifts requiring agency staff to be booked, a well-publicised challenge for all NHS organisations.

In this example, the CSM flagged that the organisation was yet to use this functionality and shared the benefits that other organisations had achieved through its use. This was discussed by the Project Board, which agreed that it was something they wanted to utilise. The CSM took the rostering team through some preparatory steps in order to assure managers that safety would be maintained when staff were allowed to book directly into duty slots. This led to discussions with nurse leaders to review the skills and rules that are built into the system to ensure safety. These preparations then moved onto steps to ensure a smooth and rapid uptake of the app after launch.

The CSM ensured the customer was able to access the tools that Allocate provide to support the launch of such an app to clinical staff, and also ensured that the customer team members were trained to support staff in downloading the app and registering for the service. The CSM also advised the customer that a Champion model was a successful means of rolling out the app's usage more widely. On the launch day, the CSM was on site with the customer to support with any questions that arose. Daily reports were generated that showed the uptake of the registrations, which then developed to show the change in behaviour of staff increasingly engaging with activity through the app – booking their leave – which saves their senior clinical managers time by checking some initial rules to ensure that not too many staff are off at the same time, as well as the chief aim, the increasing number of staff who were booking additional duties through the app. This took away a lot of regular activity from the customers bank bookings team, which meant they were able to focus on some of the historically hard-to-fill shifts that would generally have gone out to the more expensive agencies earlier.

The organisation was very happy with the process followed, with all the recommendations of best practice and lessons learnt from other organisations, as well as the impact that the project had at so many levels. The CSM was very much seen as a member of the project team by the organisation, and the impact of the project was acknowledged as a success by the Trust's CEO.

The team has moved on to a new project now, but the CSM and the customer continue to review the metrics as part of the regular reviews to ensure that activity does not slip, now that the focus is elsewhere.

KEY LESSONS LEARNED

Dods humbly points out how vital it is to properly educate or communicate to customers regarding the purpose and role of Customer Success. It has taken some time to move its clients on from viewing Customer Success as a purely reactive escalation point (e.g. raising support tickets and development issues) versus a proactive advisor. It now has an explainer document that is supplied during onboarding, which outlines the service and gives examples of actions that CSMs have undertaken with other organisations, and how the customer can get the best out of their CSM.

LOOKING TO THE FUTURE

The Allocate Customer Success Team has always set out to be proactive, noting areas of opportunity for better use of the software and drawing this to the clients' attention. It actively listens to customer feedback on how to take the strong foundation created to date and develop the Customer Success experience further.

In summary, the Allocate Customer Success Programme has demonstrated incredible creativity, innovation and a commitment by both the Customer Success teams and other functions to drive retention and growth. NPS scores have demonstrably increased over the last 2 years, and improvements have been made to the user communities and customer data intelligence. Dods concludes, 'The thing I am most proud of is my team. They're completely dedicated to supporting customers in a meaningful manner. They have turned reactive product-feature discussions into strategic-outcome conversations. And they have brilliantly championed Customer Success across the whole company, and indeed with our customers for the benefit of the patient populations they serve'.

SLACK: CUSTOMER SUCCESS AT SLACK, THE UNICORN'S UNICORN

'Slack is the unicorn's unicorn'
– Nick Mehta, CEO, Gainsight

Slack was founded in 2014 and provides a workplace community and collaboration platform. Now, with over 6 million active users and a private valuation of US$7 billion, it is characterised by an exceptional brand, a great product, and has been incredibly successful in raising funding for its company.

A year after funding, it recognised the need to build a Customer Success team. Prior to the Customer Success organisation, account managers were employed originally to maintain client relationships; however, they were not best-suited to growing adoption inside the account. The main driver for this was the sheer number of users added organically from within organisations. The non-technical users of the system especially needed help to realise the system's true value.

As Slack transitioned from a consumer-based company into the enterprise, it was critical to build a Customer Success team. This team would help customers drive adoption inside their organisations, especially as large organisations were going wall-to-wall with Slack, with the platform being used across all functions within organisations. In addition, as customers were maturing their usage with Slack, it was critical that they build integrations and workflows with core applications and use cases.

According to Christina Kosmowski, Global VP of Customer Success at Slack (Figure 6.6), 'Companies have long struggled to break down siloes. But changing culture is very hard. The role of the Customer Success organisation is to drive cross-functional collaboration in order to present a single view of the vendor to the client'.

Kosmowski and her team first set out to map the customer journey and then to understand the cross-functional touch-points across that journey. The CSMs provided the high-touch

FIGURE 6.6 Christina Crawford Kosmowski, VP, Global Head of Customer Success and Services at Slack.

Source: Christina Crawford Kosmowski. Reproduced with permission.

experience to help their customers along the journey. In addition to the CSM coverage, Slack has launched a Champion network. 'It's all about establishing a human connection inside and across customer communities', remarks Kosmowski. Slack organises meetups across cities all over the world.

The Customer Success team is incredibly strategic to its organisation. For a start, it owns both the net revenue retention (NRR) and annual recurring revenue (ARR) numbers. Given that this is perhaps the single biggest measure of company growth and success (especially in the SaaS world), this is a very telling fact. In effect, the Customer Success team has been instrumental in driving the growth of the company.

Slack continues to hire CSMs as it understands the hugely strategic importance of this role. The following job description was recently posted by Slack for a CSM. It is a beautifully simple and clear way of describing how the CSM holds the keys to orchestrating the entire cross-functional customer experience. This is a great template (see Table 6.2) for any organisation looking to run a Customer Success programme.

TABLE 6.2   Slack CSM job description.

CSM, Slack

Our Customer Success team advises and guides a wide variety of customers, ensuring they launch Slack successfully, adopt it widely and are continually driving business value from Slack. Our CSMs work closely with customers to discover their business needs and challenges and then coach them in the best ways to use Slack to solve them.

Working closely with Slack's account executives (AE), our CSMs provide strategic territory coverage, coordinating with the AEs to identify areas where existing customers could improve their use of Slack or uncover new uses for Slack. From time to time, our CSMs will work with AEs on pre-sales activities such as pilot engagements to set up a customer for long-term success.

Part coach, project manager, consultant and product expert, our Slack CSMs are continually focused on helping our customers improve their team communication and be successful with Slack.

What you will be doing:

Empathise with every aspect of customer experience, putting customers' needs first.

(continued)

TABLE 6.2 (Continued)

Guide and coach customers with a proactive Customer Success process.

Travel to meet with customers onsite to discover and understand their needs to help them develop a tailored Slack onboarding process.

Coach customers to be product experts and train their teams on Slack's best practices, so they become increasingly self-sufficient.

Maintain high levels of customer engagement and satisfaction with a focus on customer loyalty.

Identify common customer challenges to suggest better solutions.

Partner with Slack's AEs to help them drive growth.

Partner closely with other cross-functional team members to translate business needs and product requirements into new solutions for customers.

Adapt existing customer onboarding assets and work with product marketing to refine them over time.

Help drive customer references and case studies.

Source: Slack. Reproduced with permission.

Customer Success has caught the imagination of business leaders around the world. Originally emanating from the SaaS industry, it has now migrated across a range of other sectors such as healthcare, publishing and legal. The CSM's role is rapidly cannibalising the traditional account management functions, and there are many companies today that can already attribute significant business transformation and growth to their Customer Success teams. At The Customer Catalyst, we believe that the role of CSM should only increase in terms of business relevance and gravitas, and would encourage every CEO to re-divert investments from sales into Customer Success.

CHAPTER 7

HEALTH

Predict the future of customer-led growth for your organisation

C-CHANGE TAKEAWAYS

- **Customer Health measurements are objective and data-driven – use them to better understand and predict customer behaviours, wants and needs** – without even asking them! While an effective Voice of the Customer (VoC) programme is critical to understanding your customers, it represents only one side of the coin.

- **Build a Customer Health index (CHI) to objectively measure your entire organisation's company-wide impact on the Customer Experience (CX).** This index helps you better identify where to improve CX and how to mitigate the risk of customer churn or defection. Ensure this index is aligned to the customer journey you have built for your key customer segments. Set goals and compensation models for each function linked to the index.

- **Develop client-specific health scores to align your own organisation's goals according to those of the customer.** Link these scores back to the key performance indicators (KPIs) of the Customer Success teams. This will ensure that your organisation is focused on the things that matter to your customer, which will drive sustainable growth.

Customer Health is a new technique when it comes to understanding and predicting the views and behaviours of your customers. It provides real-time customer-led insight and intelligence to your entire business to drive the appropriate actions in support of sustainable business growth. It uses big data and artificial intelligence (AI), analysing multiple data sources to understand the total health of your customers throughout their entire journey with your organisation.

In the Voice of the Customer chapter, we exposed some of the drawbacks of relying solely on survey data, when it comes to understanding customers' feelings, opinions and, ultimately, actions. Customers simply get tired – especially if they see little or no positive follow-up after they have provided their feedback. Also, we considered some of the drawbacks associated with existing measurement systems such as the net promoter score (NPS). This is especially true for companies who run annual NPS surveys where responses can be many months out of date. The information gathered may represent just a small subset of 'lagging indicator' data points which do not tell the whole customer story, and will not necessarily allow a company to predict future customer behaviours.

Steven Walden, author of *Customer Experience Management Rebooted*, adds to this by stating that surveys are not always the best at helping us understand causality, sentiment or meaning with customers. Claire Sporton, CX leader at Confirmit, shares similar thoughts. Claire believes there are now tremendous opportunities to understand and, most importantly, to predict customer behaviours using other sources. These sources can include customer intelligence (whether from operational data, text or voice analytics) – and increasing AI. Indeed, Richard Owen, ex-CEO of Satmetrix, goes a step further by stating that the future is survey-less.

Despite their drawbacks, surveys are still an important part of a company's VoC measurement toolkit today. When combined with other VoC channels, it is possible to build an instant and continuous customer feedback loop, using both quantitative and qualitative data. This helps you to truly understand what customers are saying about the company and your products and services.

However, the VoC is just one side of the coin. What if companies could compare VoC knowledge with their own operational data to understand the health of every customer or consumer with which a company does business? It is already possible today to understand the health of the client base before the customer even tells a company what is happening in its commercial relationship! This is achieved by using 'big data' approaches (where data analysts can spot trends and causal links in data to reveal customer trends such as buying habits that are not apparent to the naked eye). Also, AI (where software algorithms teach themselves to 'learn' to read the data with increasing accuracy and insight) can facilitate this too. This applies equally in both B2B and B2C environments. As Clive Humby, ex CEO of leading data firm Dunhumby, pointed out, data is the new oil in the Customer Economy. It is all about how you mine the data to provide the right customer insight.

By way of further example: in a recent article in *Forbes* in 2019, Tom Taulli listed the ways in which AI will change

B2B marketing forever. He interviewed Casey Carey, Product Marketing Leader at Adobe, who suggested that AI will help:

- Better identify target audiences to deliver more intelligent customer segmentation
- Provide more relevant offers and content
- Enable the selection of the best and most timely omnichannel communication routes
- Deliver the most insightful analytics of customer and consumer behaviour.

PUTTING A CUSTOMER HEALTH INDEX (CHI) IN PLACE

In the customer experience chapter, we considered ways in which companies can map out the journeys that their customers typically take with them. Most importantly, these journeys can be normalised (i.e. standardised into a single or small group of journey types) to produce a common customer journey framework, or a set of frameworks, which allow organisations to measure customer-aligned, cross-functional data.

The example in Table 7.1 is a common journey framework, which was validated with over 50 clients, developed by Misys (later Finastra), one of the world's leading fintechs. (For more information about the Misys CHI, see the case study later in this chapter.) This Misys customer journey framework

TABLE 7.1   Example journey stages from Misys.

Customer journey stage	Primary functional owner/department
Awareness and consideration	Marketing
Customer need assessment	Inside sales
Proof of concept	Pre-sales
Partner engagement	Partners
Purchase	Sales
Product/service implementation	Services
Post-sales support	Support
Training and communication	Training
Renewal and repurchase	Sales
Recommendation and endorsement	Marketing

Source: Finastra, with permission.

comprises 10 stages, with each one being assigned a primary functional owner, as indicated in Table 7.1.

Once each customer journey stage is defined and each function owner is agreed, a KPI or a set of KPIs need to be agreed with each function for each part of the journey. The KPIs then should be weighted and normalised according to a % score, providing a health score for each journey stage and an overall score for each customer. By normalising data across many customers, it becomes possible to stack rank and compare clients against each other to understand the health of the entire business, from a customer. This is in contrast to measuring clients by the amount of pipeline they generate or their renewal value.

Operational data about customers can come from a variety of sources and systems.

One of the most important factors in determining which KPIs to choose is what data is available, as well as how complete and accurate the data is. There is sometimes a trade-off between what the perfect, customer-aligned KPI should be, what the respective department is able to measure, and what data is available. Defining the perfect KPI or set of KPIs can be challenging, even if the rewards are massive.

OPERATIONAL DATA TOO INTERNALLY FOCUSED? WHAT ABOUT CUSTOMER-LED KPIs?

In the Customer Success chapter, we pointed out that many Customer Success metrics (or measurement of client outcomes) are too internally focused, and that Customer Success Managers (CSMs) should align with the customers' measures of success. This is true, especially at an individual customer level. However, this is a complementary perspective to that of establishing a CHI using a company's own internal data sources. It would, after all, be almost impossible to normalise the customers' own measures of success across multiple clients.

In order to implement change inside an organisation, individual departments still need to make a quantifiable link between their departmental or function-specific activities and the overall CX or health. For example, customer support tickets still need to be raised and issues need to be fixed, and projects still need to be tracked and delivered (hopefully on time and to budget). In addition, sales still needs to close deals. The power of CHI is that it turns internally focused, operational data into customer-aligned information which gives the business a standardised view for each single client, so that any business leader can compare apples with apples when assessing the health of their customer base.

Often, internal operational data is only ever seen at a macro or cross-regional level. For example, solution sales teams like to see the total sales pipeline for their product and services portfolio across multiple geographies. Similarly, marketing likes to see the total pipeline supported by an entire marketing campaign. As we said in the introduction, this often distracts executive attention from the real issue, the health of the customer base – as reflected by a set of *customer-specific* cross-company KPIs. Hence, when this data is reported in this way, at each individual customer level, it becomes powerful.

CUSTOMER HEALTH SCORES: GO DEEP AND OUTSIDE-IN TO UNDERSTAND ROOT CAUSES

The CHI, described in the preceding text, helps organisations understand their entire business and functional performance from the lens of the customer. This is a key perspective,

ADVANCED HEALTH SCORING WORKBOOK

This workbook is designed to help people who attaended the Pulse Europe 18 session "how to construct a predictive health score with or without usage data."

The session highlighted three keys to building a predictive health score:
- Statistical validity beats intuition
- Beyond risk - health scoring for opportunities
- Customer ROI is the key to customer health

This workbook suggests a few areas for study in each of the three headings, prompting thought about the actions you should take.

STATISTICAL VALIDITY

TO CONSIDER	ACTION
What outcomes do we want to understand best?	
Which customer behaviours correlate most strongly with each outcome?	
What key data points are we missing and how do we fill the gap?	

BEYOND RISK

TO CONSIDER	ACTION
What are the statistically valid differences between customers that churn and customers that renew?	
How can we use that information to keep people on a renewal path?	
What are our most important expansion revenue opportunities?	
For each expansion opportunity type, what data patterns identify a high propensity to spend more?	
What interventions can we design to increase the customer's propensity to spend?	

CUSTOMER ROI

TO CONSIDER	ACTION
What are the key roles in our chosen customers?	
How does the company measure their success and how can we access them?	
What are the key tasks and challenges facing the key roles?	
For each role, what data correlate with completion of key tasks?	
What must we do to help them achieve success?	

Produced by
Charll Rogers, VP Client Success, Yext
David Jackson, CEO, TheCustomer.Co

FIGURE 7.1 Advanced Health Scoring checklist.

Source: Dave Jackson. Reproduced with permission.

especially for business leaders, so they can see the operational impact of each function's performance to customers.

However, Customer Health scores at an individual level can go deeper and do not necessarily need to include usage data. At Pulse Europe in 2018, Gainsight's Customer Success conference in London, Charli Rogers and Dave Jackson produced an 'Advanced Health Scoring' workbook. Designed to help CSMs intelligently assess how the overall health of their individual customers can be measured, they advised using health scores more than churn risk and to focus on the statistical reliability of the data components in the health score (see Figure 7.1). Most importantly, health scores should give some insights into how well the customers are achieving their goals with the product, which is the most important driver of retention for B2B SaaS customers.

CUSTOMER HEALTH: WHAT CAN BE MEASURED?

When it comes to choosing the right measures, the possibilities are (almost) endless. The Finastra CHI, described later, contained 30 data points and shows a broad selection of measurements.

In her recent blog article titled 'How do you measure CX success?', leading CX expert Annette Franz listed out many possible considerations, including more employee-related measures around more qualitative issues such as culture, employee retention and employee satisfaction. Annette's suggestions are listed in Box 7.1.

Box 7.1 How do you measure CX success?

Business

• Cost savings • Revenue/recurring revenue • Retention (employees and customers) • Profitability • Customer lifetime value • Share of wallet • First call resolution

Customer

• Net promoter score • Customer satisfaction • Customer effort score • Ease of doing business • Expectations met • Accuracy of transaction • First call resolution • Speed of resolution • Quality of resolution

Employee

• Employee engagement • Employee satisfaction • Employee happiness • Retention/turnover (overall, by manager) • Internal promotions • Learning and development metrics • eNPS

Other success metrics

• % ownership of customer issues • % employees know who our customers are • % employees who know key drivers of customer experience • % improvements implemented as a result of customer feedback • % improvements implemented as a result of employee feedback

Source: Ideas for measurements of CX success, taken from Annette Franz's blog 'How do you measure CX success'. Reproduced with permission.

While many of these measurements might be hard to implement in a pan-organisation CHI, they might be useful considerations at the customer level (e.g. by a CSM), or as macro-level, organisational metrics.

DO NOT LET PERFECT BE THE ENEMY OF GOOD

Recently, the magazine *B2B Marketing* produced a report titled 'How to measure and monitor CX'. It considered many perspectives around the metrics of companies looking at improving their CX. According to author Paul Snell:

> *'With so many metrics to track, there is the potential to go round in circles to find exactly the right dashboards to produce. The metrics are only ever an indicator and what really counts is action'.*

In other words, while it is important to do as much up-front thinking and constructive discussion about metrics, with customers and employees alike, it is arguably more important to turn these insights into action. We will consider some of the work of Hg Capital in this light.

CUSTOMER HEALTH: AI AND BIG DATA

Customer Health scores and indices have the potential to leverage a lot of data. As you will see with the Finastra and Hg Capital Customer Health programmes, significant volumes

of data and sources of data have been consolidated to produce a health score for their customers and those of their
portfolio companies. This is starting to allow companies to
develop sophisticated algorithms. In some cases, self-learning
algorithms (like AI) will help them to better predict customer
behaviours or recommend next best actions – for example,
which departments need to be more proactive in engaging with
the client.

AI AND BIG DATA: SOME WORDS OF CAUTION

In the customer experience chapter, we argued that 'human
first, technology second' was a key principle when companies
look to driving a positive experience for customers. Organisations should retain a healthy scepticism about the role
of new and emerging technologies alone being a force for
positive transformation. On a similar note, and according to
Claire Sporton, Confirmit CX leader, 'In many ways, I feel like
we've gone back years with AI. We must look at causality and
correlation and how it benefits customers before getting lost in
data. Data alone is dumb'.

CASE STUDY: MISYS CATALYSES REVENUE GROWTH
WITH THE HELP OF ITS CHI

In 2016, the UK-headquartered financial technology provider
Misys launched the first version of its CHI. The company was

combined with Canadian fintech D&H in 2017 to become Finastra. The new company brings breadth and depth across all areas of financial services: retail banking, transaction banking, lending and treasury and capital markets. Finastra has a global footprint, US$1.9 billion in revenue, 10,000 employees and over 8500 customers, including 90 of the top 100 banks globally.

CHI was the brainchild of Martin Haering, Chief Marketing Officer at Finastra, (see Figure 7.2). The company trademarked the CHI logo (see Figure 7.3) and unveiled this new technique for measuring customer centricity. As part of its ongoing strategic and operational push for customer-led growth, the CHI – together with its client engagement programme,

FIGURE 7.2 Martin Haering, CMO, Finastra.

Source: Martin Haering. Reproduced with permission.

FIGURE 7.3 CHI logo.

Source: Martin Haering, Finastra. Reproduced with permission.

Misys Connect – was a major factor in the reverse-significant annual loss of new deals to a significant increase in new deals over a 5-year period.

By launching the CHI, Misys became the pioneer of a brand-new, multi-variant, predictive algorithmic model for measuring Customer Health. At the time, Misys possessed a 2000-strong customer base, comprising mainly enterprise and mid-sized financial services organisations located across the world. In launching the CHI, Misys could measure the health of all its customers using 30 real-time, operational data points that it could derive from its CRM system, salesforce.com.

The journey to the CHI started in 2013. The company looked to the future by analysing all open sales opportunities across the globe. It turned out that the majority of all new license deals, both in terms of volume and value, were from existing customers. Adding renewal values on top, the company soon realised that over 90% of projected future business revenues and growth came from existing clients. Also, Misys analysed the average number of products per client, and it was clear that the opportunity for cross-sell and upsell was huge. According to

Haering, 'In 2013, we were losing a significant amount of net new revenue per year because of a lack of healthy, referenceable clients'. Hence, Misys set about addressing this issue.

As a forward-thinking, customer-centric marketing leader, Haering was dissatisfied with NPS and other industry-standard customer satisfaction measurements. So much so, in fact, that he even wrote a blog article in 2017 titled 'NPS is dead' (see Figure 7.4). The blog went viral, and he successfully managed to engage thousands of NPS supporters

NPS is dead!

Published on January 10, 2017

Martin Häring | ✓ Following
Chief Marketing Officer (CMO) at Finastra
34 articles

👍 3,594   💬 459   ↪ 6

FIGURE 7.4 'NPS is dead', LinkedIn blog.

Source: Martin Haering, Finastra. https://www.linkedin.com/pulse/nps-dead-martin-häring/?trk=prof-post. Accessed by Chris Adlard and Daniel Bausor on 18th June 2019. Reproduced with permission.

and sceptics in healthy discussion in the process. It was an inspired piece of brand awareness which cost nothing in programme-spend terms.

In his blog, Haering stated, 'Basing customer satisfaction on a single question is a narrow and inaccurate measurement which does not take into account the full picture and definitely loses pace in an increasingly digitalised world. The answer to that single question ['Would you recommend this company?'] is often driven by the last experience with the business, failing to give the complete view of the customer mindset and interactions that will have taken place right across the organisation'.

CHI provided an alternative that is far more suitable for a customer-centric organisation. According to Haering, 'CHI is a transformational Customer Health framework that helps businesses align internally to better serve their customers. It provides an objective, normalised measure of Customer Health based on the full customer lifecycle from the moment the customer gets aware of your business to the moment they renew or upgrade your service or product'.

HOW WAS THE CHI CREATED?

Haering's mission for his Customer Engagement team was first to establish a common customer journey comprising 10 stages. This was planned with a single business function defined as the primary owner of its respective stage of the journey. The common customer journey was co-created with a selection of customer advocates. Then, it was sense-checked with customers at the company's annual customer advisory board meetings.

CONFRONTING THE BIGGEST CHALLENGE: CUSTOMER-CENTRIC KPIs!

Each stage of the customer journey, and therefore each function, had to select three customer-centric KPIs. Haering notes, 'Choosing three KPIs sounds simple, but, in fact, it was the hardest part of building the Customer Health index. Every function had a vested interest in making their own department look good. The key was to define KPIs that provided the most balanced and insightful view of Customer Health, not ones that measured purely internal aspects of business performance'.

Once the KPIs had been defined, they were then laid out on a scale between 0 and 100, and the average of the three KPIs was built to give each function/stage a final score. Finally, all the stages were weighted. An overall CHI score could be displayed to cumulatively reflect the scores and relative weighting of all stages. The final score was between 0 and 100. The higher the score, the higher the probability that Misys had a healthy customer relationship. The following screenshots (see Figures 7.5 and 7.6) show the stage descriptions, functional

Client Lifecycle & Client Health Index – owners and KPIs – Part 1

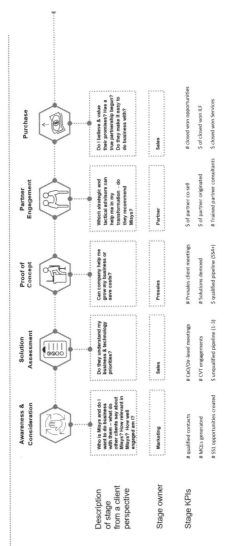

	Awareness & Consideration	Solution Assessment	Proof of Concept	Partner Engagement	Purchase
Description of stage from a client perspective	Who is Misys and do I want to do business with them – what do other clients say about Misys? How relevant in Misys? How well engaged am I?	Do they understand my business & technology priorities?	Can company help me grow my business or save costs?	Which strategic and tactical advisors can help me in my transformation - do they recommend Misys?	Do I believe & value their promises? Has a true partnership begun? Do they make it easy to do business with?
Stage owner	Marketing	Sales	Presales	Partner	Sales

Stage KPIs	# qualified contacts
	# MQLs generated
	# SS1 opportunities created
		# CxO/Dir-level meetings
		# CVT engagements
		$ unqualified pipeline (1-3)
			# Presales client meetings
			# Solutions demoed
			$ qualified pipeline (SS4+)
				$ of partner co-sell
				$ of partner originated
				# Trained partner consultants
					# closed won opportunities
					$ of closed won ILF
					$ closed won Services

⊗ MISYS
FINANCIAL SOFTWARE

FIGURE 7.5 Customer Journey, Part 1.

Source: Martin Haering, Finastra. Reproduced with permission.

Client Lifecycle & Client Health Index – owners and KPIs – Part 2

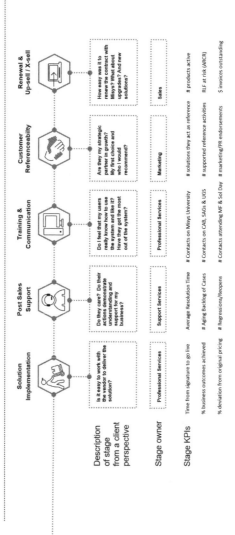

	Solution Implementation	Post Sales Support	Training & Communication	Customer Referenceability	Renewal & Up-sell / X-sell
Description of stage from a client perspective	Is it easy to work with the vendor to deliver the solution?	Do they care? Do their actions demonstrate understanding and support for my business?	Do I feel that my users really know how to use the system and like it? Have they got the most out of the system?	Are they my strategic partner in growth? My first choice and who I would recommend?	How easy was it to renew the contract with Misys? What about upgrades? And new solutions?
Stage owner	Professional Services	Support Services	Professional Services	Marketing	Sales
Stage KPIs	Time from signature to go live	Average Resolution Time	# Contacts on Misys University	# solutions they act as reference	# products active
	% business outcomes achieved	# Aging Backlog of Cases	# Contacts on CAB, SAGs & UGS	# supported reference activities	RLF at risk (ARCR)
	% deviation from original pricing	# Regressions/Reopens	# Contacts attending MF & Sol Day	# marketing/PR endorsements	$ invoices outstanding

FIGURE 7.6 Customer Journey, Part 2.

Source: Martin Haering, Finastra. Reproduced with permission.

owners and KPIs in each stage. In the following text, there is a more detailed breakdown of KPIs and their relative weightings that was used upon CHI launch.

This meant that every customer could end up with a single health score, derived from 30 cross-functional KPIs. Since these scores were real-time, the CHI score could change on a daily basis. For impact, each score was colour coded – red, yellow or green – to represent areas of risk, concern or positive performance. Figure 7.7 is an example of how the CHI looks.

CHI: Weighting and building the overall average - an example

Account: Client name

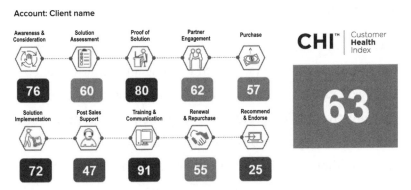

FIGURE 7.7 CHI with example scores.

Source: Martin Haering, Finastra. Reproduced with permission.

The CHI was then integrated into the company's account planning tool, Revegy. This allowed account managers (and, subsequently, CSMs) to track and improve the overall health scores of every customer to whom they were assigned. Thanks to the CHI and the customer engagement programme, Misys was able to capture the closure of significant net new revenue through a referenceable client base, thus reversing the original problem.

Since the combination of Misys and D&H, and the acquisition of thousands of new customers, Finastra is considering future iterations of the CHI that could better reflect the different customer segment groups associated with the new business.

The benefits

The CHI helps to improve the end-to-end CX – for example, to develop even more personalised and engaging marketing content; generate more senior-level customer meetings; maximise the effectiveness of customer engagement programmes; and decrease the number of outstanding invoices. The CHI table given in Table 7.2 provides a full breakdown of all the areas of improvement that CHI can help facilitate.

TABLE 7.2 The Finastra Customer Health Index

Stage	Stage weight	KPI	Definition	Health Score
Awareness and Consideration	5%	Number of qualified contacts	Number of contacts with full details who have not opted out of email	• Contacts between 0-99 = score is same number • 100+ contacts = 100
		Number of MQLs generated	Number of contacts or leads who have not opted out of email and whose lead status is "Marketing Qualified Lead (MQL)" or "Marketing Engaged Lead (MEL)"	• Contacts between 0-99 = score is same number • 100+ contacts = 100
		Number of SS1-3 opportunities created	Number of open opportunities which are currently in stages 1-3 (Plan, Create or Qualify)	• 0 opportunities = 0 • 1 opportunity = 20 • 2 opportunities = 40 • 3 opportunities = 60 • 4 opportunities = 80 • 5+ opportunities = 100

(continued)

TABLE 7.2 (Continued)

Stage	Stage weight	KPI	Definition	Health Score
Need Assessment	5%	Number of C/D-level meetings	Number of tasks / events completed in the last 12 months, where the contact has a level of 1 (C-level), 2 (Division head) or 3 (Head of business line)	• 0 meetings = 0 • 1 meetings = 25 • 2 meetings = 50 • 3 meetings = 75 • 4+ meetings = 100″
		Number of CVT engagements	Number of opportunities at the account created in the last 12 months where the CVT has been engaged	• 0 engagements = 0 • 1 engagement = 50 • 2+ engagements = 100
		$ Unqualified pipeline	Amount of all ILF opportunities which are currently in stages 1-3	• Amounts up to $5m = sliding scale from 0 to 99 • $5m+ pipeline = 100″

Proof of Concept	10%	Number of presales client meetings	Number of tasks completed in the last 12 months where the sales role is GSC (BSG) Sales	• 0 meetings = 0 • 1 meeting = 20 • 2 meetings = 40 • 3 meetings = 60 • 4 meetings = 80 • 5+ meetings = 100
		Number of demos	Number of tasks completed in the last 12 months where the sales role is GSC (BSG) Sales and the activity type is Customer Specific Demo, Generic Demo or Task Workshop POC	• 0 demos = 0 • 1 demo = 20 • 2 demos = 40 • 3 demos = 60 • 4 demos = 80 • 5+ demos = 100
		$ Qualified pipeline	Amount of all ILF opportunities which are currently in stages 4-7 (Develop, Prove, Negotiate, Committed)	• Amounts up to $3m = sliding scale from 0 to 99 • $3m+ pipeline = 100

(continued)

TABLE 7.2 (Continued)

Stage	Stage weight	KPI	Definition	Health Score
Partner Engagement	10%	$ Partner co-sell	Amount of all opportunities closed won in the last 12 months where a Partner has been used	• Amounts up to $4m = sliding scale from 0 to 99 • $4m+ pipeline = 100″
		$ Partner originated	Amount of all opportunities closed won in the last 12 months where they have originated from that Partner	• Amounts up to $0.5m = sliding scale from 0 to 99 • $0.5m+ pipeline = 100
		Has certified partner consultants	Has an opportunity closed won in the last 12 months used a Partner that has certified consultants	• Yes = 100, No = 0

Purchase	10%	Number of closed won opportunities	Number of all ILF or PS (Services) opportunities closed won in the last 12 months	• 0 opportunities = 0 • 1 opportuniy = 50 • 2+ opportunities = 100
		$ Closed won ILF	Amount of all ILF opportunities closed won in the last 12 months	• Amounts up to $2m = sliding scale from 0 to 99 • $2m+ pipeline = 100
		$ Closed won Services	Amount of all PS (Services) opportunities closed won in the last 12 months	• Amounts up to $1.5m = sliding scale from 0 to 99 • $1.5m+ pipeline = 100"

(continued)

211

TABLE 7.2 (Continued)

Stage	Stage weight	KPI	Definition	Health Score
Solution Implementation	20%	% Deviation from intended go-live	% Deviation between actual go-live date and intended go-live date on largest project in account. Defaults to 50% if no project.	• 0% = 100 • 1%-99% = 100 - KPI • 100% = 0
		% Business outcomes achieved	% Business outcomes achieved on largest project in account. Defaults to 50% if no project	• 0% = 0 • 1%-99% = score is same number as KPI • 100% = 100
		% Deviation from original margin	% Deviation between actual margin and intended margin on largest project in account. Defaults to 50% if no project	• 0% = 100 • 1%-99% = 100 - KPI • 100% = 0

Post Sales Support	20%	Average resolution time for support requests	Average solution time for support request cases closed in the last 12 months	• 3 days or less = 100
				• 4-7 days = 75
				• 8-10 days = 50
				• 11-14 days = 25
				• 15+ days = 0
		% Aged backlog of cases	% of open cases which are greater than 120 days old from all open cases	• 0% = 100
				• 1%-99% = 100 - KPI
				• 100% = 0
		% Open defects with no targeted fix date	% of all defects which have no targeted fix date from all defects	• 0% = 100
				• 1%-99% = 100 - KPI
				• 100% = 0

(continued)

TABLE 7.2 (Continued)

Stage	Stage weight	KPI	Definition	Health Score
Training and Communication	5%	Number of contacts on Misys University	Number of contacts that have attended the Misys University (Academy) programme since 1st June 2015	• 0 contacts = 0 • 1 contact = 20 • 2 contacts = 40 • 3 contacts = 60 • 4 contacts = 80 • 5+ contacts = 100
		Number of contacts on CABs, SAGs & UGs	Number of contacts that have attended a Customer Advisory Board, User Group or engaged SAG since 1st June 2015	• Same as above
		Number of contacts attending Misys Forum & Solution Days	Number of contacts who have attended a offline campaign in the last 12 months	• Same as above

Renewal and Repurchase	10%	Number of active product sets	Number of active product sets	• 10 points for every product set up to 10
				• 10+ products sets = 100
		$ RLF at risk	Amount of RLF at low, medium and high risk of loss	• $1m+ = 0
				• Amounts up to $1m, sliding scale from 1 to 100
		$ Invoices outstanding	Amount of all overdue unpaid invoices	• $1m+ = 0
				• Amounts up to $1m, sliding scale from 1 to 100

(continued)

TABLE 7.2 (Continued)

Stage	Stage weight	KPI	Definition	Health Score
Recommendation and Endorsement	5%	Number of products they act as reference for	Number of products the customer has agreed to act as a reference for	• 0 products = 0 • 1 products = 20 • 2 products = 40 • 3 products = 60 • 4 products = 80 • 5+ products = 100
		Number of supported reference activities	Number of times a client has either hosted a reference call or visit	• 0 times = 0 • 1 time = 20 • 2 times = 40 • 3 times = 60 • 4 times = 80 • 5+ times = 100
		Marketing / PR endorsement provided	Has the customer provided a marketing or PR endorsement	• Yes = 100, No = 0

Source: Misys. Reproduced with permission.

CASE STUDY: HG – TAKING CUSTOMER HEALTH SCORES TO NEW HEIGHTS

Hg is a specialist private equity investor, primarily focused on software and service businesses. Hg is committed to 'building businesses that change the way we all do business', through deep sector specialisation and dedicated operational support. This means they are interested in investing and growing businesses for the benefit of their employees, customers and investors, which, in turn, leads to medium-term growth and profitability.

Customer Health as a portfolio assessment tool

Given the nature of the industry of Hg's portfolio companies (i.e. primarily SaaS and renewal software/services businesses), Hg places significant emphasis on the underlying causes and drivers (e.g. operations, processes, systems, culture, leadership, etc.) leading to net revenue retention (NRR) growth. For this reason, the assessment of a firm's customer-centric initiatives such as Customer Success and Customer Health is of paramount importance. According to Joachim Kiefer (see Figure 7.8), Operations Leader at Hg: 'When we look at growing our portfolio, we carry out extensive due diligence around a company's philosophy and approach towards customer-centricity. Do they have a clear customer strategy, do they understand the ideal customer journey, do they have a customer maturity model? What is their approach to Customer

FIGURE 7.8 Joachim Kiefer, Principal, Portfolio Team at Hg

Source: Joachim Kiefer. Reproduced with permission.

Success? Then we go deeper into the day-to-day activities of customer-focused teams. For example, how are their Customer Success teams structured and incentivised, what is the quality of their customer onboarding?'

That is not all. Also, Hg assesses the company's capability to score the health of their customers. Kiefer continues, 'We like to know if the company in question has established a single view of the customer and whether they have executive support to drive cross-functional alignment around this single customer view. We also consider the capabilities and datasets of each prospective company to understand how a Customer Health scoring system can be layered on this single customer view. As a starting point, we always assess their net revenue retention and churn rates as key data points to understand the underlying quality of the customer base, and identify opportunities for improvement'.

Monitoring and improving Customer Health as a means of driving Net Revenue Retention

Once Hg invests in a company, they immediately make available their tools, guidance and operational experts. As part of this, Hg can put in place a health scoring system, using the Hg proprietary data analytics platform, which effectively automates NRR assessment across a business. The Customer Health scoring system collects data from a number of sources – including financial, operational, support and services systems – and maps it onto an analytics platform hosted in the cloud.

In order to accelerate the delivery of a Customer Health scoring system, Hg has a reference IT architecture that it recommends to its portfolio companies. Since platforms and data are the bedrock of all Customer Health scoring systems, Hg encourages its companies to adopt a best-practice blueprint of platforms, similar to that described in the Platforms chapter. However, this is by no means mandated – it is only encouraged, and is particularly valuable where portfolio companies have gaps in their technology. The great benefit of the analytics platform is that it is entirely flexible and can integrate with almost any system and a variety of datasets.

Hence, after just a few months' work by Hg's data analytics team, it is possible to produce a Customer Health scoring system for a given portfolio company. Once the Customer Health scoring system is in place, it helps Hg's portfolio companies drill down into the system to develop a whole host of customer-centric business insights. For example, what does the ideal client look like? Which clients should the business go after in the future? Which customers are most likely to churn? What are the next best solution sales opportunities? Even, which products and solutions are performing best with clients? The possibilities of predictive modelling across many areas of the business are endless.

Kiefer sums up Hg's view on Customer Health as follows: 'At Hg, we live and breathe NRR as the ultimate measure of success of our portfolio companies. We always aspire to see NRR of 100% plus, which means we are not only helping our companies to minimise churn and keep their clients happy, we are also helping them to grow their business with them. Customer Health scoring provides an indispensable tool in doing this. In the private equity and investment market, the importance of NRR and Customer Health scoring is only set to grow'.

THE POWER OF COMBINING VoC AND CUSTOMER HEALTH

VoC information provides an essential view of how the customer is thinking and feeling about the relationship with a company. The CHI provides operational view. When the two perspectives are merged, by aligning them around a common customer journey framework, the combination can be very powerful in terms of understanding the customer base and driving customer-led growth.

Misys also updated its customer questionnaire to include more customer-centric questions that aligned to the same customer journey framework as the CHI. The questions were tested with customers first to check if they had meaning, and effectively represented the other side of the customer measurement coin (the former being the CHI) (see Figure 7.9).

To what extent do you agree or disagree with each of the following statements?
Please answer using a scale. 10 = Strongly Agree, 1 = Strongly Disagree.

☐ **Awareness & Consideration**
My team and my organisation know who Misys is, and the solutions it provides to our company

☐ **Solution Assessment**
Misys solutions positively stand out compared to solutions from other technology partners

☐ **Proof of Concept**
Misys' solutions have been well demonstrated to us before we chose them

☐ **Partner Engagement**
The Misys partners (e.g. consultants, systems integrators) we work with provide value-add services and skills

☐ **Purchase** It is easy doing business with Misys and our account manager provides a good service

☐ **Solution Implementation** The implementation of Misys' solutions has been executed on time with committed functionality

☐ **Post-Sales Support**
We are satisfied with the quality, approach and responsiveness of customer support provided by Misys

☐ **Training & Communications**
Misys has provided high quality, regular product trainings on its solutions and products and our users are adequately trained

☐ **Recommendation & Endorsement**
We would recommend Misys to other companies looking at similar solutions

We value your opinion: Any other comments or suggestions

FIGURE 7.9 Aligning VoC to the customer journey.

Source: Martin Haering, Finastra. Reproduced with permission.

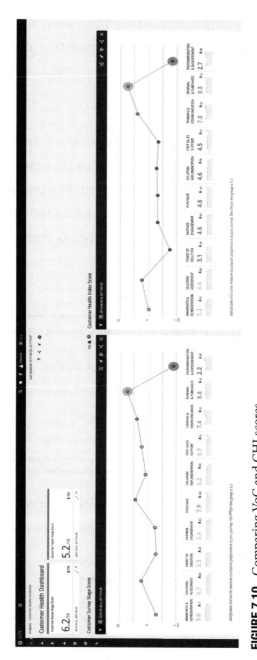

FIGURE 7.10 Comparing VoC and CHI scores.

Source: Martin Haering, Finastra. Reproduced with permission.

The following mock-up (not using live customer data) shows how Customer Health scores could be mapped to customer survey scores. This effectively meant that both leading and lagging indicators could be compared to balance the 'as-is' customer feedback against the 'future-state' likely actions. The example in Figure 7.10 shows, for example, that the customer was relatively happy today, but CHI data is showing warning signs for the future (e.g. increased likelihood of a customer to churn, not increase spend, etc.).

MAKING CUSTOMER HEALTH (AND VoC INFORMATION) ACTIONABLE

One of the biggest challenges of implementing customer-centric data is turning it into action. The CSM should be the ultimate orchestrator of cross-functional improvement to drive successful client outcomes. Therefore, embedding Customer Health and VoC information into the systems, tools and workflows of the CSMs, to trigger actions, is key.

Figure 7.11 is a screenshot of CHI (using sample data) that has been embedded into an account management planning tool (Revegy). The same principle can easily be applied in Customer Success management platforms such as Gainsight and Totango. Ultimately, one of the key roles of the CSM is to drive up health scores.

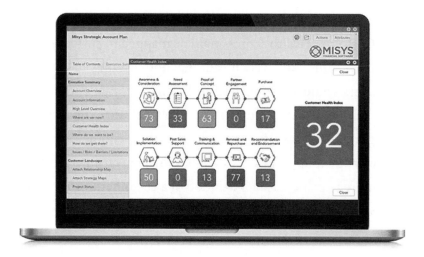

FIGURE 7.11 Embedding CHI scores into the account management (AM) or CSM workflow (screenshot showing sample data).

Source: Martin Haering, Finastra. Reproduced with permission.

CUSTOMER HEALTH AND COMPENSATION MODELS

Some companies put customer NPS into compensation plans for executives and customer-facing teams. This is a very risky approach and causes all kinds of gaming and manipulation of scores. For example, salespeople are likely to only ask for scores from happy customers or will encourage client contacts to skew their responses.

However, Customer Health scores are harder to game. Moreover, a CHI that is supported by all business functions can be more easily linked to the KPIs of ALL employees – whether they are directly interfacing with the customer or not. Everyone is ultimately part of the customer value chain, and their KPIs should align with the health scores of customers.

Therefore, as the organisation aligns more around the experience and customer journey, cross-functional team members should be compensated increasingly (either in salary or bonus terms) based on their impact on Customer Health scores. Even if this compensation is nominal, it is also an important message to the entire workforce. It says we are here to serve our customers, keep them happy and grow the relationship with them.

So, what can a CEO learn from Customer Health?

Today, organisations are generating huge volumes of untapped customer data, often packed with incredible yet unearthed insight. Often, all it takes is a data analyst, or a team of data specialists, led by, for example, a head of customer operations, to examine the data sources and compare them with the many VoC insight information sources and customer journey maps. Once they have done that, they can start building a CHI or a set of Customer Health scores.

Moreover, it is often better to assess people's true feelings and emotions based on their behaviours and actions, and not on their words. We should not assess them solely on how they respond to a survey, especially when survey fatigue is on the rise. For these reasons, Customer Health scoring and Customer Health indices will only become more prevalent in the future.

CHAPTER 8

ENGAGEMENT

How to engage with your customers

C-CHANGE GROWTH DRIVERS

- **Create a VoC-derived, strategic customer engagement pro-gramme to increase co-creation and customer advocacy.**
  Customer Engagement programmes help retain customer knowledge and protect customers for staff movements and attrition. Ultimately, the customer engagement programme will deliver tangible growth.

- **Audit existing customer engagement programmes such as user groups or customer advisory boards and test them with your target customer personas**. Ask yourself – are they all linked strategically to your customer-led, company-wide growth objectives? Appoint an executive sponsor, for example, a chief customer officer, of a pan-company customer engagement programme.

- **View account-based marketing (ABM) as a strategic component of customer engagement**, and not a tactical marketing campaign to drive short-term leads just in the current financial quarter. Work strategically with customers on ABM to inspire interactions that result in more productive mutual business outcomes.

Customer Engagement is about creating connections, via multiple channels, between the customer and an organisation. There are many customer programmes which engage customers in a particular area such as customer events or client hospitality. These are customer engagement activities that have merit. However, the real challenge in the Customer Economy lies in creating strategic customer engagement which adds value to customers and, in turn, adds value to your organisation by focusing on long-term interactions. In this chapter, you will learn how such strategic customer engagement programmes can create a 'C-change' with a clear link to your customer-led business objectives and informed by continual insight from Customer Voice (see Chapter 1).

'The ultimate aim of engagement with customers is to build a trusted, advisory relationship for mutual benefit. This is hard, especially when deployed at large scale, but can be incredibly valuable. It's easier to simply measure customer transactions in terms of sheer numbers. However, it's more important to look at how we are actually providing value and building trust with those customers when we engage with them across every aspect of the relationship,' says Rob Leavitt, Senior Vice-President at ITSMA, a global research and advisory community focused on strategic B2B marketing.

HOW DO YOU CREATE MUTUAL VALUE DURING CUSTOMER ENGAGEMENT?

Customers are looking for new ideas and approaches to meet their business challenges. So, your organisation needs to build relationships of trust and be, as Rob Leavitt says, a 'thought partner' to provide value to customers. 'In other words, we as organisations need to be relevant. We need to understand our customer's company and their business, the industry in which they operate, and their individual roles and measures for success', added Rob Leavitt.

To create this understanding of your customers before you create an engagement programme, there needs to be a combination of research and practical experience to create value. There is a proliferation of new CxO roles in the Customer Economy which are disrupting industries to create growth, such as the Chief Digital Officer and the Chief Data Officer. These new and emerging roles are defined very differently within organisations before they mature and standardise. This makes it more difficult to engage with them in a standardised way, requiring much closer alignment to your individual customers and their organisations. Similarly, within your own organisation, this forces far more consultative skills and sharing of customer intelligence that is drawn from the 10 elements of our 'C-change' model to create an effective customer engagement programme.

HAVING A CLEAR VISION AND STRATEGIC OBJECTIVES FOR YOUR CUSTOMER ENGAGEMENT PROGRAMME

First, a customer engagement programme must not be just a series of tactical initiatives; it must be backed by the CEO with executive endorsement, embedded in the culture of the organisation. The programme must be linked to your strategic priorities, which will naturally direct its creation based on sustainable, customer-led growth. Second, customer segmentation for inclusion in the programme needs to map onto these objectives. This needs to be informed by insight from the Customer Voice (see Chapter 1) and data on the macro factors of a particular industry. For example, a traditional car company could segment by millennials, who are unlikely to own a car in the future but hire one on a 'pay as you go' model. This is in contrast to, say, a customer segment for the 20–50-years age group, which will break down into sub-segments of leasing and outright capital purchase versus an early adopters' segment planning for the future of driverless vehicles.

HOW DO YOUR CUSTOMERS ENGAGE WITH YOU?

Depending on the customer persona you are interacting with, examine how your customers like interacting with their peers. Do they prefer interacting face to face rather than online and on social media? It is key to understand the profile of your customers and what their drivers are, such as 'Make me rich, make me famous' (which we will discuss in Chapter 10 on Customer Advocacy). This provides evidence with which to build your customer engagement programme.

'For effective customer engagement in the Customer Economy – especially with CxOs, it's fundamental that you demonstrate the skills of empathy. Your customers in your engagement programme need to know that you're in the relationship for the long-term', commented Rob Leavitt. 'This is because trust is a long-term issue. Customers don't put a great deal of value on a transactional relationship; they want long-term, strategic commitment'.

Prioritisation is key. Maintaining relationships at the executive level requires research and investment of time, so you need to prioritise. One of the most important factors in executive engagement is about operating at the right level. For example, if you are trying to reach CEOs, you need to tailor customer engagement programmes specifically for them. It has to be at a peer-to-peer level rather than bringing in other job roles, as people want to mix and learn from their peers. So, different engagement programmes are required to meet the needs of different customer personas.

ENSURING LONG-TERM CUSTOMER ENGAGEMENT

The professional services and management consultancy companies typically live and breathe customer engagement. It is in their nature and how they do business, because they are basically selling 'people', and they come from a partnership model where each partner is responsible for building long-term relationships for repeat business. So, there is a strong collective focus on building long-term, executive relationships. However, although customer engagement is in their DNA, sometimes these firms fall short in systematising this focus with a structured, measured approach. A good case in point is how senior partners' customer relationships often leave with them when they leave the firm. The lesson from this is how management consultancy and professional services firms are putting in place customer engagement programmes to ensure that relationships with customers are not limited to one or two partners in the firm. Programmatic customer engagement is being woven into the fabric of their organisations.

WHAT ARE THE KEY STEPS FOR AN EFFECTIVE CUSTOMER ENGAGEMENT PROGRAMME?

Once you have segmented your customers, the next step is to design an engagement programme which is tested with customer advocates and prospective customers on a qualitative and quantitative basis.

CUSTOMER RESEARCH

Look back at our earlier chapter on Customer Voice and use the research on which key customer decision-making roles you wish to focus upon in your engagement programme. Utilise primary research (from your direct face-to-face customer contact) and secondary research (from third party information – e.g. on macro factors for a particular industry) to develop a coherent strategy. The customer engagement strategy should include which roles you are targeting and, most importantly, what they care about and how they want to engage with you. Testing customer attitudes, preferences and engagement should not be a 'one-off', but built into the customer-led culture and processes of the organisation. Also, it should not be a one-way street where the organisation is asking the customer for feedback. The organisation needs to be upfront about the value which they will give in return to customers – this is the 'mutual business currency', such as co-creation, access to knowledge and senior executives and experts; that is, helping the customer to gain value and differentiate their organisation.

WHY IS CUSTOMER ENGAGEMENT DATA CRITICAL?

The real challenge for organisations is to turn data into insight and action. This is where you need to understand which customers matter most, and what types of engagement can be meaningful and valuable for customers. Then, you need to plan how best to mobilise and measure engagement with those customers. Data alone is meaningless unless you can act upon it. You need to use data from Customer Voice to inform which customer personas you are going to target in your engagement programme and how best to engage. Once the programme is operational it does not stop there; you need to channel feedback from the customers in your engagement programme back into Customer Voice – and, equally, feed in information from Customer Voice into your engagement programme.

BUILD A 'PORTFOLIO-BASED APPROACH'

Build programme elements with a 'portfolio-based approach', that is, a mix of engagement activities to achieve your business objectives and to ensure a range of opportunities to help different customers engage in ways that are most convenient, comfortable and valuable for them. For example, you could identify 1000 executives in 200 companies who are your most important customers, with roles such as CEO, CMO, CFO, etc. Across that group, you will find a variety of interests and opportunities to engage: some may prefer one-on-one meetings and briefings; others would rather gather in small groups of peers from the same industry or role. Still others are looking for large events that bring forth multiple industry perspectives. To provide mutual value across such a diverse group, you will need to offer a variety of activities. However, to get the most value for everyone, you will also need to orchestrate these different activities into a coordinated programme that creates personalised and valuable options for the executives while giving you an integrated view of the overall impact.

The following text discusses some common characteristics of customer engagement programmes.

THOUGHT LEADERSHIP

Thought leadership provides a foundation for any programme to provide valuable engagement with customers. How will your organisation and you, personally, develop new ideas and approaches that are truly insightful, valuable and relevant in order to engage with these customer decision-making roles? It is important to note that we talk about cultivating thought leadership from personal and corporate points of view. Personally, employees – *in particular, customer advocacy consultants working with marketing, sales and customer success* – need to be accountable for understanding customers and their roles and industries, and for consulting with them to provide value. Personal thought leadership can be as simple as being an expert in a particular subject matter which is valuable to your customers and relevant influencers. In addition, it may be that you enhance your personal thought leadership by commenting on social media and in the press on a particular topic. It must be noted that, if you are commenting to the press, you will need permission from your public relations function.

EVENTS

Events are a common customer engagement programme tactic which can bring results as they provide an opportunity for face-to-face engagement and relationship building. Face-to-face engagement is harder in an increasingly online

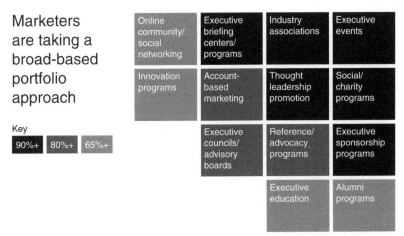

Marketers are taking a broad-based portfolio approach

Key
90%+ 80%+ 65%+

Online community/ social networking	Executive briefing centers/ programs	Industry associations	Executive events
Innovation programs	Account-based marketing	Thought leadership promotion	Social/ charity programs
	Executive councils/ advisory boards	Reference/ advocacy programs	Executive sponsorship programs
		Executive education	Alumni programs

FIGURE 8.1   2017 ITSMA Research – common customer engagement programme elements.

Source: ITSMA. Reproduced with permission.

world; so, to engage customers at events, they need to be linked strategically with other key programme elements to provide value (see Figure 8.1).

Tailoring events to a particular customer role, such as a regular forum for CFOs, offers peer-to-peer networking – as well as expertise, say on forthcoming industry legislation. In tandem, you can create a larger forum for the entire community of customers that might be held once a year globally. Salesforce does this very well with its 'Dreamforce' in the United States.

EXECUTIVE EDUCATION PROGRAMMES

Education provides value for customers in a world with an over-abundance of information. So, who better to provide education to your customers than you and your organisation as a trusted source with in-depth expertise in relevant areas? Signify (formerly Philips Lighting) has excelled in providing an engaging, global education programme for customers who specify lighting from lighting designers to architects and, increasingly, engineering consultancies: www.signify.com/lightingacademy.

Co-creation programmes for innovation

Co-creation is customer engagement at its best with the dual benefit of aiding the customer, your organisation and other key stakeholders. The practice of co-creation helps customers to imagine how their businesses and industries will evolve in the future, including concrete actions to get there. Co-creation can be highly effective to help customers differentiate and leapfrog competitors in a disruptive market (see Chapter 9 on Co-creation).

CUSTOMER COMMUNITIES

The most important ingredient for successful customer communities is empathy. Communities that work well are built around service to their constituents. This cannot happen without understanding and identifying the goals and challenges that community members are facing every day. Of course, companies that build or sponsor customer communities are in it to grow, but there has to be a balance to achieve the mutual value that we speak about in the Customer Advocacy chapter. For a successful community, you have to commit to effective service with empathy for the needs of the members, and also use research from Customer Voice to plan and test the best mix of face-to-face contact and online channels, which should be refined on an ongoing basis.

HOW DO CUSTOMER ENGAGEMENT PROGRAMMES BENEFIT YOUR ORGANISATION AND CUSTOMERS?

Insight is akin to how we described data in Customer Voice, that is, they are the high-value 'new oil' in the Customer Economy. Customer engagement programmes can provide valuable insight and understanding for your customers in the industries in which they operate. In particular, one-to-one/face-to-face engagement with executives is irreplaceable by secondary data.

Trust: Customer engagement programmes build trust for long-term relationships and customer-led growth. Most companies have some kind of an 80/20 rule where 20% of customers are delivering 80% of revenue. So, are you planning to build customer engagement programmes with the 20% who are driving your business beyond just revenue in to areas such as innovation? You can really use this 20% of customers who you need to nurture as advocates, who you will co-create with and disrupt new markets in which you can achieve exponential customer-led growth. In a nutshell, this 20% of customers will keep you honest if you have focused on an effective customer engagement programme!

Innovation: Use customer engagement programmes to drive co-creation and innovation. Build an innovation component in your programme. The common mistake is thinking inwardly about how your organisation can sell. However, the approach that should be taken is how to offer innovation to solve your customer's problems.

A FULLY INTEGRATED CUSTOMER ENGAGEMENT PROGRAMME

Figure 8.2 shows an example of the award-winning Misys customer engagement programme, which also contained a number of sub-components – each targeted at different customer personas. Note that the programme includes other value-added initiatives such as beta programmes, user communities and return-of-investment assessments.

Misys Connect

A comprehensive suite of value-driven programmes that deepen the relationship between Misys and its clients. It maximises the return on our clients' technology investments and helps them to drive competitive advantage

Executive & Strategy Leaders
(CEOs, CROs, CMOs)

› Executive Communities
› CVT & ROI Evaluation
› Executive Briefing Centre & Partner COEs
› Industry Reputation

Business Managers and Professionals
(Line of business owners e.g. Head of Lending, Head of Trade Finance)

› Business Communities & CABs
› SAG

Technology & Operations Leaders
(CTOs, CIOs, COOs)

› Engineering Collaboration & Early Adopter
› Peer to Peer Programme

Technology and Support Users
(IT Managers, Project Managers)

› User Communities
› Deployment Accelerators & Misys Academy

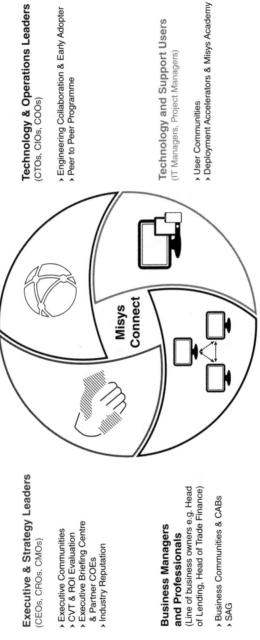

FIGURE 8.2 Misys Customer Engagement Programme.

Source: Finastra. Reproduced with permission.

Box 8.1 Giving Royal Caribbean customers back time in their vacation

The management consultancy EY has an interesting engagement programme with its client Royal Caribbean Cruise Lines to help better engage with its customers to give them a richer experience.

In 2016, EY engaged with Royal Caribbean at the CxO level with their CFO, Jason Liberty. Together, they looked at Royal Caribbean's challenge of giving holiday time back to their customers. So, EY looked at Royal Caribbean's digital strategy from every angle.

While looking for ways to innovate their customers' cruise experience, executives at Royal Caribbean worked with EY on their digital transformation. The two companies collaborated on a 5-year innovation road map, which included updating Royal Caribbean's technology and enhancing their customers' on-board experiences.

One example of successful engagement between the two companies is a recently updated mobile app that helps customers navigate around the ship, eases their check-in and even allows them to order drinks.

HOW CAN ACCOUNT-BASED MARKETING (ABM) CONTRIBUTE TO EFFECTIVE CUSTOMER ENGAGEMENT?

While there have been many positives about marketing automation, one downside has been that it often results in marketing bombarding prospects to act. This creates more noise that customers need to cut through. ABM, which is often referred to as *key account marketing*, moves from generic marketing approaches to tailor the discipline more directly to the needs of individual customers. The practice of ABM focuses on specific customer accounts and is associated with B2B.

The practice of ABM provides a strategic approach to business marketing based on designated client and prospective accounts with which an organisation communicates, as markets of one. Bev Burgess, Senior Vice-President and ABM Practice Leader, ITSMA Europe, and author of *A Practitioner's Guide to Account-Based Marketing: Accelerating Growth in Strategic Accounts*, has pioneered the practice. She sees ABM as a way to segment and focus on key customers and prospects, and to align sales and marketing. One of the critical success factors when building an effective ABM programme is to gain executive sponsorship. This helps to ensure that ABM is a business growth initiative, and not a marketing initiative. Following on from that, you need to partner with sales to identify the right accounts and build your ABM foundation, including programme objectives, metrics, funding, resources, systems and processes.

SO HOW DO YOU DIFFERENTIATE BETWEEN ABM, CUSTOMER ENGAGEMENT AND CUSTOMER ADVOCACY?

Bev Burgess believes that they are all interlinked. 'ABM often leverages Customer Engagement and Customer Advocacy programmes. In fact, these programmes are often focused on executives in ABM accounts, since these are the most important accounts for the business' future customer-led growth'.

TECHNOLOGY IS A CRITICAL ENABLER FOR ABM

When ABM emerged as a business practice back in 2003, one-to-one ABM was done without much technology. However, today, nobody is doing ABM without leveraging technology. This is particularly important to help companies scale their ABM programmes. 'Insight tools such as Agent3 are delivering intelligence on the accounts and executives within the ABM programme', says Burgess. Also, targeted marketing tools such as Demandbase are delivering personalised ads to executives in the programme, while Folloze is curating and sharing content for individual stakeholders. Then there are orchestration and measurement tools such as Engagio, which are effective at planning ABM activities across marketing and sales, as well as in measuring results and overall impact. In addition, the contact management, content management and marketing automation tools already in most companies' Martech stacks are leveraged for ABM.

SO, WHAT BENEFITS CAN ABM OFFER YOUR ORGANISATION?

ABM is an enabler for better relationships with key clients, as well as stronger reputations in the accounts that matter most. This can provide a C-change to accelerate sustainable growth. Also, within the organisation, there is a better alignment between marketing, sales and other business functions centred around the client.

Bev Burgess commented, 'To succeed in ABM, you need to avoid an inside-out mindset that focuses on the company's solutions rather than the client's issues. Also, you need that senior sponsorship to lead internal alignment around the client and to build relationships and reputation with them and to generate more, larger opportunities with a higher win rate and a shorter sales cycle. We're seeing other business outcomes from ABM accounts, including more collaborative innovation, creating new solutions to take to market, greater success with solutions that are bought, and more executives willing to be advocates'. Bev added, 'In the future, I see ABM and customer engagement evolving where they remain closely aligned, focused on the most important accounts and enabled by technology to reach more of those accounts'.

THE TOP THREE LESSONS FOR CEOs/CXOs TO ACHIEVE EFFECTIVE ABM

1. Map the marketing investment to the sales coverage model (e.g. if an account warrants an account manager, it may warrant an ABM-er too) and establish ABM as a growth initiative, with sales and marketing working in partnership.
2. View ABM as a strategic growth programme, not a tactical marketing campaign to drive leads in the current financial quarter.
3. Make sure all things ABM are built around customer insight and customised for each executive.

WHAT IS THE BIGGEST BARRIER TO CUSTOMER ENGAGEMENT?

The biggest barrier to customer engagement is time, since, by and large, most of our customers are time poor and are inundated with demands for it. 'However, often organisations are unwilling to make the investment of their own time to make engagement worth our customers' while', says Rob Leavitt. 'We try to rush and automate and minimise our own investments while somehow expecting our customers to reward us with their attention anyway. If it's not worth our time why should it be worth theirs?'

Rob Leavitt believes that *effective customer engagement is all about the four Ps*:

1. *Personalisation*: Being relevant to the customers with regard to their specific business, industry, role and situation.
2. *Proactive*: Reaching out with new ideas and approaches that can provide true value to those customers based on their specific issues and needs.
3. *People-influenced*: Working with peers and influencers who have respect and credibility with the customers that you are trying to engage.
4. *Proven*: Providing proof points to back up your ideas and approaches so customers understand you can deliver on your promise. (*We concur with Rob Leavitt on this. If you have aligned with your customer advocates on their business and marketing objectives during engagement, and then followed through with placements, you will create the valuable mutual business currency as a C-change for growth*).

Rob Leavitt argues that using the four Ps effectively, in turn, requires a heavy commitment to investing in data and insight. This means prioritising your most important customers and taking a long-term approach. In addition, it needs to be an organisation-wide commitment, with marketing, sales, service and your own senior executives all working together to ensure long-term success.

WHEN DO FAILURES WITH CUSTOMER ENGAGEMENT OCCUR?

Typically, engagement failures reflect a lack of commitment to the customer, and lack of long-term investment in customer-first approaches that are required to break through the barriers to success. Quick-hit programmes to drive web traffic, event attendance or even short-term sales often fall flat in the long run when organisations fail to sustain the investment in building relationships based on service and shared value.

HOW DO YOU MEASURE CUSTOMER ENGAGEMENT?

'Always take a Three Rs approach to measuring engagement with reputation, relationships, and revenue', says Rob Leavitt. He advises organisations to elevate their reputations with the customers who matter, build long-term relationships for insight and growth, as well as to drive sustainable, profitable revenue with their most important customers.

In the future, customer engagement will continue to grow in importance as the power shifts further towards customers and away from organisations. Rob Leavitt added, 'Deep engagement is the basis for relationships and trust, and those relationships will more and more become the primary source of competitive differentiation as digital transformation enables ever greater automation of daily business routine. And the art of designing engagement and strengthening relationships will continue even as the sciences of artificial intelligence and machine learning provide ever more opportunity to automate personal experience'.

WHAT ARE THE TOP THREE LESSONS FOR CXOs TO ACHIEVE EFFECTIVE CUSTOMER ENGAGEMENT?

1. Prioritise and segment customers who matter the most for long-term strategic growth.
2. Take the four Ps approach to engagement: personalised, proactive, people-influenced and proven.
3. Measure the three Rs: reputation, relationships and revenue.

WHAT DO LEADERS NEED TO DO TO DRIVE BEST-PRACTICE CUSTOMER ENGAGEMENT IN THEIR ORGANISATIONS?

'The organisations that are most effective with customer engagement are the ones that prioritise investment, cross-organisational collaboration and outcomes', says Rob Leavitt. 'These customer-led organisations understand that engagement is a long-term commitment, and they invest in both the programmes and the metrics to build and sustain real relationships based on understanding, service and shared value'.

Strategic customer engagement programmes mobilise customer advocates through word-of-mouth to foster loyalty and customer-led brands. As a CEO in the Customer Economy, we encourage you to make the customer engagement programme a part of your strategic plan. By doing this, you will be able to differentiate as a customer-led organisation and generate profitable growth.

CHAPTER 9

CO-CREATION

Customers: Let's go co-create!

C-CHANGE GROWTH DRIVERS

- **In the Customer Economy, collaborative models for innovation have become the norm**. Organisations should create business and technology platforms on which their ecosystems of customers, partners and other influencers can co-create. The organisations that create platforms effectively become the emperors and their networks of innovators become kings. Innovation is no longer a top-down, linear process, but instead a continuous collaborative ecosystem that benefits all.

- **The best way to achieve co-creation is for employees to be empowered and rewarded for co-creating with customers, partners and other stakeholders**. This behaviour must be linked with the tangible results of this newly co-created, customer-led growth gained by all parties involved.
- **Make customer co-creation one of your organisational values** and part of your customer vision and mission that is led by the CEO in conjunction with someone in the organisation who is accountable for leading co-creation – such as the CCO.
- **Learn from the world leader in lighting, Signify (formerly Philips Lighting), about how it co-created successfully with its customers**, Planet Farms, the largest vertical farm in Europe, and Albert Heijn, the Dutch supermarket chain.

'The most distinguishing characteristic of complete co-creation to drive customer-led growth is, unsurprisingly, the central role that customers play when they are engaged in a strategic way'.

Maarten Pieters, Head of Co-creation &
People Insight at Signify

In the spirit of The Customer Catalyst, we encourage every organisation to consider all components of the C-change growth engine. However, co-creation, like success, health and advocacy, is one of the sections that can really differentiate organisations in the Customer Economy. This chapter is all about learning to work with your customers and other key stakeholders to co-create.

In the product era, most innovation was driven top-down by individual organisations. In the Customer Economy, the model is almost completely inverted. The responsibility of generating new ideas for products and services is no longer the sole preserve of a closed- and proprietary-based, individual organisation. Instead, co-creation provides a C-change for growth with a collaborative evolution including customers, partners, suppliers and other key stakeholders.

We are seeing a move from being organisation-driven to being customer-driven. Organisation-driven is typified by the one-way 'sending' of products and services which have been developed internally and then validated by customers after production. In contrast, the Customer Economy sees the exchange of this organisation-led dominance for collaboration with customers and stakeholders, which prioritises value for customers over and above the organisation's own ends.

So, how do you define co-creation? In 2010, Professors Venkat Ramaswamy and Francis Gouillart published the book *The Power of Co-Creation: Build It with Them to Boost Growth, Productivity, and Profits*, which laid down the theory of co-creation with 'win more, win more where co-creation helps manifest benefits for the organisation, the end-users and the planet'.

In 2017, Stefanie Jansen and Maarten Pieters went on to develop their definition of 'Complete co-creation', building on the theory laid down by Ramaswamy and Gouillart:

'Complete co-creation is the transparent process of value creation in ongoing, productive collaboration with, and supported by, all relevant parties, with end-users playing a central role'.

Their premise of complete co-creation focuses on actively involving customers and other relevant parties in a development process, from the identification of a challenge to the implementation and tracking of its solution. Complete co-creation is foremost a *procedure* which may evolve into an *organisational principle* and potentially even a *co-ownership*. This thinking reinforces the concept of our C-change principles to drive customer-led growth in contrast to the rigid organisational structure and rules of the past.

Maarten Pieters highlights that collaboration provides the 'C-change' for co-creation. This comes about from complementary knowledge and skills that both companies and their customers hold. He argues that co-creation can solve challenges that impact customers directly and indirectly. The obvious application is the innovation of new products and services.

However, co-creation can work equally well for strategy development and scenario planning. For example, it could be brainstorming with customers and partners about how to evolve in the event of sustaining innovation in your market akin to what Uber brought about in the market for taxis. In such instances, customers and other stakeholders bring a unique perspective.

Maarten Pieters, Head of Co-creation and People Insight, and Laura Taylor, Innovation Design Director at Signify, have pioneered co-creation within Signify – more of which we will share later, including how the company has co-created with two of its customers: Planet Farms, a new vertical farm in Milan, Italy, which is using LED lights to grow lettuces and other fresh produce; and Albert Heijn, the supermarket chain using Signify's 3D printing technology to co-create bespoke lighting to continually reinvent the lighting and look of their stores with sustainable materials.

'The Co-Creation Transition Model' – which features in the book *The 7 Principles of Complete Co-creation* by Stefanie Jansen and Maarten Pieters – sums up this power shift and the change in behaviour that successful customer-led organisations need to adopt (see Figure 9.1).

Power in the hands of customers results in greater personal-isation and choice. Being able to create individual value for

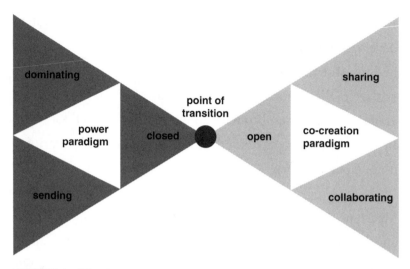

FIGURE 9.1 'The Co-creation Transition Model'.

Source: The 7 Principles of Complete Co-creation, a book by Stefanie Jansen and Maarten Pieters. *Reproduced with permission.*

customers is a predictive factor for customer loyalty. As a result, there is an acknowledgement that organisations in partnership with their customers and other stakeholders can co-create together to better meet the needs of customers. This means better products, services and a stronger customer experience. The consequence is that the way of working is changing to become more collaborative in contrast to the past, one-dimensional pursuit of profit and growth by large organisations where a higher purpose has often been absent. Today, customers want to see how organisations work on a day-to-day basis, what their values are – and, importantly, how they go about creating value for their employees, buyers and suppliers. This is in contrast to organisations who try to dominate by holding onto their knowledge and not collaborating with key stakeholders, which results in trust in them being eroded.

'For customers, trust is now based not on money and power but on value, honesty, authenticity, involvement, transparency and empathy. You need this first before entering into a co-creation partnership', says Maarten.

Insight from customers – from both a personal and corporate perspective – with their deeper motivation, aspirations and fears provide the answer to unlocking market differentiation. The decision-making processes of customers and their view of your competitors is highly valuable during co-creation. Customers who enter into co-creation with you are usually customer advocates. However, those who are not advocates at the start typically become customer advocates after going through the process, importantly sharing this positive customer experience via word of mouth. This includes telling their peers about the new product development process before a product or service is developed, providing the added benefit of giving a boost with customer advocacy when it is launched.

LAYING DOWN CO-CREATION PRINCIPLES TO MAKE THE 'C-CHANGE'

Leaders must develop their own complete co-creation strategy with guiding principles that meet the needs of the organisation (see Figure 9.2). These principles will develop from customers, partners and other stakeholders being involved in different ways – from organisational processes such as innovation through to their supply chain and customer service. This means that customers and these other interested parties have a direct and indirect influence on decision-making and the development of newly co-created products and services. Also, it is highly significant that the complete co-creation process is

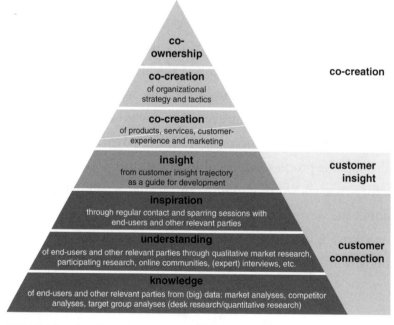

FIGURE 9.2   Co-creation story: Signify and its customers co-creating for business growth.

'Customer Connection Pyramid' from '*The 7 Principles of Complete Co-creation*' book by Stefanie Jansen and Maarten Pieters.

Source: Signify. Reproduced with permission.

bringing new meaning to marketing. As a result of the direct connection with customers from co-creation, the needs of customers are being met far better.

Maarten Pieters (see Figure 9.3) argues that activities that focus on value creation, which fail to involve customers, do not qualify as complete co-creation. Customers can augment the process of co-creation in different ways, both face-to-face and online. Look at how you can explore active participation for customers in co-creating: product and service optimisation sessions, creative brainstorm sessions and customer advocacy marketing, through to creative design, product innovation and packaging briefs.

FIGURE 9.3   Maarten Pieters, Head of Co-creation and People Insight at Signify.

Source: Maarten Pieters. Reproduced with permission.

When used strategically, co-creation can really enhance customer-led growth, which Pieters and Jansen illustrate well in the 'Customer Connection Pyramid'. In summary, organisations that maintain continuous contact with their customers, face-to-face and online, gain a firm grasp of unsatisfied needs which is at the very heart of marketing in the Customer Economy. This enables organisations to be agile and meet customer needs in a far more relevant way to gain competitive advantage – in contrast to competitors who are less connected to customers.

SIGNIFY: CO-CREATING FOR INNOVATION AND GROWTH

The story begins in 2016 when Philips Lighting separated from its Dutch parent, Royal Philips, to be a stand-alone organisation listed on the Euronext stock exchange in Amsterdam, forging its own way as the world leader in lighting. Then, the company created its own identity in February 2018 as 'Signify', with a clear customer-led purpose centred on the word 'signify' and the meaning that it has for businesses and consumers. Signify is the world leader in lighting for professionals and consumers, and lighting in the Internet of Things (IoT). Its Philips products, Interact connected lighting systems and data-enabled services deliver value to businesses and transform life in homes, buildings and public spaces for customers.

The company has reinvented itself in the lighting industry by driving multiple waves: first, the move from conventional lighting to energy-efficient LED lighting; and now the wave to connected lighting, bringing value by linking real-time data with other connected devices via the IoT. The more digital and connected lighting becomes, the more it becomes possible for Signify to deliver more personally relevant and meaningful experiences.

'It used to be about making "one size fits all" where one product was manufactured for everyone, that is, light bulbs. Now customers expect products and services that feel like they are tailor-made for them. Signify has responded by innovating connected lighting systems, luminaires and services which are co-created with customers. For example, to create dynamic lighting experiences for both businesses and consumers, we've seen the pioneering development of "light recipes" and customised luminaires', says Laura Taylor, Innovation Design Director at Signify.

Initially, product development did not change much when the market transitioned from conventional lighting to LED. 'The real change came when lighting became connected digitally and started being part of a much larger IoT eco-system, opening huge possibilities in how technology meant that we could co-create with customers and IoT partners. This makes it the most exciting era in lighting – after the discovery of fire and electrification of light', added Laura. 'This new era of lighting is about tailoring lighting with applications that create unique experiences for people'.

For example, with Philips Hue from Signify, consumers can personalise the lighting in their homes, syncing light with their own music, movies or games (see Figure 9.4). Meanwhile, the company is developing Interact Office, its IoT-based lighting system and applications, with the associated data and services to meet the needs of customers' businesses. All of this is facilitated by co-creation, and means that people can use

FIGURE 9.4 Philips Hue outdoor lightstrips shown in the photo are a product of co-creation.

Source: Signify. Reproduced with permission.

personalised lighting to better connect to the spaces they are in – whether at work or in their homes.

Designing lighting experiences and IoT applications using lighting has become more complex. Signify is working with stakeholders such as workplace innovation (WPI) experts, heads of real estate, facility managers, architects and IT managers, and using co-creation to connect lighting with digital technology, enabling more choice with fast availability. Co-creation is fundamental to Signify's own transformation, linking firmly back to one of its core organisational values of 'Customer First'.

OVERCOMING BARRIERS TO CO-CREATION

One of the biggest barriers to co-creation is fear. Change is needed for co-creation, but change brings fear of the unknown within the organisation – fear of not having the awareness, skills and experience to go through the change. There is fear of becoming obsolete, and fear of not being able to step out of the usual way of doing things to embrace co-creation. Finally, there is fear of not being able to deliver results or to work towards customer- or co-creation-related key performance indicators (KPIs). Employees at all levels tend to cling onto what they know and not step outside their comfort zone. They may not recognise it, but they do need to know they can do it; that is, that they can achieve successful co-creation. Also, there are many people who do know that they can achieve co-creation and embrace it from the start.

To create a customer-led culture, organisations need to nurture a trusted work environment by empowering employees to co-create with their leaders. This shows employees the way to facilitate working in a co-creative way. It is not easy to do this when you consider how most organisations are structured with pressure to deliver short-term financial results. Leaders need to step outside of that with agile working.

Signify has used Maarten Pieters' co-creation principles, which have been embraced in the company's global design function. This has helped the organisation to create space in which co-creation can happen, so that people can have confidence. Think about the co-creation principles: how you can continually involve customers in all processes of development, and how you can break through your organisational siloes with cross-functional teams to enable the process of co-creation.

An example of this is that Philips Lighting's design department often helped in hosting visits by leading global architects to experience early stage lighting demos. The department wanted to get in-depth feedback from architects and to discuss which directions to develop in. To get to this level of dialogue, they needed to rethink how they co-created with customers. So, Laura looked for new ways of co-creating, and was introduced to Maarten Pieters via a colleague to come in as a consultant. He helped get real conversations started with the architects. 'We changed the format to workshops, which architects rated as a highlight of their visit to Philips Lighting. The workshops were also much more useful for the designers', said Taylor. Maarten had a deep-held, customer-led perspective to see customers as partners rather than just sending information one way to them. Maarten later joined Philips Lighting in 2014 to lead people in research activities, and has, over the last 3 years, evolved his role to lead co-creation within the company. Philips Lighting has now transformed to become Signify, a stand-alone business separate from Royal Philips.

During 2014, in his first full year with the business and working on the programme, Maarten's vision was to make the organisation 'co-creation-ready' by getting understanding and traction of what was possible with co-creation. He coached 'co-creation champions' who could act as the customer catalyst for co-creation pilot projects from which to experiment. In addition, the team conducted research studies in conjunction with customers and stakeholders. These projects acted as proof points from which to build upon. One of the first hurdles was to get employees to see that it was not hard to work with customers and partners. These projects demonstrated the benefits to employees in multiple ways, with a clear focus on creating a connection with the customer, communicating the tangible results of the pilot projects which benefited customers and the organisation. Maarten points out that the change process involves continuously taking small steps, and years of lobbying different decision-makers and gaining employee and customer inclusion in projects, followed by continuously repeating the process of co-creation.

A good example of co-creation was in the Philips Hue home segment. Maarten suggested bringing customers into a one-day creative product concept development workshop at the global headquarters in Eindhoven in the Netherlands. The aim was to develop thinking for new, connected lighting products for the home, which culminated in the development of the innovative Philips Hue Outdoor Lightstrip. By bringing in Dutch consumers and key stakeholders from research, design and marketing, it fundamentally changed the whole dynamic of the workshop. From this seed of co-creation, impressive results were achieved. The Philips Hue Outdoor Lightstrip is a consumer lighting innovation with a patent submitted for its design. It has won numerous awards (2018 CES Innovation Award; ID Design Award), in addition to generating a 4.6 rating (out of 5) on Amazon, which is the highest rating for a Philips Hue product at the time of writing. In addition, as a result of the co-creation of design, less silicon was needed in production, which in turn reduced the overall product costs by 10%. Overall, customers love Philips Hue Outdoor Lightstrip, substantiated by the fact that over 85% of positive reviews relate to the product design.

Within Signify, co-creation has been acknowledged as an intrinsic way of how the company wants to work with customers. Maarten and Laura talk about part two of their journey being about getting 'co-creation to be owned, driven and ingrained into the company's DNA'. This is a great segue to Signify's Ignite 2019 global leadership conference with the top 180 leaders from all over the world. As part of the move to be a customer-led organisation, Signify wanted to share its leading co-creation story – and there was no better way of doing this than through leading by example. The following are two fascinating co-creation stories with Planet Farms from its agriculture business and Albert Heijn supermarket chain from its retail business.

Signify sees co-creation not just as an activity in isolation but as part of a cultural change centred around the customer. As part of this cultural change, Maarten undertook an internal change programme called 'Let's go co-create', educating the organisation and its employees on the power and benefits of co-creation. This was spearheaded with a session at its Ignite annual leadership conference – alongside stories from Planet Farms and Albert Heijn on how it has been done with tangible results. The 'Let's go co-create' initiative is a catalyst for leaders to explore co-creation projects in their respective countries, supported by a 'Let's go co-create' digital playbook for all employees (see Figure 9.5).

FIGURE 9.5   From left to right: Remco Duchhart, Store Design Format Manager at Albert Heijn; Daniele Benatoff, Co-founder of Planet Farms; Maarten Pieters, Head of Co-creation & People Insight at Signify; and Luca Travaglini, Co-founder of Planet Farms.

Source: Frank van Beek. Reproduced with permission.

WHAT FAILURES HAVE YOU EXPERIENCED IN DEPLOYING CO-CREATION, AND WHAT HAVE YOU LEARNED FROM THEM?

Maarten shared that there are co-creation failures. However, organisations need to avoid looking at these as failures because everybody learns something from each part of the process, which delivers incremental improvements to benefit customers and the organisation. One example is that Maarten often assumes that certain aspects of co-creation are easy to do, such as facilitating groups of employees, customers and partners in a co-creative way where they take ownership of the process. However, there is a significant number of people in any organisation who find this difficult. The net effect is that you can start a co-creation project where stakeholders end up doing things in the same way that they have always done and know. Maarten led a smart city co-creation project where the aim was to understand the main customer drivers to buy connected lighting systems and luminaires. The team was organised in a very traditional way where the members of the team were not actually acting together as a team. So, while there were a lot of meetings, there was little collaboration. The next step was a co-creation workshop in the Netherlands where Signify invited smart city experts from a national government, customers, consultants, Signify Design, R&D as well as business groups. The workshop went well, because there was a lot of interaction among the different stakeholders. However, 'co-creation is never just one workshop': it was very difficult to evolve the output of the workshop and continue the co-creation process. This was because the Signify project team could not change its way of working as they were not committed as a team. In addition, leadership did not support the project – plus, there was limited awareness of what working in a co-creative way meant. Also, prior to the workshop, there was not enough time to break through their way of working. The lesson here is that, if you really want to effect change, people have to be open and willing to move to a co-creative way of working. This is in contrast to the perception of 'just getting the workshop done' to tick an entry off their to-do list.

PLANET FARMS: GROWING CO-CREATION FROM THE GROUND UP!

Daniele Benatoff (see Figure 9.6), co-founder of Planet Farms, says, 'Co-creation for us is approaching a joint project or negotiation – putting everything together into a set of shared beliefs to create the optimal outcome where everyone is on the same page – from how we work with technology partners and, fundamentally, how we operate the company which allows co-creation to happen'.

FIGURE 9.6 From left to right: Planet Farms co-founders Daniele Benatoff and Luca Travaglini.

Source: Frank van Beek. Reproduced with permission.

In May 2018, Signify announced its collaboration with Travaglini FarmTech, a new business division of Travaglini S.p.A., an Italian food manufacturer. The aim is to build Italy's first vertical farm plant research lab in Milan to serve the Italian market as the first step of a global strategy. However, that belies a larger scene set to create a pioneering, new global business called Planet Farms. The company has a vision to build Europe's largest vertical farm, but equally important is the human story behind it, which was the spark for this powerful co-creation story.

Luca Travaglini is the third generation of this Italian family business, which, after being founded in the 1920s, has become the global leader in the manufacturing of drying, smoking, and ageing systems and industrial automation for cured meat, fish and cheese. He had always been interested in the environment. However, it was not until he was diagnosed with skin cancer in 2015 that he re-evaluated his life and started looking for a different direction alongside the family business. In 2017, Luca reconnected with his childhood friend Daniele Benatoff at a mutual friend's wedding. Daniele had been in finance for 15 years and yearned for a change too. He had explored and invested in interesting businesses including biotech and had realised that much of this involved food.

With the growing scarcity of food, Daniele started reading about vertical farming. This is where food and medicine can be grown and produced in vertically stacked layers in structures from offices and warehouses to shipping containers. It contributes to a solution to help solve the global problem of food scarcity. In partnership with Signify and its position as the world leader in lighting, Planet Farms will use 'LED light recipes' to grow crops to achieve sustainable, efficient and fully controlled '*clean*' cultivation. This means avoiding the use of pesticides and herbicides, with 95% less water than required for traditional cultivation. In addition, there is the benefit of a 10–20-fold reduction in the amount of land mass required as compared to traditional agriculture too.

Luca was looking at this new business through the lens of food manufacturing, while Daniele was interested from a financial investment perspective. They began co-creating from the very start and thought about buying a vertical farm, but realised that the industry was in its infancy and believed that it needed greater structure. As a result, it made them decide upon the ambitious vision to build their own end-to-end vertical farms (see Figure 9.7). This was no mean feat where they had no experience owning and operating vertical farms. In the near future, Luca and Daniele will have gone from a business which did not exist, to literally planting the seed, through to growing and selling the final leafy greens to consumers from their vertical farm.

FIGURE 9.7   A horticultural technician working with leafy greens under Signify's LED lights.

Source: Signify. Reproduced with permission.

WHAT WAS THE CO-CREATION PATH FOR PLANET FARMS?

First, they both had to decide on the '*co-creation business principles*' – note the same use of the word 'principles' to create their 'C-change' and give them flexibility in the Customer Economy. This is in contrast to rigid organisational planning and 'rules', highlighting a parallel with the guiding 'C-change principles' to meet agile customer needs, which we discussed in Chapter 2 on customer-led culture.

Luca and Daniele locked themselves in a room to co-create together the vision and mission of their new organisation, which was to become Planet Farms. This included researching potential countries to operate in, as well as the business boundaries of what they wanted to do. They bought their first, highly visible location in Milan, right next to the main motorway that comes into the city. While there is a lot of technology from Italy, Daniele acknowledges that it is one of the hardest countries to do business in, owing to its high energy and labour costs. However, they both had big ambitions and had the 'Google Moonshot factory' in mind; that is, make a dream and see how they could make it happen. Also, they shared a belief in doing your hardest challenge first, from which they could learn and then replicate successfully with the aim of creating a competitive advantage.

They decided as a key part of their vision not to create everything themselves but instead go for an *open architecture*, and finding the right investors. 'So, the plan for our Planet Farms' shareholder structure from the start was to find co-creative investors who shared our ethos and had complementary skills – rather than purely from a financial investment perspective', said Daniele Benatoff.

First, Planet Farms outlined its vision for the largest vertical plan in Europe with a large utility company, RePower, which has a very 'green' ethos. Luca and Daniele chose RePower because they needed electricity to power the new Planet Farms' vertical farm. Daniele added, 'We co-created "tri-generation" with electricity to power the LED lighting from Signify to grow the crops. This is where the heat from LED lighting is used to control the temperature in the plant from which there is a perceived, harmful product CO_2. However, we've used CO_2 for photosynthesis to grow plants such as leafy greens, that is, the product which we are selling'. Fabio Bocchiola, RePower Italia's general manager, is one of the key shareholders on the Planet Farms board where the company has proved to be a real co-creator on a continual basis.

Also, the Bonadeo and Serapian families, where Riccardo Bonadeo is the leading force behind 'One Ocean Foundation', equally shared Luca and Daniele's vision and have co-created the Planet Farms business strategy. This has included advising on where to locate their first vertical farm in Milan as well as environmental and geographic analysis for potential future locations.

Following the selection of investors, Planet Farms began the search for strategic partners to co-create with. Signify was the natural choice for LED lighting, owing to its extensive experience in the horticulture and agriculture sectors. The company has worked together with Planet Farms, providing specific plant knowledge and co-creating tailored 'LED light recipes' from its innovative GrowWise Centre in Eindhoven, the Netherlands. Planet Farms is gaining significant learning and experience from co-creation with Signify's customers. This has had a significant impact on co-creating with Daniele and Luca for their new business. Signify is helping to optimise crop yields on the 12,000 square kilometres of the Planet Farms vertical growing surfaces (see Figure 9.8), which is forecast to produce a staggering 1000 tons of leafy greens each year, once production starts in 2020.

'Travaglini FarmTech is going beyond crop cultivation to investigate the optimum factors for processing and packaging crops grown in a vertical farm using LED light', said Roel Janssen, Global Director City Farming at Signify. 'This is an important project for Signify because this vertical farm focuses on a new market segment, the food processing segment in Italy, where open field farming and taste are king. It shows how rapidly vertical farming is growing and evolving. It's an exciting time to be involved in vertical farming, and we are excited to help shape its future'.

FIGURE 9.8 Planet Farms' new vertical farm in Milan, Italy.

Source: Signify. Reproduced with permission.

Another interesting co-creation partner is Sirti ICT. The company provides hardware technology that delivers blockchain technology via wearable devices to ensure employee safety across Planet Farms' fully integrated supply chain. From seed to final grown product, Planet Farms will have full traceability of all of its leafy green produce at its fingertips for today's high customer expectations for food provenance. Also, the technology will allow them to do predictive maintenance – all based on their 'open architecture'. Daniele said, 'Blockchain technology is giving us the assurance of where every food source has come from and where our final produce is going to. This is highly valuable, quantifiable knowledge and gives us statistical information to feed into big data and AI (Artificial Intelligence) and deliver machine learning. We'll be able to create continual efficiency from this data'.

'Co-creation was a necessary step for us as we were creating something new. We didn't want to compromise – we want to be pioneers in vertical farming and not settle for second best', commented Daniele Benatoff.

HAVE YOU HAD ANY FAILURES DURING CO-CREATION?

Daniele Benatoff shared one example, 'We thought we were co-creating with one partner over the course of a 3-month period – but the final product was definitely not a product of co-creation: it was a product which the partner already had and just wanted to sell us'. He added, 'What the partner was saying about co-creating was not true. So, when it came to the final output, it was clear it wouldn't deliver what was planned'. Luca Travaglini and Daniele Benatoff knew that they needed the project to be done in a different way with genuine co-creation. So, they acknowledged this failure. Consequently, they began the search for a new partner who shared the same vision and who they knew they could work with to deliver the right result for the business.

PLANET FARMS' TOP THREE CO-CREATION LESSONS

1. *Have a clear customer-led business vision*: Be very clear on what your business vision is to set the stage which helps you to focus on taking on board only those partners who share your vision.

2. *Do not be an information hoarder*: Get over the natural approach of holding on to information and know-how for fear of it being stolen. This enables you to start with an open, co-creative approach.

3. *Co-creation is a continuum*: Co-creation does not happen in a single moment and then it is complete. Ensure that your co-creation process is a continuum with fluid communication. For example, Planet Farms' partners are dispersed from the Netherlands to Portugal and Italy, but that does not

matter: you just need to have formal and informal ongoing communication to co-create successfully.

'Successful co-creation is a whole ethos to continually improve production and productivity with combined benefits for our consumers, partners as well as improving sustainability. Ultimately, what excites us is that we're turning co-creation into reality', concluded Luca Travaglini, co-founder of Planet Farms.

SEEING THE LIGHT TO CO-CREATE THE IN-STORE CUSTOMER EXPERIENCE AT ALBERT HEIJN, THE DUTCH SUPERMARKET CHAIN

Albert Heijn is the Dutch supermarket brand of Ahold Delhaize, the global retail conglomerate with global sales in 2018 of €63 billion. It has 37,000 employees in 6700 stores, serving 50 million people in Europe, the United States and Indonesia. Remco Duchhart is the store format design manager for the Albert Heijn chain and is the brains behind an amazing co-creation story with Signify (see Figure 9.9). Duchhart has an interesting background as a tax lawyer who got into retail, working for department stores and in design agencies before joining Albert Heijn. The whole ethos of the Albert Heijn brand is to bring fresh inspiration to its customers every day, which brings us to the beginning of the co-creation story in 2016.

FIGURE 9.9 Remco Duchhart, Store Design Format Manager, Albert Heijn supermarket group, speaks at Signify's Ignite Leadership Conference in the Netherlands.

Source: Frank van Beek. Reproduced with permission.

The challenge was to rethink the design of the stores in the Netherlands which had been built to last for 15 years with their dark brown floors. However, this look was too dark and dominant, and out of step with shoppers. So, they moved to building a store shell with neutral colours on the floor and ceilings. The aim was to future-proof the stores, the effect of which would last 20–30 years, as a neutral colour that could be transformed with lots of additional, different colours to inspire customers. The difference now though is that the store has a modular format for every shopper category. This means that there is a consistent look and feel, but local stores can adapt quickly according to their size and taste in the highly competitive retail sector.

One of the biggest opportunities is to develop brand pro-grammes for particular stores. In Philadelphia, there is a large store with 60,000–70,000 square feet area, but there is a store in the city centre with only 10,000 square feet, more self-service and a smaller product range. On the shop floor, they work with different types of equipment such as chillers for frozen food, and have developed 'clickables' which can be changed quickly, such as the product tables to show off merchandise as well as the lighting.

'Customers in retail now expect change every week, which meant that we had to find a way of reinventing our stores to keep pace with this customer demand. They are inspired and fed by fashion stores where they now expect constant change to satisfy them in store', said Remco Duchhart. 'This is where we started co-creating with Philips Lighting (now Signify) on our reinvention concept to our 900 Albert Heijn stores across the Netherlands and Belgium to drive customer-led growth'.

WHAT IS YOUR DEFINITION OF CO-CREATION?

The Albert Heijn chain believes in two types of co-creation: (1) developing better and more flexible stores, which we can do bet-ter in conjunction with our partners; and (2) co-creation for a specific task. The story with Signify to co-create dynamic store lighting at its global headquarters at High Tech Campus Eindhoven, the Netherlands, is a great example of this second type of co-creation.

> 'Our customers are time-poor so when they come in they haven't had time to think what to eat. So, we want them to be surprised, delighted and inspired when they come into our stores. Co-creating with Signify, we knew that dynamic LED lighting could be an integral part of our in-store customer experience to help and inspire them', said Remco Duchhart, Store Format Design Manager for the Albert Heijn supermarket chain.

Remco knew that lighting could inspire customers in-store. He had heard from Signify that luminaires (which are the lighting units with one or more light bulbs and wiring) could be 3D printed to quickly and sustainably create a different ambience in stores. Signify and Albert Heijn's real estate department began discussing this radical way of reinventing stores. Signify arranged a tour of its Global Lighting Application Centre at the company's global headquarters in Eindhoven, the Netherlands, to begin the co-creation journey for the stakeholders at Albert Heijn and to see what was possible. They saw a whole range of innovative and inspiring lighting technologies, such as LED lighting for vertical farming, 3D-printed luminaries and retail in-store positioning. As a next step, Signify suggested a retail co-creation innovation day to develop a new in-store lighting experience using 3D printing. The innovation day brought together a team of experts from Albert Heijn from real estate, in-store realisation, a store designer and a buyer – alongside Signify's 3D printing expert, a lighting designer and a customer account manager. The combined team explored ways of creating 3D-printed luminaires in multiple colours and designs which could take customers on a journey to inspire them.

They took this to the next stage to test the new 3D-printed luminaires (see Figure 9.10) as part of a new store format in

FIGURE 9.10 3D-printed luminaires co-created with Signify and the Albert Heijn supermarket chain to differentiate stores.

Source: Signify. Reproduced with permission.

Albert Heijn's XL (extra large) 35,000-square-meter stores in Leidschendam and Purmerend near Zaandam. 'This really helped us scope our new ideas balanced with practical guidelines of what we could do in-store', said Remco.

The next step for the team was to work together in the subsequent 2–3 weeks on 3D-printed, durable, plastic luminaires with different textures for the Albert Heijn store (see Figure 9.11) in Rotterdam in the Netherlands. The material is highly sustainable and can be recycled, and then reused for new-look luminaires to engage customers. At this point, Remco and the team went to the Rotterdam store and literally tested different colour shades, shapes and how easy they were to install – as well as with different connected light bulbs which showed different levels of light. This had a positive knock-on effect on the co-creation process, where they learned a great deal – for example, sometimes there was too much light on the products. Remco added, 'All of this made a difference in the ambience and atmosphere. We were conscious that we didn't want light to dominate but to complement the products. What was good was that we could see the immediate reaction on the faces of our customers in the store'. He continued, 'Our customers gave us positive feedback instantly, which reaffirmed our co-creation strategy'.

Customers and staff in the store gave a very positive, immediate reaction to the new lighting, because it was a dramatically

FIGURE 9.11   Albert Heijn supermarket.

Source: Signify. Reproduced with permission.

different visual experience in the fresh fruit and vegetable produce section. It was fashionable and brought warmth into the department, in contrast to the more rational, simple lighting that was in place before. This instant customer feedback guided the team to refine the in-store lighting experience in a number of ways: not to use too much light; use fewer shapes for luminaires; use fewer colours (reducing the number from eight to two); and last, to limit the number of different textures (reducing the number from five to three).

After only a few months, Albert Heijn and Signify were in a position to work together to integrate a new category of lighting into the overall real estate store plan. Then, Signify took just a few weeks to refine a lighting design plan to help Albert Heijn with the steps required for the production of coloured luminaires for the Rotterdam store, which were installed in October 2016.

'Within a matter of months, we managed to co-create and design a whole new connected lighting format from inception through to production – which for two large, multinational companies like Albert Heijn and Signify is impressive!' com-mented Remco Duchhart, Store Design Format Manager at Albert Heijn supermarkets.

The following year, Albert Heijn introduced the 3D-printed luminaires into the bakery and flower section in the Amster-dam store. The next step was to roll out the luminaires into over 200 stores that are being remodelled, as well as to the remaining stores. This innovative co-creation project has made a major contribution to the new inspirational, in-store experience at Albert Heijn supermarkets, in addition to improving the company's net promoter score (NPS), which has increased by 10–20% in the newly remodelled stores.

The Albert Heijn leadership team fully supported this co-creation initiative, because it has been an integral part of the company's strategy for continual in-store innovation. Furthermore, the 3D-printed luminaires are highly sustainable, as the luminaries can be recycled and reused back in the store, which is a compelling message for customers.

HOW DID CO-CREATION COME ABOUT WITH OTHER PARTNERS: WHO AND HOW?

'We have learned a great deal from the co-creation process by bringing together an innovative team from Albert Heijn, Signify and our customers. This has been a really fluid, energising process and resulted in a much faster way of working, with significant results within a matter of months', concluded Remco Duchhart.

OUR TOP THREE CO-CREATION LESSONS AT ALBERT HEIJN

1. *Say it!* Get the organisation to stake a claim on co-creation and create a 'change' to foster a co-creation movement. This is how the organisation needs to commit to co-creation, where 'we don't just do co-creation' *but* co-creation is how 'we do what we do'. It is all about taking the final step of mature co-creation.

2. *Work on building your co-creation stakeholder relationships early on* and spend time with them as a team. This can yield great results in a short time.

3. *Be open with information sharing.* Also, do not assume that some information might not be useful for others just because it is not useful to you.

Co-creation gives the organisation and your brand a C-change to be implemented in all functions – from R&D, design and HR to sales and marketing – to achieve customer-led growth.

Maria-Letizia Mariani, Chief Strategy and Marketing Officer at Signify, pointed out, 'The magic of co-creation in Signify has come from radical collaboration internally between departments, from R&D, marketing and sales to HR, as well as externally with customers, like, for example, on the product roadmap. Signify has moved to a situation where there is now an increasingly deep partnership with our customers. Equally our leaders and employees are on board and we're gaining continual insight from customers in different countries to introduce stronger co-created products which meet their needs'. This is what marketing in the Customer Economy should be. She added, 'We are succeeding in building trusted relationships with key stakeholders and in strengthening a way of working strongly based on the principle of a radical collaboration'.

WHAT DOES THE FUTURE HOLD FOR CO-CREATION?

So, what does the future hold for co-creation? Steven Walden, author of *Customer Experience Management Rebooted*, believes that, currently, a lot of co-creation is focused on crowd-sourcing and implementing innovation labs. 'Co-creation is not yet institutionalised within firms where there is equity based on creative co-creation. The practice of co-creation needs to move from piecemeal to be instilled into the strategy of the organisation'. Going forward, there is a significant opportunity for co-creation to capitalise on the move to trusted infomediaries and value from digital platforms. For example, car companies are changing to become 'mobility services companies', driving a need to blur boundaries and be interconnected with technology to enable this blurring. This makes co-creation vital to create the 'C-change' for this customer-led digital transformation. Another example is Laing O'Rourke, which is moving from being a construction company to being a group of facilities managers balancing multiple stakeholders. These organisations will not be able to achieve sustainable growth in the Customer Economy without co-creation. Walden added, 'This will necessitate a cultural shift to co-creation which will be re-enforced socially by Generation Z, who will form the new majority of customers. Generation Z is so much more predisposed to co-creation in contrast to previous generations'.

EMPERORS AND KINGS

In some sectors such as fintech, we are now already seeing co-creation as the defining principle of the industry itself. Companies working in the financial services sector such as Finastra and Virtusa have launched their own open innovation platforms on which customers, partners, developers and consultants across the globe can co-develop new financial products and services. Both the challenger banks (such as Starling and Monzo) and the established financial players (such as Barclays) are doing the same. Organisations that own the platform are the emperors, and their network of customers and partners can become kings. Much of this principle started with the launch of salesforce.com, supported by its ecosystem of platform partners. The open innovation world in fintech is even helping to drive wealth creation in hitherto untapped and undeveloped markets, especially across the African continent. Fintechs are springing up all over Nigeria, Kenya and Rwanda – and this, in turn, is helping in the mission to bank the unbanked. The Vodafone M-Pesa example was just the start – many countries across Africa are working quickly towards a truly cashless economy. This trend is only set to continue.

CO-CREATION: A WORD OF CAUTION

In The Customer Catalyst, we advocate that a balanced use of all C-change growth drivers become the norm. While co-creation is an essential component of this model and will increasingly define every industry we work in, it has the potential to fragment the customer experience. For example, the more organisations involved in innovating new products and services, the harder it might be to ensure a connected customer experience. This is especially true when it comes to technology platforms and data (i.e. the more intermediaries, the more data sources, and the harder it might be to establish a single customer view). Organisations should never lose sight of why co-creation exists, that is, to drive customer-led growth. Any co-creation initiative should always be linked back to the company's customer vision, customer-led cultural values and, indeed, customer-led growth targets.

In summary, we are only just scratching the surface with what is possible with co-creation. In the Customer Economy of today, it is impossible to imagine any organisation that is serious about customer-led growth not adopting the C-change principle of co-creation. Within 5 years, we believe co-creation with customers, partners and other stakeholders will be the norm rather than the exception.

CHAPTER 10

ADVOCACY

Let your customers do the selling

C-CHANGE GROWTH DRIVERS

- **Customer advocates are the most effective salesforce your company will ever recruit.** It is far better to invest in great customer experience, led by cross-functional teams and customer advocates, than it is to spend inordinate money purely on recruiting and training expensive sales teams.

- **Customer Advocacy is the result of implementing the C-change growth engine**, and it helps create customer-led brands and drive sustainable, profitable growth.
- **Customer Advocacy creates a cultural C-change.** It does this by galvanising the organisation around listening directly to insight from customer advocates (this is a key part of Customer Voice) to co-create more targeted products and services that meet their needs, as well as by customer advocates telling their story in a far more authentic way. This is done at every stage of the customer journey to drive organic growth (i.e. with existing customers) as well as to engage prospective customers.

TALKING ABOUT A CUSTOMER REVOLUTION!

Since the launch of the Internet, the floodgates of information have opened, leading to greater transparency for customers. We have seen the breakdown of control by 'corporations' over the buying process. We have gone from having a captive audience with customers to a situation where their attention is now scarce. This means that companies now face the challenge of spending disproportionally more money for a land grab for the remaining attention of time-poor customers. Customer Advocacy, if executed well, spans both marketing and sales to accelerate growth. Also, it represents a smart way to capture customer attention.

Bill Lee, author of *The Hidden Wealth of Customers* and founder of the Centre for Customer Engagement, commented, 'For me, firms like HubSpot, BMC, Marketo (an Adobe company), Salesforce, Finastra, and Microsoft have stand out capabilities for creating and leveraging customer advocates and influencers. Led by smart people, they often build relationships with the firm's best customers more effectively than anyone else in the organisation'.

Now, the customer has the power over the buying process and their journey. This is especially important when you consider that, according to Forrester, up to 90% of the buying process in B2B is done before a business makes a sales call; hence, hearing from customer advocates online and offline as credible sources of information are very important in driving growth. In this chapter, there are fascinating examples of Microsoft in the technology sector and LCH (formerly London Clearing House) in the financial services sector on how marketing and sales skills are blurring in the quest for organisations to be genuinely customer-led.

The Internet and the advent of social media have brought transparency and ubiquitous access to information. However, they bring with them a whole new set of challenges. While it allows businesses of all sizes to sell their wares to the world, how can potential customers determine those who will really deliver

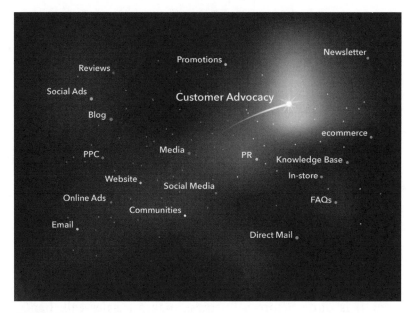

FIGURE 10.1 Customer Advocacy is the shooting star in a galaxy of information.

Source: Famous4CustomerAdvocacy. Reproduced with permission.

against their well-crafted promises? This brings us to highlight the twenty-first-century customer journey (see Figure 10.1), where the buying process has shifted from a linear model. In this context, customer advocacy represents a shooting star in a galaxy of information.

CUSTOMER ADVOCACY IS THE SHOOTING STAR IN A GALAXY OF INFORMATION

In the past, customers had to go through a fairly uniform number of linear steps before purchasing products and services.

Typically, a customer would have little choice other than to accept information given from organisations. They would only have a limited number of alternative, independent sources of information, such as their peers, industry associations and the press, on which to rely before buying. In the twenty-first century, customers and prospective customers are bombarded with an abundance of information via multiple channels including the web, smartphones and tablets, through to events, direct messaging, social media and review sites. All of this has brought us full circle. Word of mouth, perhaps the oldest form of communication, is still today the most effective way of sorting the wheat from the chaff. As customers, we seek out those who we respect and trust, and so we will trust products and services endorsed by these individuals and organisations. The smart organisations in today's market are letting their customers do the talking.

They are helping them to do it with customer advocacy to drive awareness, engagement, business development, sales – and, ultimately, more meaningful, customer-led brands. It is all about nurturing your customers in the Customer Economy as genuine champions or 'advocates' to tell their stories in their own words online and offline. Organisations should work closely with customer advocates tell these stories tightly, following along the customer journey to help you cut through the noise and drive sustainable growth.

The answer to achieving this lies in the careful joint business and marketing planning with customer advocates which we term '*mutual business currency*'. This provides credible, authentic content combined with strategic, targeted customer advocacy marketing and sales placements to appeal to decision-makers on their buying journey. We know this works and that it provides tangible returns on investment.

In this chapter, we will also share how customer advocacy can provide a 'C-change' for leaders and employees to evolve into a customer-led culture. Also, customer advocates are a key part of customer engagement and demand-generation programmes. Customer advocates are known and trusted and help drive a higher quality and value of leads, as well as higher conversion rates, in shorter timeframes. This chapter discusses the customer advocacy programme implemented by Microsoft, and the amazing results they have achieved.

SO, WHAT IS AN ADVOCATE?

'*An advocate is a person who supports or recommends on behalf of another. Further to that, customer advocates are more likely to spend more with your organisation and more frequently. With their emotional attachment to your customer-led brand, the possibilities to work with customer advocates are infinite in terms of driving long-term business growth*'.

We define four types of customers, culminating in the highest level being the customer advocate, to which companies should aspire in order to accelerate growth. By adopting the C-change growth engine, companies can catalyse the number and quality of customer advocates.

1. *Customer negative* – where a customer has a negative perception of the brand from their own experience, or influenced by a trusted source such as a colleague, family member or the views of an opinion former or influencer – such as vloggers in business-to-consumer (B2C) (e.g. James Charles, the American make-up artist). It is worth noting that there is an opportunity to turn 'customer negative', or what Mark Organ, Chairman of the Board at Influitive, calls 'Badvocates', into advocates. In fact, they can often become the best advocates.

2. *Customer neutral* – they are customers who are agnostic in their attitude towards your brand and organisation and have no strong emotional attachment to them. This represents an opportunity to nurture them and move one step closer to the customer advocacy bullseye. However, 'customer neutrals' can be the hardest to turn into advocates.

3. *Customer positive* – is where the customer has positive perceptions of your brand but a passive relationship. Therefore, they have insufficient emotion towards the brand to instigate action and customer advocacy. Many organisations make

the mistake of thinking they have customer advocates who want to work with them. In fact, these customers are often 'customer positive', where they have to be given some inducement such as a financial discount for them to endorse the organisation. This is not a customer advocate.

4. *Customer advocate* – where the customer has an active and emotional relationship with the brand and is willing to be an ambassador for the organisation. The aim of every organisation should be to reach the Customer Advocacy Bullseye (see Figure 10.2). This brings an enhanced customer relationship and improved loyalty, which results in increased brand awareness, profitability and market share. The customer advocate does not need to rely on financial inducements to endorse your organisation. They will tell their story with you because they have an emotional attachment to you, owing to which they will go to extraordinary lengths to be your advocate. This is hugely powerful.

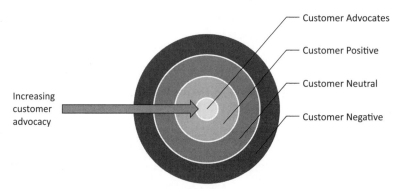

FIGURE 10.2 The Customer Advocacy Bullseye approach.

Source: Famous4 CustomerAdvocacy. Reproduced with permission.

THE NEED FOR NEW SKILLS: THE RISE OF THE 'CUSTOMER ADVOCACY CONSULTANT'

The Customer Economy requires new skills to meet the far more demanding needs of the customer who is information-rich and in control of the buying process. As a result, the roles of the traditional salesperson or marketer from a siloed department with constrained skills and limited access to the knowledge needed to satisfy more sophisticated customer needs are under threat.

With the fight to capture customers' attention, the customer advocate marketer needs to be adept at being creative to engage and nurture customer advocates. Meanwhile, they need to be good at data with a disciplined, scientific approach to testing messages, customer-led issues and campaigns that resonate with other customers. Mark Organ, Chairman of the Board at Influitive, a software and services company, ranked 87th on Deloitte's Technology Fast 500™ (fastest-growing technology, media, telecommunications, life sciences and energy tech companies in North America), says that the reason why there is a scarcity of customer advocacy consultants doing it well is because there are few people who are creative while possessing scientific and data skills. The best customer advocacy consultants need to combine the 'one-to-one' empathy and love for customers typical of Customer Success departments with creative 'one to many' marketing campaign skills. Traditional marketers prefer to segment the market and deliver campaigns to a large number of people and are conversely less inclined to build one-to-one relationships.

Mark Organ continued, 'The Customer Advocacy marketer is both a creative artist and a scientist. They balance *creativity* such as the application of what, how and where a customer advocate tells their story, as well as *psychology*, gut feelings, and emotional intelligence for relationship building, plus hard data, facts and statistics to track ROI'.

In addition, there is an emergence of leaders and vice-presidents of customer marketing both 'selling to' and 'selling through' customers, nurturing customer advocates for organic growth as well as new customers. It is a sector that is growing in maturity, with impressive people moving into these roles who love customers, including tech companies in business-to-business (B2B) as well as in B2C, examining converting leads into lifetime value customers. Now, there are examples of tech companies with teams of up to 200 people working in customer marketing globally. Typically, the role reports into the CMO and looks at how to make the customer journey more satisfying. For example, the hospitality industry with Ritz-Carlton and Disney is innovating guest experience with direct input from customer advocates in the form of 'guest advocates'. Typically, customer marketers are taking responsibility for a number of areas from customer advocacy communities, nurturing customer advocates as references with prospects, getting them to speak at events to drive organic growth and new business. This is all in pursuit of becoming what Mark Organ describes a 'customer-powered enterprise', competing on the basis of the relationships with customer advocates. As a result, we are seeing the customer becoming central to marketing within organisations, and, conversely, sales teams are becoming smaller because the cost per head is high. The corollary of this is that customer marketing will continue to represent an increasingly larger proportion of the company budget, because it has increasingly proved the success of integrating successfully into every part of the organisation from sales to experience.

The best customer advocate marketers share these skills with growth hackers who bend rules to find new ways of engaging customers while, at the same time, having incredible discipline. Mark Organ added, 'Influitive is investing in training dozens of people every month to develop this rare combination of creative and scientific skills – as we know, the demand is there in the Customer Economy'. Calling CEOs and CxOs, you need to cultivate these skills in your organisations in order to drive profitable growth.

Box 10.1 LCH (Formerly London Clearing House) Redefines the Role of Sales with Customer Advocacy

The LCH is a leading global clearing house, providing proven risk management capabilities. The company was established in 1888 as an industry-owned clearing house. In 2013, the London Stock Exchange Group (LSEG) became a shareholder and has increased its shareholding in LCH to in excess of 80%. LCH is a great illustration of how the traditional, often siloed, sales skills are changing to work across different functions to better serve clients in the Customer Economy. In short, the organisation has used customer advocacy to turn traditional sales into consultative sales.

The 2008 financial crisis turned the financial services sector upside down, including LCH's core derivatives market. The G20 group of countries and financial regulators across the world wanted to make the over-the-counter (OTC) derivatives market more transparent. So, the regulators standardised OTC trade derivatives in the clearing houses.

At the time, there was little competition. LCH was the only clearing house via Lehman Brothers trading OTC derivatives, which accounted for 5% of the overall market for the product. In contrast, now over 80% of OTC derivatives are handled via clearing houses. When these new global G20 financial regulations came into force in 2012, each country had to work out how to implement them, which was a huge change. There was even a question mark over whether the OTC derivatives market would survive and cope with the increased risk, not to mention how all parties would comply with the new regulation from LCH as the central counterparty (CCP); regulators; and customers, that is, banks' 'sell side'/'buy side'.

To overcome this, LCH had to adapt to the industry and its clients. LCH already had an existing service and extensive experience, but the new regulation applied not to just one country but globally, which made it complex. It was key to keeping the overall market open and allow trading across borders. LCH worked with US and European regulators to protect their clients, ensuring that the new regulation was in the best interests of the industry. This included regulation not being too prohibitive for banks. Also, LCH had to educate clients on how banks were centralising their risk with a CCP such as LCH – so transparency was key. 'This necessitated LCH fundamentally changing from a straight sales relationship between the salespeople and their clients to consultative selling bridging sales and marketing skills', said Marcus Robinson, Head of Group Business Development at LCH.

LCH had to design new client workflows as a result of working closely with banks, and intermediaries called futures commission merchants (FCMs), so they could efficiently connect to clearing houses to meet the regulatory obligations and clear funds. Marcus had worked in London, Sydney and Tokyo, so knew that it was key to working with local markets as part of its global strategy. So, for example, LCH developed a working group in Sydney with Australian banks, getting their feedback and co-creating risk management products and services that their market wanted to use. As a result, LCH engaged in this new global market by evolving the way it sold its financial products. The sales and marketing function has blurred, where salespeople have now adapted to consult and provide an educational and relationship-building approach – with a view to working together over a period of years. In doing so, LCH was building stronger customer partnerships and a large base of customer advocates who could help the organisation drive growth.

'In the past, LCH never had to focus on its brand and had product-led sales roles, whereas now the company has developed its brand centred on innovating client experience and advocacy – our tagline is "LCH, the Markets' Partner" to enable global growth', commented Marcus Robinson. He added, 'Our salespeople are multi-skilled with sales, marketing and Customer Advocacy skills'.

Now, in the OTC market, there is no exchange, so LCH acts as a clearing house and does not do settlement or execution. However, there is far more competition, which has meant a considerable change in the way of working. 'From a sales and marketing perspective, it's very much about relationship management where it's become a team sell. We've created a hybrid sales, marketing and relationship management role called "OTC Derivatives Sales and Relationship manager," which is customer-led and is helping us to achieve sustainable growth', added Marcus Robinson.

A client such as a bank will work with LCA's 'OTC derivatives sales and relationship managers'. They will bring in different financial services subject matter experts from risk, operations, legal and compliance to meet their needs.
Typically, the 'OTC Derivatives Sales and Relationship manager' will work on
at least four levels with the client, aligning with their respective subject matter experts. In doing so, LCH is able to drive customer engagement across
the entire customer ecosystem, which has helped it develop new OTC products and services. An example of this includes the first time LCH created a
non-clearing product, which it called "Swap Agent. This is a financial service to facilitate the transfer of bilateral margin (where banks have to pass
financial margin on cash or securities). The 'OTC Derivatives Sales and Relationship manager' has developed new technical knowledge as well as understanding of the capital and operational drivers of their clients, which was
not necessary before. The introduction of these new customer advocacy-led
skills has enabled LCH to differentiate its business as a 'leader in OTC derivatives revolution' says Marcus Robinson. LCH has expanded its operations from
London to the United States and Asia, achieving significant growth over the
last 10 years.

CUSTOMER ADVOCACY TO DRIVE GROWTH

One of the main issues facing organisations and a key accusa-
tion levelled at marketing is how to generate leads which are

short-term and diminish the perceived value of marketing. Of paramount importance is to change the tactical conversation of marketing's ability to create leads to a strategic one about mapping customer advocates onto the business objectives, mission and vision of your organisation to drive measurable, sustainable growth. Read our four stages of Customer Advocacy as a framework to deliver success for you and your customer advocates.

STAGE 1: LISTENING TO YOUR CUSTOMER VOICE TO INFORM YOUR CUSTOMER ADVOCACY STRATEGY

First, you need to listen to your customer advocates to determine their traits from the Customer Voice data (see Chapter 1), from which you can nurture 'Customer Neutrals and Customer Negatives'. This will inform and shape your Customer Advocacy strategy.

Bill Lee added, 'I think it's important for practitioners to use Customer Voice to inform the development of Customer Advocacy programmes. My advice would be: transparent, authentic conversations between customers and prospects is the true "Voice of the Customer" and the best sales tool you have in today's world. In the early days of Salesforce, Marc Benioff found (to his surprise) that bringing prospects together with existing customers at local events simply to have conversations drove growth. 80% of prospects who attended such events eventually became customers'.

STAGE 2: PROFILING YOUR CUSTOMER ADVOCATES

Customer advocate profiling needs to take place with CxO involvement. This is where the customer advocacy programme leader's consultancy skills kick in. They need to work with CxOs, the CEO and heads of sales and marketing to build on the data from Customer Voice and identify existing and potential customer advocates. The profiling of these customer advocates will be aligned to the business growth plan and also will involve consultation with the client directors or CSMs. The customer advocacy programme leader needs to sell the benefits and value of customer advocacy to the client directors and CxOs for them to have confidence in opening the next stage of direct contact with the customers.

STAGE 3: MAPPING YOUR CUSTOMER ADVOCATES ONTO YOUR BUSINESS STRATEGY AND PLAN

Map your customer advocates onto your business plan, so that they can be embedded in every area of the business as well as at every touchpoint on the customer journey. Working with customer advocates can be a positive business disrupter, driving a quantum leap in organic growth; that is, with retained customers as well as in forging new business.

This is not a one-off process of gleaning information but a dynamic, two-way process with your customer advocates. For example, if your business strategy is to focus on certain horizontal products and services with say, 40% of planned revenues in financial services, 30% in retail and 30% in manufacturing, then the next step is to map potential customer advocates proportionately on those respective business areas. This is a pivotal business planning process which needs to bring together CxOs, including the CCO, CMO and chief sales or revenue officer, and customer experience.

> 'Select customer advocates as if they'll become your most important growth asset – because if you do so, they will', pointed out Bill Lee. 'Don't limit your choices to your existing customer base. Look at the whole market, and ask, "Which prospects out there would make the best advocates for us?" Make it a priority to win their business. By the way, your "best advocates" aren't necessarily the biggest logos'.

STAGE 4: JOINT CUSTOMER ADVOCACY AND ENGAGEMENT PLANNING – NURTURE, NURTURE, NURTURE!

Individual customer advocate programme planning needs to take place with the client directors, or, increasingly, the

CSMs, to develop customer engagement (also, see Chapter 8 on Customer Engagement). This should include several initial, target sales and marketing placements that are likely to deliver 'mutual business currency'. This needs to be mutually beneficial for both customer advocates as well as your organisation. Importantly, this process should be led by 'What's in It for Me' (WIFM) for your customer advocates. 'Ultimately, the best customer advocates need to feel valued, not just valuable', says Mark Organ, Chairman of the Board at Influitive.

We see two financial and emotional drivers for customer advocates from both an organisational and personal perspective: 'make me rich' and 'make me famous'. 'Make me rich' is obviously a financial driver. For example, the customer advocate may achieve a financial bonus as a result of the customer advocacy programme promoting their business and driving growth. Conversely, 'make me famous' involves tapping into the social media and selfie age for personal promotion. Now, in the Customer Economy, customer decision-makers – even if they are introverts – realise that they need to promote themselves to build their careers. Customer advocacy is an enabler for this – which is powerful, as it is an independent, third-party endorsement. What's key is for the customer advocacy programme leader and consultants to identify and tap into these drivers to create 'mutual business currency'. This is highly effective as a C-change to drive success for your customer advocates as well as profitable growth for your organisation.

GETTING ENGAGED WITH YOUR CUSTOMER ADVOCATES

Profiling and nurturing your customer advocates are symbiotically linked with effective engagement programmes (see Chapter 9 on Customer Engagement) that marry your customers' business and marketing objectives with those of your organisation to drive the 'mutual business currency', which we have spoken about.

Primary data and feedback from your customer advocates will shape your customer engagement strategy and tactics. A good example is asking what media and information sources your customer advocates consult on their journey which prompts them to act and buy. Most customers have a profile on social media from LinkedIn to Instagram that can be easily researched. This is valuable information on which to base customer advocacy placements that meet and exceed their needs. Once created, your customer advocacy leader must test and refine the programme continuously. This is a classic example of where the hybrid creative and scientific skills of customer advocacy leaders come to the fore. Read the Engagement chapter to explore the most powerful elements of a customer engagement programme.

However, trust has been challenged with, for example, an abundance of fake reviews for consumer tech products on Amazon, where companies have manipulated reviews. It is not long before the truth comes out with telltale signs such as a high number of unverified, five-star ratings posted in a short space of time – indicating inauthentic reviews. The important point here is the one we made in Chapter 2 on culture, where transparency and authenticity from the inside show up on the outside. In 2019, those organisations which manipulated customer reviews on Amazon got found out by consumer champion, Which? This had the knock-on effect of damaging the product brands of those organisations and diminished their sales – in addition to tainting Amazon's brand too.

THE BUSINESS BENEFITS OF NURTURING CUSTOMER ADVOCATES

A company that has genuine customer advocacy will possess a customer-led brand and will, therefore, be much more trusted. Taking that a step further, such a company with high levels of customer advocacy typically has a response rate that is four to five times higher than a company that is not trusted.

'Companies can create a virtuous circle of advocacy and growth. A company with high levels of customer advocacy can more easily augment and improve the customer experience. In doing so, it is then able to further drive customer advocacy, which can propel the company to market growth and dominance. If you have an army of unpaid customer advocates who are helping to convert existing customers and prospects through the funnel, how can you not win?', commented Mark Organ.

This contrasts with companies which look at NPS in isolation, where NPS is only the propensity to recommend, versus actually tracking if the customer has advocated, that is, by using the customer advocacy placements that we have discussed in this chapter. In the simplest terms, customer advocacy tracks these placements and, essentially, evidence of why customers love your product or service.

HOW CAN YOU USE CUSTOMER ADVOCACY TO POWER SALES ENABLEMENT?

The job of sales enablement is to equip sales with tools to improve their effectiveness and productivity. So, getting the right customer-led evidence at their fingertips at every step of the customer journey is fundamental to winning market share in the Customer Economy. A company with a smart customer advocacy strategy and assets will drive sales enablement. This is all about giving salespeople specific customer advocacy assets such as customer reviews and stories in video and in the press to help drive awareness and sales. This can be tracked with platforms (see the Technology chapter) and often cuts sales cycles in half. This is not the old-fashioned sterile case study, but storytelling on how the product or service has improved the business and the life of the customer advocate.

CREATING A VIRTUOUS CUSTOMER ADVOCACY CIRCLE

The organisation needs to think of Customer Advocacy programmes as a virtuous circle, feeding a pipeline of customer advocates to maintain momentum and growth. Also, customer advocates will leave the programmes, often because they are leaving a company, which represents a growth opportunity. On many occasions, the customer advocate will move to a new organisation, which can be a new prospect. However, companies need to ensure they have enough advocates in their pipeline to achieve the organisation's business objectives.

CASE STUDY: MICROSOFT AND ITS CUSTOMERS DOING THE TALKING!

Claire Grove (see Figure 10.3), Head of Customer Advocacy and Storytelling, Microsoft UK, says, 'I am convinced I have the best job in Microsoft: I get to go out and talk to customers, learn what's important to them and create win-win scenarios. It is a privilege to share their stories'.

Claire Grove has been a leader in the practice of Customer Advocacy for over 20 years and has seen it become a strategic

FIGURE 10.3 Claire Grove, Head of Customer Advocacy and Storytelling, Microsoft UK.

Source: Claire Grove. Reproduced with permission.

weapon in driving sustainable growth for organisations. She has led customer advocacy and storytelling for over 5 years in the United Kingdom for Microsoft. Her role is to meet with key customers, not just by spend, but according to their innovation and alignment with Microsoft's growth areas. It is interesting to note that companies that are successful at driving customer advocacy to achieve growth for themselves as well as their customer advocates have a deep-seated, customer-led culture, as well as the other elements of the C-change growth engine. Microsoft is no exception and makes no secret of its customer-led mission, 'Our mission is to empower every person and every organisation on the planet to achieve more'.

Microsoft is a customer-obsessed company that believes in 'Customer First', which is led from the top by Satya Nadella, its CEO, who is an inspirational and highly successful customer-focused leader. This has had a positive impact on the company's customer advocacy function which, interestingly, in the United Kingdom, has been moved from marketing to a 'Customer and Partner Experience' function. Customer Advocacy at Microsoft starts with the Customer Voice, which echoes what we said earlier in this chapter about it informing which customer advocates to nurture.

In the past, Microsoft customer references were driven out of the business groups with a tendency to be internally focused. However, with the 'One Microsoft' approach, there has been recognition that customers do not typically go out and buy one product or service from one business group; that is, that customers do not follow our business groups, and that we need to be more customer-focused and bridge organisation siloes.

Claire's role was created to bridge all of the four business groups – Intelligent Cloud, Modern Workplace, BizApps and Devices – to pursue Microsoft's business goal to help drive digital transformation. 'This is because when we talk to customers, we want to represent their full story rather than telling it in isolation just from one particular business group', said Claire Grove. This is about driving value for customers, driving business results and Microsoft's 'Tech for Good' approach, which helps customers across three areas: AI for Accessibility, AI for Earth and AI for Humanitarian Action.

The role of customer advocacy in Microsoft aligns to customers in these and other business priority areas, to understand their business objectives, helping them to tell their story in an impactful way, and then representing VoC information back into Microsoft to provide a better customer experience. Claire Grove pointed out, 'At Microsoft, we mean what we say when we talk about empowering our customers. It's not about the product – it's about how we drive our customers to achieve their business objectives. My role is to communicate internally and externally as to how we're doing that through customer advocacy and storytelling'.

Of the utmost importance is for Claire to understand the business objectives of Microsoft's customer advocates and what they are fundamentally trying to achieve. Claire says, 'Customers don't go out to just buy cool technology for the sake of it – they want to address a need, now or are anticipating a need in the future. So, they're looking to effect change for their customers and/or employees, which Microsoft technology can enable'. This reinforces our point of finding the 'mutual business value' for your organisation and customer advocates, which is the secret to successful advocacy.

There has been a company-wide approach to drive value to customers as well as Microsoft itself via storytelling. When Claire started in 2014, her vision was to show impact on customer advocacy as soon as possible and approach it in a different way. 'I do see people in this field who focus on a single dimension of the old-fashioned case study and challenge, solution, benefit approach. Customers see this as asking for a favour because it's about you. However, if we ramp up storytelling to be truly about the customer and our role in their success, we can effect change. If our customers use our storytelling assets in the course of their own business, that's a key endorsement and measure of success'.

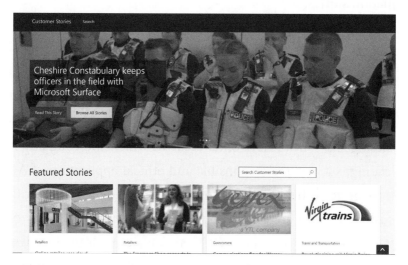

FIGURE 10.4 Microsoft's Customer Advocacy portal.

Source: Microsoft. Reproduced with permission.

The Microsoft culture is very open, where everyone is behind the ultimate aim of providing value for their customers and being customer-focused. 'At Microsoft, you have permission to fail and to learn from that. So, we have the backing to try new things with our customers'.

SO HOW DOES MICROSOFT'S CUSTOMER ADVOCACY PROGRAMME OPERATE?

As part of the Customer Experience and Partner team, Microsoft's Customer Advocacy programme works with specialist creative agencies to help tell customers digital transformation stories.

Step 1 – Identification of customer advocates: At the beginning of the financial year, the business vision and goals are clearly identified and communicated by Microsoft's CEO and COO. The Customer Advocacy programme then aligns to these goals – from horizontal areas in which the company is leading, such as the responsible and ethical application of AI, through to vertical markets. For example, Claire will work with customers who are embracing AI and look at the quality of the story. Claire and the team then connect with the business groups, comms, marketing and sales to plan target customer advocates that Microsoft would like to work with. 'At Microsoft, everyone understands the value that the Customer Advocacy programme can deliver. As a result, we have a healthy pipeline of opportunity', commented Claire.

Step 2 – Customer advocacy listening and planning: Claire is very close to Microsoft's business and planning process and uses data from Customer Voice to drive value through the Customer Advocacy programme for both customer advocates as well as Microsoft. A customer advocacy framework is built aligned to the business focus areas. There is a customer advocate nomination process *internally* from the business groups, marketing and sales – as well as externally, with nominations from partners and the customers themselves. Claire and team embark on customer listening, identifying which customers could be advocates. 'There is consultation with the internal Customer Account and Success teams, where conveying the benefits to our teams and our customers is vital'. Then, there is an introduction to the customer, but Claire says, 'It's not about "asking for a favour" – it's about delivering real value: helping customers reach their business and marketing goals. For example, understanding the audiences they want to reach from PR, events and social media'.

Step 3 – Customer advocacy engagement: Claire effects change from the Customer Advocacy programme for both Microsoft and its customers by looking for stories that really resonate with the target audiences of both parties. Ambionics (www.ambionics.co.uk), a pre-revenue start-up providing prosthetic limbs to children, is a great story which had incredible results for its founder as well as Microsoft's Devices business group. Ben Ryan, a self-taught engineer, started Ambionics after his son, Sol, had to have his arm amputated at just 10 days of age. As a result, Ben found out that, if young children were not given prosthetic limbs at an early age, the likelihood of them taking to using them lowered significantly. This, in turn, potentially limited their movement and choices in life. Ben set out on an inspiring journey to build the Ambionics business and help other families in a similar situation and open up opportunities for children such as Sol.

AMBIONICS: BORN TO ENGINEER

Ambionics was reliant on donations, so Microsoft gave Ben a Surface Pro, which he used to work alongside a second-hand Kinect and 3D printer to develop a 3D prosthetic limb for Sol (see Figure 10.5). Also, Ben needed awareness to garner support from other organisations to bring his 3D printed prosthetic arm business into operation. This involved scanning a child's body accurately and providing a fully functioning 3D-printed prosthetic arm.

Microsoft spent time with Ben and his family, told the story in a video clip which was promoted within Microsoft to employees and externally online, in the media and via social media. Ben shared the story at Microsoft's Partner Conference too.

FIGURE 10.5 Microsoft–Ambionics case study.

Source: https://customers.microsoft.com/en-gb/story/726957-ambionics. Accessed: 18th June 2019. Screenshot by Chris Adlard and Daniel Bausor.

As a result, from being in a precarious situation in terms of the future of his venture, the global awareness generated has helped Ben to turn Ambionics' future into a thriving one. This is a great example of a 'Tech for Good' story where Microsoft has added value to people's lives by 'empowering people'. This shows how the power of storytelling can be applied by any size of organisation. For Microsoft, this was not about selling; it showed how technology could effect change and illustrated the art of the possible.

Step 4 – Customer advocacy – measure, measure, measure!
Claire and her team recommend embedding the Customer Advocacy programme in marketing, sales and across the whole organisation, so that there are multiple placements with clear and transparent measurement. Microsoft has multiple

measures for customer advocacy: there is customer advocacy content, which provides resonance at the top of the marketing funnel; customer assets on the Microsoft website (https:// customers.microsoft.com); and the use of social media to share customer stories, where click-throughs, engagement, scroll-depth and dwell time are measured. This measures how much time is spent watching a customer video, including the written content alongside it. The number of unique and returning visitors is also measured. Customer stories and assets can be tracked on the customer journey, including the PR coverage generated and the use of customer speakers at events. Also, all of the customer content is integrated via marketing, so that Microsoft has a clear audit trail on where the customer content has been placed.

Microsoft's commitment to customer advocacy is epitomised by its website, where the URL says it all: 'Customers.Microsoft .com' – this is the showcase for customer advocates and their stories. The company's Customer Advocacy programme typically generates 700 customer assets every year from around 80–100 enterprise customers (public sector and health, to the private sector). This is from social media content, audio descriptors as well as customer video subtitles to meet Microsoft's accessibility goals. The diversity of Claire's job with customer advocates is enormous. On any day, she might be in a London law firm climbing a ladder with a hard hat, getting a great photo of the firm on the London skyline; or, she could be on a dairy farm in North Devon, telling the story of a retailer specialising in selling agricultural goods where she had to be hosed down by the farmer before getting back into her car! In addition, wherever possible, Microsoft will always look at their customers' customer – so that they are truly customer-led.

HAVE YOU HAD ANY FAILURES WITH CUSTOMER ADVOCACY?

'I've had failures with Customer Advocacy: particularly early in my Customer Advocacy career, I took a defensive view to Customer Advocacy where we would ask the customer to become a reference – thinking of the value to our business rather than benefits aligned to our customers', said Claire Grove. A lot of organisations do this, which causes sales and their customers to miss the value of the Customer Advocacy programme. For Claire, this resulted in one-dimensional customer references who were not genuine advocates. She added, 'You have to develop a Customer Advocacy programme based on value for your customers. We have to make it easy for customers, and you really have to understand the customers' drivers and their business priorities. It's Marketing 101 – understand your customers and address their needs'!

Daniel Langton (see Figure 10.6), Head of Customer and Partner Experience, Microsoft UK, concluded, 'We know that Customer Advocacy resonates – it drives customer engagement via

FIGURE 10.6 Daniel Langton, Head of Customer and Partner Experience, Microsoft UK.

Source: Daniel Langton. Reproduced with permission.

our digital and social channels. Also, it helps bring to life just what the right technology can do to help our customers transform in a context that's relevant to them'. He continues, 'Our customer storytelling is supporting our sales teams by providing invaluable proof points that give confidence and accelerate the sales cycle. Above all, Customer Advocacy is driving sustainable growth for Microsoft and our customer advocates'.

While there is overwhelming evidence that customer advocacy provides far more authentic and credible customer-led marketing, its use by organisations still remains the minority rather than the norm. IDC's customer experience practice conducted a study as part of its loyalty marketing and advocacy marketing barometer to chart the progress being made to support customer advocacy marketing efforts across the industry. In its 2016 Five Key Competencies for Modern Marketing Assessment, only 10% of B2B IT vendors surveyed had advocate marketing programmes in place. In 2017, this increased to 67%, a 570% increase year over year. While this is only in the IT sector, it highlights the value of customer advocacy and its rise in importance within marketing. Customer Advocacy programmes need to be adopted strategically at the top of the organisation while aligning customer advocates onto the business plan for sustainable growth in the Customer Economy. It is important for customer advocates to be linked dynamically across the whole organisation – for example, guiding the overall customer experience from customer advocacy Councils to Customer Voice – and fundamentally as an integral part of the customer-led culture that we spoke about in Chapter 2.

Above all, trust is fundamental to the success of Customer Advocacy. The greater the trust between customer advocates and the organisation, the deeper the relationships and a greater potential for mutual business currency. As Mark Organ says, 'Customers will discover your flaws anyway, so it's better to be open and transparent, which is a cornerstone to foster Customer Advocacy. Trust is a key differentiator between the successful and unsuccessful companies in the Customer Economy'.

Greater trust leads to achieving the planned customer advocacy marketing and sales placements to achieve the business objectives of both the customer advocate and your organisation. Some companies like Salesforce are even using a trust URL to be transparent on who they are and how they operate (https://trust.salesforce.com). What is significant about this is that customers can see key information on all of Salesforce services. Salesforce even tells you when their system has not been available. So, it gives a prospective customer a new level of information about what it would be like to work with Salesforce on a day-to-day basis, which previously was not available. Buyers do not want to spend ages during the buying process. So, with a move like this to openness, and rationalising the whole process, the buyers are more likely to buy. Furthermore, they are far more likely to buy more quickly.

TAKING CUSTOMER ADVOCACY TO THE NEW FRONTIERS

Customer advocacy – just like the customer experience as a whole – will have differences, often subtle, from one region to another: differences in the best ways to recruit advocates, to engage them in advocacy efforts and to communicate advocates' experiences to your market. Bill Lee makes the point that 'Many companies make the mistake of transferring a model of Customer Experience that succeeded in their home country to other cultures – even the smartest companies make this mistake'. He added, 'For example, Walt Disney's Euro Theme Park, Eurodisney TM, (located in Paris) was a disaster in its first few years because of a failure to adapt the "formula" to French sensibilities'. He argues that the solution to overcome this is to have both HQ representation and local representation in a global Customer Advocacy programme. The HQ representative keeps things focused on corporate strategy, while the local representation adapts initiatives to the local culture.

Bill Lee makes a valid point concurring with us on the blurring of customer advocates into other areas of the C-change model – notably, co-creation. He states, 'Current approaches to the customer experience are failing badly. Companies that *are* succeeding at improving the CX are moving away from *creating* the CX *for* customers to *co-creating* the customer experience *with* customers. And they're doing this *throughout* the customer journey'. He added, 'The most prolific co-creators tend to be what we now call customer advocates or customers in related engagement initiatives like your customer community and customer advisory boards. These customers will no longer be *supporting* traditional marketing, sales and other customer-impacting functions. They'll be *driving* these functions, and eventually the entire customer experience'.

TOP THREE LESSONS OF CUSTOMER ADVOCACY PROGRAMMES

1. *Integrate customer advocates into the heart and soul of your organisation.* Make advocate marketing a corporate initiative that is embedded in the customer journey, where

there is a shared mission to nurture and retain successful customers. For many organisations, this will mean moving from a one-dimensional customer reference programme to a strategic customer advocacy and engagement programme. Customer advocates inform with insight and value at every step of the customer journey and should be integrated into your organisation – from a customer-led brand and messaging to new product development. For example, work with your customer advocates to test your messaging and brand, through to your go-to-market strategy.

2. *CEOs need to cultivate customer advocate marketers' combination of creative and scientific skills* to drive best-practice customer advocacy and engagement for growth.

3. *Getting customer advocacy storytelling right* will be key to success in the Customer Economy. This involves blending creativity, science and planning. Propagating customer advocacy video clips via social media is highly effective, and not just the high-production, corporate videos but more conversational, human stories planned with different decision-makers. This can deliver exponential ROI in driving awareness and customer-led evidence early in the buying process.

We believe the companies that put their customer advocates at the heart of their business – so that it guides their culture, mission and their entire raison d'être – are the ones that will win in the Customer Economy.

SOME FINAL WORDS

Creating the Customer Catalyst has been a labour of love for us. Our respective careers have been built on the firm belief that organisations live to serve their employees; the ecosystem of partners, suppliers and the community around them; and, ultimately, their customers. We have practised what we preach. Everything from the title of the book, to the 10 chapters which comprise our customer-led C-change transformation, have been co-created in partnership with the pioneering customer-led leaders and organisations actually doing it. We thank these leaders and organisations for sharing their vision and learning on how to achieve sustainable customer-led growth. In today's Customer Economy, organisations face a stark choice: either fully embrace a customer-led mindset – or, ultimately, face extinction.

We hope you have enjoyed reading this book and will be able to apply the C-change growth engine to your organisation, and that you may encourage your leaders, managers and employees to embrace it. The C-change growth engine will deliver some quick wins, but its real impact will only be felt over the subsequent months, quarters and years. We believe that good, ethical businesses do the right thing by their customers – repeatedly over time – to drive sustainable growth.

We appreciate that the pressure to increase sales and continuously drive short-term growth is immense. This train will never stop. However, we encourage CEOs and the entire C-suite to – in parallel – rigorously champion the C-change growth engine and drivers across the organisation. Create a customer-led mission, vision and set of values and act accordingly. Do not merely pay lip service to any of this, because your employees will smell it from a mile away. Mean it, do it and watch the positive impact over time. Treat these initiatives with the same level of commitment as the need to drive short-term revenue and profitability.

Finally, we reiterate our call to action: Encourage your organisation to get on board the Customer Catalyst movement. Promote the C-change growth engine and drivers across your business. Encourage your teams to join the Customer Catalyst community. The community allows teams across the C-change growth engine to share ideas and best practices about how to drive growth, and how to bridge the division across its respective communities.

We encourage you and your team to sign up now to the Customer Catalyst community (www.theCustomerCatalyst.com).

Chris & Daniel

INDEX